TRAVELING
THE
EXOTIC

Other Books by Glenn W. Ferguson

Unconventional Wisdom, A Primer of Provocative Aphorisms,
Pen Art Productions, Tempe, Arizona, 1999, (out of print).

Americana Against the Grain, a Collection of Essays,
Pen Art Productions, Tempe Arizona, 1999, (out of print).

Tilting at Religion, Prometheus Books, Amherst, New York, 2003.

Sports in America, Fascination and Blemishes, Sunstone Press,
Santa Fe, New Mexico, 2004.

TRAVELING
THE
EXOTIC

Distinctive Experiences in Twelve Unique Countries

Glenn W. Ferguson

SUNSTONE
PRESS

SANTA FE

Cover photograph by Carl D. Condit

Sunstone books may be purchased for educational, business, or sales promotional
use. For information please write: Special Markets Department, Sunstone Press,
P.O. Box 2321, Santa Fe, New Mexico 87504-2321.

Library of Congress Cataloging-in-Publication Data:

Ferguson, Glenn W.
    Traveling the exotic : distinctive experiences in twelve countries
Glenn W. Ferguson.
    p.cm
    ISBN 0-86534-461-2 (hardcover : alk. paper)
    1. Voyages and travels. 2. Ferguson, Glenn W.—Travel. I. Title.

G465.F465 2005
910.4—dc22
                                    2005029090

Published in
Santa Fe

WWW.SUNSTONEPRESS.COM
SUNSTONE PRESS / POST OFFICE BOX 2321 / SANTA FE, NM 87504-2321 /USA
(505) 988-4418 / ORDERS ONLY (800) 243-5644 / FAX (505) 988-1025

To Patti

A devoted wife; a delightful traveling companion, and my best friend

CONTENTS

PREFACE

Evelyn Waugh and Kingsley Amis are cited as xenophobic travel writers. Having read several of the travel pieces of both writers, the word is used with precision: "unreasonable fear or hatred of foreigners or strangers or of that which is foreign or strange." Few travel writers are xenophobic.

In contrast to Waugh and Amis, it is unusual for a travel writer to present a negative view, or even a balanced view, of a foreign locus. To guarantee a free ride, a contemporary travel writer becomes a figurative agent of the host. The writer who incorporates a balanced appraisal in a travel piece may be declared persona non grata in the country or at the resort of infraction. For the writer who derives supplemental income from published pieces about the world abroad, an honest approach is tantamount to professional suicide.

Between the xenophobe and the sycophant, there is a narrow band of opportunity to write about foreign travel with a modicum of perspective. I have attempted to endorse that principle.

During the past half century, I have lived, worked, or traveled in more than one hundred countries. In most cases, I was catching my breath while en route to a permanent overseas assignment; discharging a short-term consultative role, or paying my respects with a brief commitment to the environment.

Regarding five countries, my wife and I were residents for several years while discharging a professional assignment: the Philippines, Thailand, Kenya, Germany, and France. With the exception of subsequent visits to Kenya, and a weekend in Thailand, the countries of residency are not included in this book.

In my early career, my impressions were not submitted to writing. In 1981, I started preparing a daily entry in a personal journal. Rather than resorting to a basic diary of events, matters of substance have been covered in essay form: travel, foreign affairs, politics, satirical essays, culture, and aphorisms.

For twenty-five years, that discipline has been honored. The essence of the material in this book has been derived from my journal entries.

I am convinced that travel writing must reflect a purpose more profound than sightseeing. I have selected a dozen countries in which I discharged a meaningful role. The point of departure is usually professional. In a few cases, I have relied upon an avocational interest, birding or the environment, which transcends the typical travel piece. In reporting on each country, there is a "twist" that, in my judgment, provides depth, balance, and at various times, insight.

Most contemporary travel writing concentrates on countries which are comparable, in accommodations and in outlook, to the conditions and attitudes which the author left at home. I have attempted to select a dozen countries that are exotic, different, complex, and which portray uncommon learning opportunities.

There are two countries which are covered in greater depth: India and Kenya. India is a complicated study. In 1984, we were in Calcutta at the time of the assassination of Prime Minister Indira Gandhi. In order to convey the nuances of local, national, and international affairs, a one-month visit was marginal. At the same time, with the exception of Kenya, India is projected in greater depth than the other ten countries.

Regarding Kenya, the short visits which I have attempted to capture occurred fifteen years after a three-year assignment as American Ambassador. The "flashback" technique has been employed to integrate essential background. With the exception of the capital of

Nairobi, most of the locations presented are "off the beaten track." For the other eleven countries, I have also included "flashbacks" of relevant experiences.

In each of the country chapters, there are references to birding. For a lifetime, birding has been an occasional, but sustained, leisure time pursuit. I am hopeful that the references will serve as an introduction to remote locations and as an innocuous comparative approach. A brief comment regarding capitalization may also prove useful. In citing birds and animals, the standard professional approach is utilized. For a single species, both the species and the family are capitalized (e.g., African Fish Eagle). In denoting a family per se which may include more than one species (e.g., eagles) the family name is not capitalized.

Since I have spent a significant segment of my life traveling and residing overseas, when I write about my experiences abroad, my fundamental bias, by choice, is to project positive impressions. At the same time, based on experience, I feel that I have an obligation to reflect a balanced approach.

If travel is to be broadening, it must encompass a fragment of pain. I am hopeful that an occasional light moment will assuage any discomfort which I may cause the gentle reader.

INDIA

The Assassination of Indira Gandhi and the Immediate Impact

October 26, 1984 / Frankfurt to New Delhi, India:

A few months ago, as I was completing my assignment as President of Lincoln Center in New York City, I received a call from the United States Information Agency in Washington, D.C. asking me to undertake a lecture tour in India. In late August, the tour was confirmed. Two weeks prior to our departure for New Delhi, Pakistan, and The Sudan were added to the itinerary. The approved topics were freedom of information, the performing arts, and higher education.

After an absence of twenty-five years, I was anticipating a return visit to Pakistan. In 1959, while serving as Assistant Dean of the Graduate School of Public and International Affairs at the University of Pittsburgh, I participated in an International Cooperation Administration project in India and Pakistan. A four-man consulting team conducted a six-week public administration survey. The trip included a visit to Dacca in East Pakistan and in West Pakistan, to Karachi (our base); Lahore (where the Zam Zam cannon was memorialized by Rudyard Kipling in *Kim*); the new capital of Rawalpindi, and Peshawar and the Khyber Pass near Afghanistan.

A few weeks prior to our departure on the current speaking tour, the Pakistan commitments were canceled without explanation. The flight to Delhi included a stop in Karachi, and I was delighted that a brief reunion would be possible. Upon landing in Karachi, we were informed that the Pakistani authorities would not allow transients to disembark. The explanation was "security." After a three-hour wait, the captain announced that "we had a mechanical problem, and we will be underway in five minutes." Obviously, given the deteriorating relationships with India, Pakistan did not want to accommodate transients en route to India.

Arriving at the Delhi Airport from Karachi at 4:00 a.m., we were met by a United States Information Service (USIS) officer. At the Maurya Sheraton Hotel, we were notified that two additional lecture topics had been approved: "The U.S. Presidential Debates" and "Private and Public Management—Comparisons." Bhopal had also been added to the itinerary to supplement Calcutta, Hyderabad, Madras, Bombay, and New Delhi.

October 28 / Calcutta:

The Air India flight from Delhi to Calcutta afforded an object lesson in airline cuisine. Delicious lamb and bean curry were served. After the bland Pan Am bill of fare, the taste treat was delightful.

At Dum Dum Airport ("Dum Dum" bullets were invented in Calcutta prior to World War II, and the new airport, and its predecessor, were saddled with the appellation), we were greeted by a young USIS officer who was born in Peru.

After living overseas, I did not believe that impoverished conditions could affect my equilibrium. In riding to the Oberoi Grand Hotel from the Dum Dum airport, I was shocked.

Nothing about Calcutta seemed familiar. Waves of penniless Hindu refugees from East Bengal arrived following the partition of Pakistan. Subsequent waves of Hindu and Muslim refugees migrated from former East Pakistan after India's successful effort to create independent Bangladesh.

At the end of World War II, the population of Calcutta was approximately three million. In 1984, without the benefit of a corroborating census, the population exceeded ten million. The natural procreative proclivities of the Indian population have also contributed to the crunch of humanity. Since 1977, the elected Communist government of West Bengal (Calcutta) had been unable to cope, especially with the Central Government in Delhi ignoring the plight of the former British capital in India.

The corrupt National Congress Party had not been perceived as a viable option. Last year, the Communists were reelected. Because Indira Gandhi has refused to solicit loans from international banking agencies, the combination of circumstances in Calcutta has been devastating.

British and American business interests departed. The remarkably beautiful British-inspired buildings and gardens had deteriorated. Essential services were disappearing, and the local government lacked the financial and personnel resources to cope.

With the public relations impact of a Communist regime, tourism had fallen off appreciably, jobs were being eliminated, and anarchy loomed. The traffic was dense and undisciplined. Dust, filth, disease, deprivation, and despair constituted a way of life for millions of indigenous Bengali and millions of homeless newcomers who shared a shrinking pot.

October 29:

Reflecting typical American overseas values, US Government employees in Calcutta live in luxurious ghettos and make little effort to learn about or understand the host nationals.

For my first speech at the Indian Chamber of Commerce, the USIS control officer informed me that I should stress private support for the performing arts. In contrast, the local program assistant suggested that I emphasize the role of nonprofit corporations in American society.

During a courtesy call on T.R. Malakar, Station Director of All-India Radio, the unique problems of a government-controlled radio network were discussed. The central Indian government dictates basic policy and delegates a modicum of programming responsibility to the states.

Prior to the Indian Chamber of Commerce speech, R.S. Lodha, the president, asked me to stress the taxation realities for Indian charitable trusts and the American nonprofit corporate entity. Although

I was unable to present any insights concerning tax problems in India, the group was interested in US nonprofit management.

After a lifesaving nap, we trotted off to a dinner hosted by Sri (Mr.) B.D. Sureka, an industrialist who serves as the President of the Padatik Art Center. The Center presents theatrical and dance performances. The guests included industrialists from the afternoon Chamber of Commerce presentation; a journalist from the *Telegraph*; a traditional dance star; a film director; two classical Indian singers, and several performing arts devotees. The vegetarian meal was superb. The guests were gracious and interesting. I was impressed by the articulate, attractive Indian women. The Marwaris (the so-called "Jews" of India) who originate from arid Rajasthan in Western India, and who control most of the significant business interests in Calcutta, are major patrons of the arts. They are charming, but it was disconcerting to realize that representatives of the Bengali majority are seldom successful in the arts or in industry.

October 30:

A morning appointment with the director of the government-controlled television monopoly did not stress freedom of the media. The national network owns one operational camera and controls one studio. The office and studio space are limited. Scarce financial resources and limited local programming responsibility prevail. In desperation, the television monopoly is attempting to recapture a bored and disillusioned audience with *Different Strokes*, *I Love Lucy*, and a bombardment of sports events.

In the international freedom of information debate, including the New World Information Order, India has assumed the leadership in attacking the media of the United States for alleged cultural imperialism, colonialism, and insensitivity to Third World developmental needs. The ultimate irony is that the Indian government is voluntarily featuring the least educational commercial television programs from the United States in attempting to increase the television audience. Indira Gandhi has launched a crusade for the need for "balance" in worldwide media reporting, but *Different Strokes* is not the solution. That series will bring a few minutes of unintelligible light and color to the local viewers who will not be informed, educated, or even entertained. The United States' commitment to freedom of the press will continue to be misunderstood.

A midday visit to the Kali Temple (Kali, the Goddess of Death) was a shattering experience. Hundreds of maimed paupers inundated the premises waiting for free meals which were distributed by the temple staff. Kids (goats, that is) were being slaughtered to gain points with the deity. Beggars inside and outside the temple were omnipresent. The filth was indescribable. The crunch of humanity was frightening. There was no discipline, no ostensible sign of authority, and no indication that Kali religious practices mean anything more than a sanction to kill goats, to pollute, and to sponsor a limited feeding program for a few handicapped people who reside on the sidewalks surrounding the temple. Christianity may be irrelevant; the Moslems may preach bellicosity, but there is not any indication that the Kali Temple has long-term positive impact on the lives of its adherents. Mother Teresa, who was awarded the 1980 Nobel Prize, resided one hundred paces from the Kali Temple.

The communists who control Calcutta are disillusioned pragmatists who were convinced that the corrupt practices of the Congress Party constituted a greater evil than the British colonials. As local communists without ideological baggage, or ties to Moscow, they represented minimal hope for the survival of Calcutta. To date, they have failed to guarantee subsistence, much less employment. India is confronted with another irony. Indira Gandhi, the product of a discredited political system (the National Congress Party) has accepted some tenets of the jingoistic brand of Russian communism as a guideline. At the same time, the local indigenous communists in West Bengal ignore Moscow, and Indira Gandhi, while they attempt to lead the devotees of Kali from inevitable chaos.

Today's luncheon guests included Ananda Shankar, the son of Uday Shankar. Uday applied lessons learned from Anna Pavlova to traditional Indian dance and created a modern art form. Ananda Shankar has formed his own dance troupe which recently returned from a tour in the United States. Ananda is a rival of his Uncle Ravi who is the leading sitar player in India and a folk hero in the United States.

The guests included the granddaughter of Berla, the Indian

counterpart of the elder Rockefeller, who runs the family art gallery in Calcutta. The gallery is seldom visited by Bengalis. We also met a pediatrician who plays western classical music twice per year in local piano concerts, and who serves as the only media music critic in Calcutta.

My afternoon speaking commitment, "Corporate Support of the Arts" (USIS asked me to be prepared to discuss "The Status of the Performing Arts"), was delivered to an audience of four, each of whom was more concerned about delivering a speech than engaging in a dialogue. The sponsor (Seagull Empire) is not aware of Jonathan but bases its origin on a huge drug caper in Calcutta. It has become a respectable, under-funded art group which sells books for profit, arranges a few folk exhibits (e.g., wood-cutting), and covets a building and a "sugar daddy." The founder of Seagull is anxious to obtain additional grants from the Indian Tobacco Company. A representative of the ITC was invited to attend my non-speech to gain credibility for a grant pitch. USIS sponsored the event. Obviously, public relations rather than grantsmanship should have been the priority. With the Indian Chamber of Commerce and Seagull under my belt, I am now ready for Madras and my initial exposure to Indian higher education.

October 31:

Early this morning, I received a call from the representative of the Voice of America (USIS) in Calcutta. She was surprised to learn that we were leaving and disappointed that an interview would not be feasible. It is remarkable that the USIS staff had not informed her of the dates of our itinerary.

Since May, the relevant USIS posts have been in possession of my credentials and schedule. They received photographs, a press release, and additional background information. Yet, upon our arrival in India, the local USIS employees were surprised that I had discharged senior assignments, and that my schedule in India was flexible. They appeared to lack essential contacts and to be incapable of creative programming. Taped interviews and press conferences were not contemplated. Higher education was ignored as a topic until after our arrival in India. Patti's relevant experiences have been totally ignored.

For the first time, the USIS junior program officer has been meeting senior Indian officials to discuss my schedule.

Americans abroad have a unique opportunity to make a fundamental contribution, particularly in developing countries. In spite of the meaningful Peace Corps experience, we have not learned essential lessons concerning the quality of overseas representation. We continue to assign inadequately trained, poorly motivated personnel to foreign assignments which require sensitivity, expertise, and language facility. Most of these American representatives live in affluent foreign ghettos and maintain their domestic USA lifestyle with the assistance of the Post Exchange and the Commissary. There are remarkable exceptions. Unfortunately, those exceptions are limited.

In 1954, while I was serving as an external programmer for official Department of State foreign visitors, I arranged the professional itinerary for a leader grantee named Himendu Biswas. At age 29, Himendu was a university student leader in India. He gave me an inscribed copy of the "Sayings of Ramakrishna." After a gap of thirty years, we met for coffee at the Grand Hotel.

Himendu is Dean of Students at the University of Calcutta and an elected member of the University Council (Governing Board). He plans to retire in two years, and he has lost his activist zeal. We offered Himendu a ride. As we departed, we were told that Prime Minister Indira Gandhi had been shot by Sikh members of her Security Guard in Delhi. According to initial media reports, she received sixteen bullet wounds in her chest and stomach and was not expected to live. In spite of the shock, we took Himendu to the University of Calcutta and proceeded to a luncheon which was hosted, in our honor, by the widow of Uday Shankar.

In the course of the luncheon, our new friend, Supreo Bonnerjee, a USIS program advisor, received several telephone calls updating the reports from Delhi. We were notified that Mrs. Gandhi had died, and that violent retaliation was anticipated against Sikh communities in major urban areas. Before the luncheon concluded, we were advised that the USIS office in Madras had canceled our lecture commitments because of rioting in the streets.

Following Prime Minister Gandhi's dismissal of former movie star Rama Rao as Prime Minister of Madras State, and his subsequent resurrection by popular demand, Prime Minister Gandhi had not been admired. In Madras, it is more likely that there would have been dancing in the streets rather than rioting. Cinema stars with the initials "RR" seem to excel in elective politics.

Since senior politicians in India are gravitating to Delhi to pay their respects to the departed prime minister, and since airplane travel is proscribed for foreigners, our schedule has been placed in limbo.

In Calcutta, cars and buses were being burned on the major streets. Traffic was barely moving. The police disappeared, and we were not able to return to the hotel. It was suggested that we stay temporarily at the guesthouse at the American Consulate compound, and we readily agreed.

In June, 1984, the government of India alleged that the Central Intelligence Agency had been intimately involved in the training of Sikhs who participated in the Punjabi insurrection. The Delhi Foreign Office was telling the world that CIA personnel, and funding, had been instrumental in maintaining staging areas in Pakistan. The Delhi news release was not encumbered with facts. Every major news source in the West, and certainly in India, carried the story.

Since the advent of the Nixon administration, the CIA undertook a series of major efforts to destabilize selected governments in the lesser-developed world. After the election of President Reagan, the allocation of funds for overseas covert intelligence purposes was increased appreciably.

Given the deteriorating relationships between Delhi and Washington, CIA funds may have found their way into Sikh hands in Pakistan. Direct involvement with the Sikhs was unlikely. Since the assertion was believed in India, without refutation, the truth of the allegation was unimportant.

Compounding a felony, the Reagan Administration did not issue an official denial of the Punjabi caper. There was not even a policy statement pertaining to US neutrality in the Sub-Continent. The only denial from US sources emanated from the American Embassy in New Delhi. The denial was ignored by the Indian government which was obviously using the allegation to support domestic political objectives.

President Reagan should have considered an immediate denial from Washington which simultaneously proclaimed friendship with

India and Pakistan, neutrality in the Sub-Continent, and continuing US developmental assistance in the region.

In the absence of an effective US foreign policy pertaining to the Third World, the distinction between historic US concerns for democracy, and covert programs in the Sub-Continent, has eroded.

For the next several days in Calcutta, and in India, every Sikh will be considered a prime target. In addition, every person who appears to be American will be identified as an agent of the CIA. Prior to the assassination, Americans were thought to be friends of Pakistan rather than India. Now, with Sikhs allegedly involved in the assassination, there will not be any doubt.

Since the American Consulate compound is located in reasonable proximity to Amala Shankar's residence, where the luncheon was held, we left the luncheon immediately.

The traffic in every direction was heavy. Young men, in every form of conveyance, were lured to the downtown center. The Indian principle of "darshan" (approach greatness as closely as possible in the moment of need) is attracting them to potential injury through the violent acts of an irrational mob. There was an air of expectancy roughly comparable to walking to a football game in a college town. Without any disrespect for the deceased prime minister intended, a festive spirit was manifested coupled with a hint of adventure. Unthinking human insects were being drawn to the light of anarchy. We were concerned that the crowds would spot the "farangs," the Thai word for foreigners, in the backseat and decide to sacrifice our spirits to the intemperate Kali Goddess.

Supreo made a "Press" sign for the front windshield, and I extracted my National Press Club identification. Neither device would have deterred angry Hindus seeking revenge. At the same time, marginal acts provided a false sense of security and led us to believe that we were controlling our destiny.

A car passed with both the front and rear windows shattered. We were aware that the violence was escalating. Arriving at the American Consulate compound, we felt secure in the presence of the US Marine guard contingent and the high walls with barbed-wire trim.

In the few hours since the prime minister's assassination, not one Hindu whom we met has suggested that the loss of Mrs. Gandhi will affect India adversely, that Mrs. Gandhi was a popular leader, or that she will be missed. At the luncheon, one guest had a momentary display of emotion, and then suggested that the prime minister was the only Hindu political leader who supported the arts.

The prime minister did not generate affection. She never emulated the popular heritage of Gandhi and Nehru. Her left-oriented, pro-USSR, anti-USA, pro-Castro, undemocratic public stance won few admirers. Her policies ranging from detonating of a nuclear bomb through curtailment of press freedom produced a divided, chaotic, unhappy India.

We were instructed that a cable had been sent to the USIS headquarters in Delhi requesting guidance regarding the dispensation of the American visitors. The Public Affairs Officer in Calcutta was convinced that our lecture tour will be canceled, and that as soon as air travel is considered safe, we will be evacuated to another country.

The period of mourning will last for approximately ten days. Government offices and schools will be closed. Virtually all public events, including informal social gatherings, will be canceled or postponed.

Our USIS liaison officer disagrees with that conclusion. She feels that the Madras and Hyderabad commitments will be eliminated, and that we will continue the schedule in Delhi next week.

Under the Indian Constitution, which the prime minister chose to ignore frequently, the acting prime minister will be chosen by the ruling Congress Party within an unspecified period of time. To the surprise of no one, Mrs. Gandhi's son, Rajiv, was selected as her successor. Rajiv discloses a tabula rasa. Few pundits are willing to predict what political credo he will endorse.

Incredibly, during the evening after the prime minister's death, the Halloween party at the American Consulate compound proceeded on schedule. Guests were confined to residents of the compound. I was appalled by the insensitivity in failing to cancel the event. We decided to attend to assess the reaction of American government personnel to the assassination.

The death of the prime minister was not a topic of conversation. A secretary stated that all non-career US ambassadors (I happened to fall in that category) while assigned overseas, continue to discharge roles as active political partisans in the United States. She opined that there was nothing unethical when twenty-two of President Reagan's non-career ambassadorial appointees endorsed US Senator Jesse Helm's reelection campaign in North Carolina. I rose to the challenge, but failed to convince her that career and non-career ambassadors are held to the same level of performance which precludes politically-oriented action while representing the United States overseas. The topics of conversation reflected interest in US television programs, recent rest and recreation trips inside and outside of India, and the latest fashions. The spouse of a senior member of the consulate staff arrived yesterday and attended the party. She did not want to join her husband in India, and expressed disdain for her new life before she has experienced it.

November 1:

How is the credo of a politician communicated? Most of us are dependent upon the print media for substance and the electronic media for demeanor, style and personality. In spite of these modern "crutches," our judgments are formed in a subjective vacuum. The lessons of history are subject to periodic revision.

Prime Minister Indira Gandhi is illustrative. As a youngster, she sat at the feet of Mahatma Gandhi; attended secondary school and Oxford University in England; visited the USSR before the USA, and in sections of India, she is known as a spokesperson for the "rich."

As prime minister, she personally orchestrated the defeat of the elected Communist government in Kerala; negotiated a treaty of peace and friendship with the USSR; and allowed the Russians to train, supply, and advise the Indian defense establishment.

As the leader of the nonaligned countries, she condemned freedom of expression, US "imperialism," and world capitalism. In the West, she was usually perceived as the epitome of a left-wing activist and as an apologist for the USSR brand of communism.

In Calcutta she was despised because of the corrupt political party she represented. In the Punjab, she was deprecated for her totalitarian response to Sikh dissident efforts to attain increased autonomy. In Madras, she was pilloried for her heavy-handed usurpation of states' rights. In the field of communications, she was condemned for her repressive treatment of journalists and publishers. In the business community, she was considered a radical. In the student community, she was branded as a reactionary, and in the Moslem community, she was described as the Devil incarnate.

Subject to inevitable historical revisionism, it would appear that Indira Gandhi was the ultimate pragmatist who desired to remain in office and who realized that objective.

I arrived in India endorsing the stereotype that Indira Gandhi was clearly identified with a left-wing political philosophy and with elements of the Russian brand of communism. After five eventful days, I realize that the prime minister was a very successful politician who eschewed causes, per se; ignored visionary beliefs and programs; and survived by changing course rather than centering on a distant star. Most successful politicians are pragmatists. Prime Minister Gandhi could have taught the course.

November 2:

The prime minister died at approximately 9:30 a.m. on Wednesday, October 31st. Because there was uncertainty regarding succession, the official government of India announcement of her death was not released until 2:30 p.m. Domestically, government information sources did not issue a statement until a few hours later. In fact, All India Radio did not carry the initial announcement of the assassination until 5:30 p.m.

Following the assassination, the first English-language newspaper distributed on the streets of Calcutta at 2:00 p.m. carried the story that President Reagan had extended his condolences. This was one-half hour before the government of India official release.

The Russians will cite the CIA as the culprit. Congress I (Gandhi's national congress party faction) will endorse that contention, and the opposition parties will allege that Madame Gandhi enjoyed a secret alliance with the capitalists. The real culprit is the Ronald Reagan band of ideologues who fail to grasp the realities. International expertise is important. Political philosophy is secondary to effective working relationships. The Third World is not a pagan, illiterate wasteland, but a powerful moral force that may constitute a critical balance of power in an increasingly polarized world. Without thinking, the White House released the death announcement prematurely.

For three days, Patti and I have been under "house arrest." It has been strongly advised that we not leave the compound. Transportation is unavailable. The shops are closed. There are no television or radio programs. Newspapers have not been distributed at the compound.

During our confinement, we have been reading extensively about Calcutta. Several contemporary authors have captured the depravity and hopelessness of Calcutta and the necessity to accept reality in the presence of individual and collective suffering.

The "bustees" of Calcutta (temporary slums) are located on large tracts of land owned by very successful Indian businessmen. The landowners charge rent for a few square feet of land on which the residents place several pieces of cardboard and rags and construct putative homes. The rent is collected regularly by overseers who reside in two-story stone buildings which provide electricity to the tenants and which are spaced in the "bustee" areas like sentry towers in a concentration camp. Failure to pay rent in timely fashion necessitates immediate forced evacuation. The Bengali intellectuals, ignoring the "bustee" areas, are preoccupied with the poetry of Tagore; the eternal wisdom of Aurobindo, and the ethereal and ineffectual leadership of their primary historic hero, Bose.

The USIS program officer shared the rationale for failing to schedule a variety of lectures in Calcutta prior to the assassination. The program staff could not understand, based on my credentials, why I had been selected as a speaker during the Reagan Administration tenure, unless my views were reactionary. She did not want to expose the Bengali audiences, particularly the college age clientele, to my assumed conservative positions regarding student movements and voluntary service. The fact that I had served as one of the early Peace Corps staff members, the first Director of VISTA (Volunteers in Service to America), and president of three universities was lost in translation.

As a result, the innocuous performing arts topic was selected for the business executives who were affiliated with the Indian Chamber of Commerce.

Even if the USIS evaluation of my political proclivities had been correct, it would have served the interests of the United States to allow me to express diverse views in India. One of the objectives of the speakers' program was to expose audiences in lesser-developed countries to the complexity of democracy in action.

Before retiring, I tempted fate by taking a short walk outside the consulate compound. The streets were relatively free of traffic. I walked several blocks to the Maidan, a large, well-manicured park which surrounds the Queen Victoria Memorial.

The military, the police, and the mobs, had disappeared. Pedestrians were nervous, and they were interested in a white foreigner walking the streets. I admit that I took an occasional quick glance behind me, and that I was aware that sunset was approaching. There were few people in the park, but even during an emergency, "peddlers, beggars and dogs" honored the British-inspired signs which proscribed their presence in the Maidan.

In returning to the compound, I took another route which highlighted overturned vehicles, burned buses, several courageous street vendors, and a few knots of surly young men which I did not attempt to untangle. Subsequently, we were informed that the rioting and looting in Calcutta had been extensive.

For a few brief moments at the park, in the eye of the hurricane, I enjoyed a pocket of colonial metropolitan planning which represented the jewel of India in the imperial crown (the Raj).

This afternoon, the leadership of the USIS posts in Bombay and Calcutta, without involving US Embassy or USIS officials in New Delhi, decided that we should be evacuated to Bombay. Allegedly, violence in the Bombay region had been minimal. In the absence of policy guidance, the plan represented good sense.

After dark, we departed for Dum Dum Airport in a small van with only a consulate-assigned driver. The main roads were inundated with standing and walking groups and abandoned automobiles and buses. Police and security forces were not represented. After an eight hour delay, which was understandable under the circumstances, we departed for Bombay. In Bombay, we were informed by USIS personnel that the violence in Calcutta was extensive during the past evening, and that we should not have been authorized to leave.

November 3: Bombay (Mumbai)

In 1959, when I first visited Bombay, at 2:00 a.m., hundreds of residents were sleeping on the sidewalks in thin, white cotton sheets which gave the appearance of myriad corpses. Scores of sacred cows walked aimlessly on the sidewalks and streets. A long walk included the Gate to India, Raja Bai Tower, and Bombay University.

On this occasion, at 4:00 a.m., the streets were relatively clear. We went directly to a hearty breakfast at the Taj Mahal Hotel. The building was constructed in 1905 in anticipation of the arrival of the British heir apparent. After a lengthy nap, the USIS Program Officer told us that because of the national period of mourning, our official schedule would not resume until November 13th. We were advised not to leave the hotel because of actual and anticipated violence in Bombay, including the previous night near the airport. Evidently, the United States Information Service was dealing with a paucity of information or we would never have been authorized to leave Calcutta.

For two days, we vegetated at the hotel. Another form of "house arrest" produced a very negative psychological impact. Normally, several days at a modern hotel, without commitments, should be considered a vacation. If you are forbidden to leave the premises, that vacation becomes suspect.

November 5:

Without any communication from USIS, we took a walk in the area surrounding the hotel. The harbor and small islands in the Bombay Archipelago were inviting. The Gateway to India, which was constructed to commemorate the Prince of Wales visit, and which became the port of embarkation for the British troops following the independence of India in 1947, created a vision of colonial history. During the short walk, we were accosted by beggars and hawkers, propositioned by the omnipresent moneychangers, and stared at by the permanent residents. These incarnations of urban India would have been present at any time. Today, the atmosphere appeared to be charged without evident sparks.

November 6:

At the restaurant in the hotel, I ordered Thali which featured ten small cups of the hottest Indian curries. The tastes were delightful until I was overcome by the fire emanating from my throat and stomach. Within a few minutes, the conflagration led to a volcanic eruption accompanied by a few indescribables. For twenty-four hours, I drank hot tea and vowed to heed the warnings of my non-Indian stomach.

November 7:

At the American Consulate in Bombay (a former palace which includes offices and the Residence), we met the newly-appointed Consul General. He was surprised that we had been advised to remain at the hotel. Since the speaking commitments will not resume until November 13th, he suggested that we travel in the interim.

At the Branch USIS office, we received the news that the French Cultural Center across the street had been notified, via telephone, that the USIS building would be blown up. Five minutes before our arrival, all personnel had been evacuated from the building. The police had not yet arrived. We were ushered into the office of the Branch Public Affairs Officer. Two hours later, the all-clear signal was received from the bomb squad. It is not reassuring that a single unconfirmed telephone call can create an emergency and that appropriate procedures for such an emergency are nonexistent.

Since this was the day following the presidential election in the United States, the leaders of the Bombay community were invited to the USIS auditorium to watch the results unfold. In 1968, as US Ambassador to Kenya, I had used the same technique in Nairobi. On both occasions, although the results of the elections did not reflect my personal choices, the local citizens who were invited to attend were most receptive. Maps and charts depicting the major local and state results were updated frequently. The early returns showed that President Reagan was assured of decisive victories in every state in the East and Midwest. The District of Columbia was solidly for Senator Mondale. Reagan was leading in Minnesota. Senator Percy was losing in Illinois. As we watched, Minnesota swung marginally to Mondale, and the Southwest and West illustrated the magnitude of the Reagan sweep.

Utilizing the format of a US presidential election, every four years US overseas missions have a unique opportunity to expose host country leadership to the contents of the library; American personnel concerned with education and culture; the diversity and efficiency of the American media; and the meaning of free democratic elections.

Based on the telephone call, on the morning that the election results were made available to the community, guests were turned away at the door of the consulate offices. Members of the general public were informed that the building was closed. The impact of the exercise was marginal. The evils of international terrorism have just begun. It would appear that official American offices abroad are unprepared for the ordeal.

The forces of destruction, overt violence, and disinformation, are making it difficult for America to tell its story abroad. To correct the imbalance, it will be necessary for the President of the United States to acknowledge the threat; to devise a rational response including improved security measures, and to educate the American people regarding the magnitude of the threat.

In India, the average citizen now believes that the United States is imperialistic, capitalistic, militaristic, racist, prejudiced against the Third World, disinterested in foreign affairs, affluent, and incapable of launching effective international educational and informational programs.

President Ronald Reagan has won an unprecedented victory. The American people have been misled. In four more years, unless a meaningful security program is inaugurated it will be extremely difficult to take significant corrective action.

My sense of discouragement is palpable and broader in context than Indian curry. The realistic and generally effective foreign affairs programs of the 1960s have been replaced by conservatism, jingoism, insularism, and the pursuit of materialistic objectives.

The American people have not been told the truth about the world in which we live. The trend began with Richard Nixon. He has been ably assisted by Vietnam, Watergate, Gerald Ford, Jimmy Carter, and now President Reagan.

Following the assassination, all USIS Branch Chiefs were summoned to Delhi. For three days, their expertise was not utilized in creating a responsive information program. At Prime Minister Gandhi's funeral, three former US Ambassadors to India paid their respects. In India, the public information impact was ignored. In-depth interviews concerning their reactions could have been arranged. Radio clips could have been prepared reflecting their reactions to India after a gap of years. Following an appropriate waiting period, television tapings could have been aired reflecting the genuine concern and goodwill emanating from the American people.

Another opportunity has been lost to bring the attributes of the world's most significant democracy to the attention of the mass of overseas citizens who must rely upon misinformation for their views of the United States.

At the Taj Mahal Hotel, we attended a special performance of Indian classical dancing. Mime is the point of departure for all classical dancing. In contrast to the "free flow" of modern dance, or even post-Balanchine ballet, each motion and facial expression of the dancer conveys the elements of a story. The tales usually relate to Lord Krishna, the Child God, and his encounters with creatures of fantasy in a juvenile world.

The bare feet of the dancers are ugly and omnipresent. The female dancer is invariably obese. The costumes are the antithesis of feminism accentuating a more than generous derriere. Compared to Thai dancing, the stylized hand, facial and head movements are jarring, repetitive and monotonous.

Indian musical instrumentation is the premium offering in the performing arts genre. The music incorporates a distinctive "beat." Percussion provides occasional rhythm, but other instruments share the load. As a former drummer, I am intrigued that the Indian counterpart is released from the obligation to keep time. Drums are utilized for solo parts and for improvisation. The drum heads are finely tuned with a small hammer and protected from the elements by cotton "comforters." The harmonium provides the beat: a box that looks like a simplified accordion, requires minimal training or expertise, and does not even qualify as a musical instrument.

The drummer emulates the rhythm of the dancer's feet. The percussion rudiments are more numerous and more complex than those in Western drumming.

After the evening's performance, I chatted with the drummer. He has studied percussion for ten years. He is deriving his stimulation from a substance that he chews and/or injects.

When I was ten years old, I participated in a Gene Krupa drum contest at the Eckel Theater in Syracuse, New York. As a winner, I was presented with a pair of autographed drumsticks by the master himself. At that time, Mr. Krupa was also securing his inspiration from a substance that he chewed or injected. Percussionists must require special stimulation.

The assassination of a national leader condemns a security system. Widespread subsequent violence condemns a nation. The sustained violence following the death of Mrs. Gandhi has produced innumerable deaths, injuries, and looting throughout Northern India, particularly in the Delhi and Calcutta regions. From garbled press reports, it would appear that the Congress I (I for Indira) Party has instigated many of the violent attacks on the Sikh communities.

India is a land of ultimate contrasts: vegetarianism and Kali-cult bestiality towards animals; deliberate peaceful resistance to authority and mindless or premeditated violence; religious sensitivity and the epitome of religious dogmatism; ultra-sophistication in the performing arts based on centuries of exemplary tradition; abject poverty coupled with the absence of caring leaders, and innate common courtesy in the same arena with gross public behavior.

Undoubtedly, the unprecedented pressure of population creates a boiling point of irritability. It might be expected that a diverse culture which begat Mahatma Gandhi: the graceful namasté greeting of respect; the principle of nonviolence, and the inner peace of premeditation, could manifest a modicum of concern for the plight of the homeless, the hungry, the impoverished, the ill, and believers in other deities. I recognize that India is not the exclusive culprit, but the scale of the problems in India is frightening.

The funeral service for Indira Gandhi represented a poignant example of ambivalent India. Stoically, the remaining son, Rajiv, the newly-appointed prime minister, applied the flaming torch to his dead mother's face which ignited the oil, ghee, garments, and wood comprising the funeral pyre. While family, friends, and Indian dignitaries paid homage to the deceased by circling the pyre, uniformed and non-uniformed public servants roughly handled those who approached the pyre without the requisite credentials and beat back the teeming masses hungering for a dash of "darshan." Helicopters intruded on the sanctity of the classical Hindu service. Priests dressed in white attire poured additional oily ghee over the remains. Empty cans were left within a few feet of the deceased. Scores of people were allowed to throw flammable debris on the former prime minister to insure that her soul would enjoy a swift ascent into the Hindu version of heaven.

Looking bewildered and discomfited, the dignitaries sat in several rows at a considerable, and safe, distance from the pyre. The representative of the Holy See, in his irrelevant robes and beads, seemed to exemplify that bemusement.

The Indian government television network covered the festivities exclusively. The camera shots were carefully controlled to avoid closeups of crowds, of people being trampled to death, distant smoke resulting from anti-Sikh violence, or the evidence of anarchy which surrounded the relatively peaceful "eye" of the funeral pyre. As the controlled camera panned the leadership of the world, the British expatriate providing the English-language audio stressed the presence of Third World and socialist block representatives. The delegation from the United States was not mentioned or shown. That delegation included Secretary of State Schultz and former Ambassadors to India, Galbraith, Goheen, and Moynihan.

Subsequently, twenty urns of human ash, generously supplemented by the cinders from the cord of wood, were dispatched with haste to major urban areas and to the Andaman Islands. Following a decent interval for regional mourning, the remains will be consolidated in Delhi.

On the day following the funeral, Prime Minister Rajiv Gandhi, a former airline pilot, while wearing an oxygen mask, threw several parcels of cremated maternal remains from the open bomb bay of an Indian Air Force transport plane over an extensive area of the majestic Himalaya Range.

The ritual has been concluded. The leadership of Congress I, wishing to maintain political power, has arbitrarily anointed the son. This act perpetuates the dynasty until the elections scheduled for December 24.

Government of India releases concerning post-assassination violence, have been inaccurate and misleading. The intent has been to curb further violence through propaganda and to assign the unsubstantiated blame for the death of the prime minister to alleged foreign conspiracies including the specifically cited Central Intelligence Agency. Without exception, the Indian media have relied upon the government of India pap. By reading the Indian newspapers, it would appear that the violence was limited to a few minor incidents in the Delhi region. Twenty-four hours later, when an edition of the *International Herald Tribune* arrived at the Taj Mahal Hotel newsstand in Bombay, we were exposed for the first time to news of widespread violence, death, and pillage.

The first authentic report in an Indian newspaper (we were reading several newspapers every day) appeared in the *Indian Express* on November 16th. It incorporated an *Express* News Service release from New Delhi, dated November 15th. The release stated that the violence had produced a total of 1,277 deaths in Delhi and 518 deaths in six other cities and states, including Calcutta. One hundred and sixty-seven places of worship had been attacked. Thousands of people had been evicted from their homes and were now residing in temporary refugee camps.

At no time, including the November 16th story in the *Indian Express*, has the word "Sikh" been used. Repeatedly, the government of India, and major elements of the Indian press, have been attacking Western news agencies, particularly in the United States, for reporting a biased view of post-assassination violence which allegedly portrays India in an erroneous (read, unfavorable) light. These allegations have been accompanied by uncorroborated reports suggesting that the CIA actually instigated the dastardly act.

A group of lawyers (unnamed) accredited to practice before the Indian Supreme Court, alleged that the CIA had masterminded the death of Mrs. Gandhi. The report was not labeled as a rumor. There have not been any subsequent news reports clarifying or retracting the story.

If, on the day following the assassination of President John F. Kennedy, a group of unnamed lawyers accredited to practice before the US Supreme Court, had alleged that the KGB was responsible for the death of the president the allegation would have been subjected to stringent and prolonged press scrutiny.

Innumerable news stories have appeared in the last few days which illustrate the lack of expertise and integrity of Indian government and private media representatives. It is deplorable that India has assumed Third World leadership in denouncing the alleged tyranny of the Western media and the need for "balanced" (read, government controlled) media coverage. The New World Information Order must be exposed as a brake on freedom of the press. Given the perversion of this concept in India, it is unfortunate that freedom of information, and the New World Information Order, were deleted from the list of lecture topics.

Indira Gandhi was a clever mortal who wielded political power for personal motives. Following her death, she has been converted into a veritable saint. Overnight, she has been identified as a bird-watching conservationist, a lover of classical music, a warm supporter of the Girl Scouts, a satisfied wearer of Bata shoes, and a close friend of every person who saw her at a distance.

It is axiomatic that deceased celebrities become Jacks and Jills of all trades and attributes. While they were alive, many of them were fortunate to be cited for living. We tend to assign Olympian stature to the notorious deceased who were merely human.

Human beings impute undeserved attributes to the dead and withhold earned tributes from the living. Death eliminates competition. It is foolish to envy the deceased. Since the ultimate triumph is living, even without purpose or distinction, it is somewhat reassuring to be a survivor.

It is relatively easy to pay a meaningless tribute to the dead by suggesting that they endorsed what we believe and seldom practice.

November 8 / Karnataka State

After arising at 3:00 a.m., we left Santa Cruz Airport in Bombay. Following a succession of evening flights, it was a special treat to step off the plane in Bangalore in bright sunlight, with a cool breeze, and a relatively temperate climate, at an elevation of 1,500 feet.

Bangalore is southeast of Bombay and has been designated the capital of Karnataka State. In a few years, it has become a large, urban, modern, industrial complex. The new enterprises include the only American entrepreneurial venture in India (which manufactures jet engines for Indian military planes). In the midst of sprawl, colorful flowers and trees bloom in profusion. The streets are broad. Basic public services are operational. Although poverty exists, there is the expectation that a growing economy will foster a short-term improvement.

We hired a car and a driver named Krishna. As we left Bangalore, Krishna asked whether his girlfriend could join us for the lengthy trip. In prior years, before our exposure to the lesser-developed world, we would have acquiesced. Now, with the experience to identify a con game, we vetoed the proposal.

Following national highway number 49 west, we competed with myriad cows, goats, pigs, donkey carts, jitneys, buses, bikes, bullock carts, trucks, and waves of humanity on the main artery between Bangalore and Bombay (nine hundred kilometers away). With the possible exception of the coastal route in Portugal, I have never felt as vulnerable in an automobile. Unless you drive at excessive speeds, you seem to stand still. Wrecks of assorted trucks and buses dotted the landscape.

At Tunkur, we turned further west on the main road to coastal Mangalore. The scenery was diverse and interesting, and reminded us slightly of the Rift Valley in Kenya. Other views were more tropical and roughly comparable to the Philippines with water buffaloes bathing in the canals and the populace planting rice in the well-irrigated paddies.

The rural villages in the area are bleak, crowded, and devoid of charm; however, a few of them are appealing from a distance.

The tempo is related to subsistence. The children smile at strangers. The food supply appears to be adequate. There is local pride in the admixture of a rice culture coupled with cattle and goat-herding. Color is restricted to an occasional blue or red sari or the white and pastel temple facades.

The open spaces are glorious. The sunsets are exquisite. The vibrant full moon can only be replicated in the tropics. In contrast to other regions of India, which can only be improved through extensive mandatory sterilization, the children of Mysore can glance to the future with a semblance of hope.

Arriving in Hassan in mid-afternoon, we checked into the Hassan Ashok Hotel. The ambience approximates rural Thailand except for the absence of klong jars and commodes that are flush, if you will pardon the reference, with the floor.

After a brief pit stop, we headed for Belur and the Chennakasava Temple which was constructed by King Vishnuvardhana (an excellent "spelling bee" word) in 1116 AD. When you consider that Angkor Wat was built by the Kymers in Cambodia in the fourteenth century, the temple in Belur is truly a historic relic. In contrast to Angkor Wat, the restoration is primitive. Although the original design and craftsmanship were precise, the style is too "busy" to be architecturally or esthetically pleasing. The horse and elephant figures are commanding, but they are not integrated with the basic structure. There is no indication that in the twelfth century, the residents considered the temple part of their daily lives.

The beggars and hawkers, of variable ages, were persistent, offensive, and disturbing. It is difficult to enter a public arena in India without having your senses jarred by the prevalence of disease, the degradation associated with the beggar-hawker trades, and the crushing mass of humanity. The rude, constant, physically-oriented sales pitch of the beggars and hawkers thinly disguises a latent violence. Everywhere in India, where more than two people gather, with the possible exception of the private homes and clubs of the affluent, the seeds of violence are lurking. When I am exposed to a single individual in India, I am mesmerized by the warmth, the gentleness, and the countenance of human concern. India is not only a land of contrasts, but it is also the ultimate in the conflict between love and hate in the same milieu.

Beating a hasty retreat from Belur, we took the side road fourteen kilometers to Halebid and landed at the Hoysaleswara Temple, which was dedicated to Lord Siva in the tenth century.

In contrast to Belur, the original temple (except for a recently-affixed cement roof) is surrounded by flourishing lawns and gardens which generate the proper perspective.

For a few moments, I was able to walk in privacy. I exulted in the independence, the lovely scenery, the profuse birdlife, and the sense of peace. As dusk approached, I enjoyed wagtails, mynahs, parrots, swallows, bee-eaters, egrets, hawks, vultures, crows, shrikes, flycatchers, and rollers all vying, successfully, with Lord Siva for my undivided attention.

Returning to the hotel at dark, Patti retired with the inevitable "bug" associated with the lesser-developed world. Krishna retired to the backseat of his automobile. I retired to write with the assistance of a seven-watt bulb. The feeble result was one day's journal entry which attempted to convey the complex, misunderstood, exasperating, enervating, fascinating environment known as India.

November 9 / Mysore:

After a dawn start, we arrived at the Gomateswara Statute on Indragiri Hill at the Jain religious retreat at Shravanbelgola. If we were asked to repeat that location in a geography quiz, none of us would have completed the sixth grade.

After hurdling the inevitable beggars, we took thirty minutes to climb the 665 steps to the summit where Gomateswara presides amidst detritus, graffiti, chanting priests, and unattractive wooden structures which serve as barriers from visitors.

The statue is cut from a single stone. It represents the antithesis of art. Although the sculptor intended to create a replica of man, the result is grotesque. The huge, prominent penis resembles the reproductive organ of a gigantic bull. If the approximation of a human figure possessed horns, I would still disparage the artist's mastery of basic human figures.

Every twelve years, the Mahamastabhisekla Festival is held at Shravanbelgola. The festival would be held more frequently, but the spelling of the name precludes timely invitations. At the festival, fortunes in ghee, precious stones, and other valuables are poured over Gomateswara's head by Jain devotees. Unfortunately, nothing remained from previous outpourings of devotion to disguise even partially the dominating penis.

The next stop was the summer palace of Tipu Sultan which is located sixteen kilometers from Mysore at Srirangapatna. Tipu Sultan, a Muslim potentate immortalized in the West by Rudyard Kipling, was one of the most powerful rulers in Indian history. Through a series of impregnable forts, he effectively controlled the southern half of the

Indian sub-peninsula. He was feared by the British. With French support, he waged many successful battles against the Redcoats. In the final battle, Tipu's fort and palace were destroyed. He was killed and the British gained control of the empire. For the next century, the rebuilt palace became the residence of a series of British commanding generals.

The grounds of the palace are lovely. Although the main building has enjoyed minimal maintenance, the opulent, and yet tasteful, style of the Sultan has been captured. If Tipu had been victorious in the final battle, and his progeny had avoided significant battles with the British and the French, Southern India might now be a distinct country without British-style marching bands or the legacy of the National Congress Party.

In midday we arrived at the Lalitha Mahal Hotel in Mysore. Built in 1921, the structure was the guest palace for visitors of the Maharaja of Mysore. In 1974, it was converted to a hotel. The marble halls are elegant. The terraced gardens, now in disarray, must have been superb. The view of Mysore and the main palace, eleven kilometers to the west, are worth the daily hotel rate.

I have now been poisoned twice by poorly screened Indian food. Since Calcutta, I have been exposed exclusively to overly-spiced cuisine. Temporarily, the hot spices tend to disguise the less than hygienic ingredients.

Based on a lifetime of comparative exposure, and a willingness to try virtually any dish which is designated as "food," I have eaten in scores of village "cafes" in the Philippines, Korea, Thailand, and Kenya without a day of illness. In contrast, I am finding it difficult to consume a meal in India which is palatable, digestible, or adaptable for my internal combustion.

The maharaja's palace, built in Indo-Saracenic style, projects excessively bright and less than complementary colors. The garish decor is uninspiring, but the lovely grounds reminded us of the Nymphenburg Castle in Munich. If the beggars, and self-designated guides, were excommunicated, a tour of the estate would be splendid.

On the Carivery River, twenty miles from Mysore, we spent two stimulating hours at the Ranganathittu Bird Sanctuary. Three small islands comprise the preserve. Although the breeding season precluded the boat trip to the islands, we identified water birds from the shore. Several species were abundant including the White Ibis and the Openbill Stork. School children were present in generous supply. It is reassuring that the Indian government is encouraging the next generation to enjoy the priceless flora and fauna.

Returning to the hotel, we stopped at the Brindavan Garden which incorporates a series of terraces and fountains at one of the oldest and largest dams in India. A motion picture was being produced in one of the gardens. It was novel to have the crowds ogling the cinema stars rather than entertaining two foreign travelers.

November 10:

After driving for two hours to the Bandipur Wildlife Preserve, we were notified that the premises were open to the public from 6:00 a.m. to 9:00 a.m. and from 4:00 p.m. to 6:00 p.m. Since it was noon, rather than returning to Mysore, we decided to cross the border into another state, Tamil Nadu, which is the southernmost state of India. Our driver convinced the border guard that we should be allowed entrance without a permit.

At the Mudumalai Wildlife Sanctuary, located ten miles beyond the border, the premises were also closed until 4:00 p.m. I took the Gaur (an Indian bison) by the horns and decided to make a personal plea. I flashed my National Press Club and National Audubon Society identification cards. In spite of that confrontation, we were allowed to enter. An off-duty guide agreed to take us for a nature walk upon payment of a ridiculous fee. The walk was delightful. We uncovered a Greater Flameback (woodpecker) and a Blackhooded Oriole.

Our guide was a gold mine of suspect commentary. A tiger was seen yesterday. That chilling sound was a Giant Squirrel. A Guar can withstand a tiger's charge. The largest species of python swallowed a Sambur (large deer) at this spot last week. The python was unable to move for three days. Panthers are frequently observed in the sanctuary.

In real life, our game viewing was restricted to several small Spotted deer and a bevy of black-faced, silvery-grey, common Langur monkeys.

We returned to Mysore through fertile, irrigated, farming country which displayed greater affluence than our previous exposure to rural

India. In Mysore we climbed (in the car) Chamundi Hill which is the highest elevation in the region. At the pinnacle, we found the inevitable Hindu Temple. There was also a massive, black statue of Nandi the Bull. Nandi is considered the reincarnation of Lord Siva. Fortunately, the Hindus are not as explicit as the Jains in depicting certain parts of the anatomy.

Before dusk, I took a long walk in the vicinity of the hotel. The sunset was grand. I was not followed or importuned. The birds were responsive to the cooler air, and I was temporarily at ease with my fickle friend called India.

November 11 / Mysore to Bangalore to Goa:

With the exception of a few commercially-inspired, self-serving paid announcements in the local newspapers, there is not any indication that the state of Karnataka (Mysore) is particularly concerned about the death of Prime Minister Gandhi. Government flags are placed at half-mast. Official functions have been canceled or postponed. From every quarter, it is clear that Mrs. Gandhi was seldom revered or cited with approbation.

It seems ludicrous, but we are spending more for drinking water than for food. In five different locations in India, we have purchased the only brand (Bisler) of bottled water in the same unmarked bottles except for the brand name followed by "Acqua Mineral." The actual contents, weight, locus of bottling, and company name are not displayed. It is conceivable that the water emanates from the nearest tap.

The price range varies appreciably. To pay from $1.00 to $2.00 for a small bottle of ostensibly potable water seems insane. On the other hand, the alternative to insanity is untenable.

Arising at 3:00 a.m., we caught the dawn flight from Bangalore Airport to Goa. At the Goa Airport, we met a former Kenyan Asian (Indian) who was representing the Bogmalo Beach (Oboroi) Hotel. Based on his representation, we were deposited by hotel van at the door. After a distasteful luncheon, a swim in the pool, a nap (interrupted by children's screams beneath our window), a four-mile run on the sandy beach, another swim in the pool, a move to a quieter room, and early retirement, we were prepared to cope with the former Portuguese colony.

November 12:

This morning we took the hotel-provided bus into Panaji, the principal urban area of Goa. We passed through the former city of Goa which was deliberately destroyed by fire following a cholera epidemic.

Goa enjoys 62 miles of coastline, 40 miles inland, and is located on the Indian Ocean 250 miles south of Bombay. For several centuries, Goa served as the capital of Portuguese India. In 1947, following independence, the Indian government sponsored myriad incursions in an effort to wrest control from the colonial power. In December, 1963, Indian military troops invaded the territory. A year later, Goa was incorporated into India.

Walking through the main streets of Panaji, we visited a sixteenth century Catholic Church which was built from lignite (a locally-mined soft coal) and named in honor of St. Francis Xavier whose remains are permanently displayed.

The church was constructed with the generous support of a ship captain who became a lifetime friend of the Saint. The exterior of the church is ugly. The interior is grotesque. The cheap, nonprofessional paintings of a bleeding Christ make the goat-killing Kali worshipers in Calcutta look like Boy Scouts.

I have never been impressed with the Portuguese as colonialists (my first-hand knowledge is confined to Macao and Mozambique). Courtesy of Henry the Navigator, the Portuguese became superb sailors, and obtained colonies throughout Asia and Africa. When they departed, they did not leave behind any moral or governmental structure except an enervating church. They did not establish an indigenous educational base or a social ethic. As in Africa, the Portuguese departed from Goa without creating a positive heritage.

In contrast to the Mysore region, the inbreeding in Goa has produced a lethargic strain. Civic pride is nonexistent. The Indian invasion spawned inadequate financial support from the central treasury in New Delhi. Four centuries of Portuguese control created a malaise, which includes a generic hostility toward strangers.

The "Rome of the East" bears no relationship to the metropole unless you consider the omnipresent and omnipotent Catholic Church as a redeeming feature. Where the British colonialists left bad feelings and solid civic institutions, the Portuguese merely left.

After an hour on the dismal trek through Panaji, we bargained for a taxi. Paying the same fare as if we had not bargained, we arrived at the hotel in time for lunch. Patti "bargained" for a pair of "rare" Rajistan quilted tablecloths (small) from a hawker on the beach. We later discovered a large quantity of the same rarity at a local market.

At Calangute Beach at the northern end of Goa, the main drawing card was a gaggle of foreign, nude, hippie bathers. Fortunately, the natural beauty of the seacoast was not blighted by this notable attraction. We were intrigued by a movie crew photographing two emaciated white males who were wearing bikinis. If you travel, you are bound to reap memorable rewards.

The "back road" return to the hotel revealed attractive rice paddies, relaxing ocean views, and crumbling former Portuguese estates, which established a sense of balance in our evaluation of Goa.

November 13 / Goa to Bombay:

After a morning devoted to nursing colds and the packing ritual, we departed for Bombay. With an hour to spare, I departed for the United States Information Service in Bombay to deliver a lecture, "Performing Arts in the United States." The audience was composed of artists, musicians, art patrons, representatives of the media, and businessmen and housewives who are addicted to the performing arts. The brief lecture was converted into a roundtable discussion which stressed the training of creative talent and the public and private funding prognosis for performing arts ventures.

The Consul General hosted a dinner in our honor at the residence. The attendees included the Chief Justice of Bombay, the editor of the *Illustrated Weekly* who was also a poet, and the Director of Bombay Television.

The Parsees of Bombay are an intriguing leadership component. Of the 90,000 who live in India, the overwhelming majority reside in the Bombay area.

Several centuries ago, the Parsees were driven from Iran because of their Zoroastrian religious credo which included fire worship. Through good works and diligent effort, the Parsees have become respected by all political and religious factions in India. Because they do not represent a political threat, they have been allowed to amass great wealth from commercial pursuits. Zubin Mehta, the former maestro of the New York Philharmonic, which is resident at Lincoln Center, is the most renowned overseas Parsee.

In Bombay, the "Towers of Silence" constitute the Parsee center for disposing of the dead. Nonbelievers are forbidden to visit the grounds. Airplane pilots have been alerted to avoid overflights. Even Parsee devotees are prohibited from observing the sanctum where the burial rites are performed.

When a Parsee dies, his or her remains are placed in the sanctum, in the open air, for the vultures to consume. Lenin was wrong. Religion is much more than an opiate. Distributing cremated ashes over the countryside reflects a form of poetic justice. Leaving the non-cremated remains for the vultures lacks judicial appeal. Mankind has certainly devised mysterious ways in which to observe the tenets of religious myth.

November 14 / Bombay to Pune:

We arose at 5:00 a.m. and departed from the Bombay station on a train that is inappropriately called "the Deccan Queen." Decca is a large plateau in Central India. In the first-class cars, the names of the passengers, and their assigned seats, are posted on the exterior surface of the car near the entrance. In my humble opinion, this represents an invasion of privacy, and in the present emergency, a minor security problem. Every passerby, including the beggars and hawkers who are allowed free access to the train, can learn which individuals are taking the train and which seats they will occupy.

The five-hour ride to Pune south of Bombay in Maharashtra State was noisy and tedious. The "express" is in reality a "local" and to characterize this particular train as a "queen" does not capture the essence of royalty. A delicious omelet was served on a small section of wax paper, and the queen's dignity was restored.

At the Pune station, we were met by the Chief Administrative Officer of the Tata Management Training Centre and escorted to our spacious accommodations at the Centre Guest House. The Centre is responsible for middle-level training for the highly-diversified Tata conglomerate. For example, seventy percent of all heavy trucks sold in India are manufactured by Tata Industries.

The Centre's curriculum is modern, pragmatic, and emphasizes the group dynamics methodology which was created by the Bethel Experiment in Maine. The instructional approach is antiquated, but the 6:00 a.m. compulsory devotionals adds a unique requirement. The choice is restricted to Yoga or Transcendental Meditation.

Upon arrival at the University of Poona (the differentiation in the spelling of the city and the university is correct), we visited the Vice Chancellor (President) whose offices are located in the residence (palace) of the former British Governor. The Vice Chancellor is a physicist as are virtually all of the senior university officials whom we met. The Graduate Physics Department at the University of Poona enjoys the reputation as the premium department in that discipline in India.

The Vice Chancellor is responsible for administering more than twenty separate undergraduate campuses which serve the needs of 100,000 students. All graduate programs for this system emanate from the Poona central campus.

After a luncheon at which we met the deans and graduate department heads, we visited the Physics, Biology (which includes Zoology), and Computer Science departments. In each department, groups of graduate students recited their rote lines for the temporary guests.

During the past twenty years, I have visited (as the president of three universities) innumerable university facilities where I was expected to ask basic, friendly, noncontroversial questions about an infinite variety of esoteric subjects. The litany of questions can be resurrected from memory, but the answers have been lost in antiquity.

After "tea" with the members of the graduate faculty and selected graduate students on the open roof of the Communications Department building, I addressed the Academic Forum on "Evolving Higher Education Objectives in the United States." The Forum was composed of all members of the graduate faculty. Approximately four hundred students and academicians were present. The questions stressed opportunities for blacks in the United States, the preparation of teachers, and tenure criteria and practice.

At the evening dinner at the Tata Centre, we met Tata managers from all over India. They were an impressive group with sustaining entrepreneurial objectives.

The city of Pune is crowded, industrial, and depressing. For us, the one ray of hope was the visit to the Kelkar Museum. The museum was created by the ninety-one-year-old Raja Dinkar. It includes an impressive array of Indian antiques: massive mahogany doors, a treasure trove of drums, tapestries, lamps, and icons.

November 15 / Pune to Bombay:

We boarded the Deccan Queen for the return trip to Bombay. Today's version of royalty was "the fast train" not the "express." We were deposited in Bombay in three and one-half hours. Once again, we were served remarkably delicious cheese omelets on wax paper. The cost of the omelet was fifty cents. Amtrak should take lessons from the Indian Railway System.

Following our return to the Taj Mahal Hotel for the third time, we visited the offices of Jamshed Bhabha, Chairman of Tata Services Ltd. Mr. Bhabha is an Anglo-Indian by culture, a Parsee by religion, a businessman by profession, and a charmer by training. He is responsible, under the pro forma policy guidance of the only surviving Tata, for the operations of the entire Tata empire. Mr. Bhabha prefers "interests" to "empire".

After Mr. Bhabha's lecture about the wonders of private enterprise, we returned to the hotel as luncheon guests of the Tata "interests." Since Mr. Bhabha happens to be the creator, principal donor, and Trustee-in-Charge (Chairman of the Board) of the National Centre for the Performing Arts, we were conveyed to the Centre in Mr. Bhabha's Mercedes.

The Centre is impressive. It was designed by Philip Johnson who was responsible for a major component of the architecture at Lincoln Center in New York City. The acoustical work was completed by Cyril Harris who also did comparable work at Avery Fisher Hall which serves as home for the New York Philharmonic at Lincoln Center.

At the Centre, the Tata Theatre, which seats 1,000, is beautiful. The art museum is exciting, and the waterfront location—on filled land—is breathtaking.

In late afternoon, I visited the Vice Chancellor of the University of Bombay, M.S. Gore, whose field of expertise is Indian family life. Dr. Gore is a charming scholar who controls the destiny of 150,000 students on forty campuses for one of the premium universities in India. His office is also located in a former palace of a British governor who knew how to enjoy life in the colonies.

Dr. Gore is completing a three-year term which is not subject to renewal. Previously, he was Director of the Tata Institute of Social Sciences. Without success, and with acute frustration, he is attempting to decentralize the university. As I learned as Chancellor of Long Island University, which combined three discrete campuses at three disparate locations with three distinctive student bodies, and three vastly different communities, once centralization occurs, it is virtually impossible to wrest authority from the core. Even when the rationale for centralization is faulty or outmoded, power is seldom amenable to rational change.

En route to the hotel, I detoured to the Bombay Museum of Natural History. I was hopeful that I might pay my respects to the 81-year-old distinguished ornithologist, Dr. Salim Ali. Unfortunately, Dr. Ali only appears at the office for a few hours each morning. I was able to tour the unadorned, prestigious museum and to obtain a copy of Dr. Ali's field guide to Indian Birds.

In the evening, as the guests of Mr. Bhabha, we attended a special performance of Indian classical dances featuring Dr. Kanak Rele and her troupe.

The acoustics at the National Performing Arts Center were perfect. The seats were superb. The music, which included a unique male duet, was acceptable. Compared to our previous exposure to the medium, the dancing was mediocre. Since all Indian classical dance is based on the Ashta Rasa (mime) which depicts the eight human sentiments (love, laughter, sorrow, anger, courage, fear, disgust, and surprise), the basic drama was intriguing.

When a dancer attempts to capture intricate emotions, through precise facial expressions, only a few sentiments can be captured with accuracy. Nuances tend to be lost, and the distinction between a grimace and a smile may be illusory. Unless the dancers are particularly skillful, Indian dancing may become a potpourri of unattractive grimaces.

In the Ashtapadi Dance, I enjoyed the portrayal of Lord Krishna (based on the Bhagavad-Gita) playing ball, swimming, and dancing with ecstatic abandon. As usual, the percussion section was exemplary.

The versatility was astounding. The vina (a southern India relative of the sitar) performer played a creative and haunting rhythm which was barely audible.

November 16 / Bombay to Bhopal:

After three hours sleep, we left the Bombay Hotel at 4:00 a.m. The flight to Bhopal was punctuated by a pit stop at Indore. In Bhopal, we were met by the Chief Administrative Officer of the Bharat Bhavan (House of India) Arts Center who took us to the Jehan Numa Palace Hotel overlooking the city.

Bhopal, the capital of the state of Madhya Pradesh (meaning the center of India) is northeast of Bombay and south of Delhi. It was built around two lakes by a succession of Begums. It is known as the city which was constructed and ruled by women.

The Taj-ul-Masajid is one of the largest mosques in India. From a distance, the exterior facade is architecturally pleasing. The interior main hall and huge courtyard are drab and intimidatingly cold.

On a brief tour of the city, we admired an elephant carrying building supplies, noted the impossible human crunch of another Indian metropolitan area, and visited the Archeological Museum.

At the museum, we wandered through a replica of the Bhimbetka caves. The caves pinpoint rock wall paintings from the Stone Age. We acquired a facsimile of a Buddha head which was cast at the museum. At least, it will be easer to transport than an antique wooden door.

Ashok Vajpayi, the founder, mentor, and director of the Arts Center, and a prominent official in the state government, conducted a personal tour of the center. With a vision, and supreme self-confidence, he had convinced the state to build an arts complex at a choice location overlooking Upper Lake. Permission was granted with the caveat that the center would not impede the view of the governor, who lived above the site. Honoring that edict, a "non-building" was erected which is a congeries of four large underground buildings with a total footage of 100,000 square feet. At the surface, only four small domes are visible.

The building was inaugurated by Prime Minister Gandhi. It serves as the situs for the first repository of tribal art in India; the finest collection of contemporary Indian art; the most celebrated library of Indian poetry, and the most distinguished array of drama scripts and posters. Of paramount importance, the center trains young musicians in classical Indian instruments, provides a forum in which renowned poets from many countries interact, and plans and directs an annual series of national and international plays which draw special guests of the caliber of Peter Brook.

That evening, at the Bharat Bhavan Center, I delivered a lecture, "the Status of the Performing Arts in the USA." The audience included visual and performing artists, students, poets, patrons of the arts, and interested citizens from Bhopal.

Speaking in a sunken theater, with the audience on three sides, I used a series of "straw vote" questions to ascertain the level of English facility. Reassured that I was being understood by the majority, I presented a summary of current performing arts trends in the United States and attempted to correlate those trends with contemporary developments to which we had been exposed in India. I asked Ashok to join me in fielding questions.

At a dinner following the presentation, at which each of the guests sat on the floor, the conversation ranged from Czechoslovakian fiction, to the University of Iowa creative writing program, to indigenous Indian folk music. The educated Indian loves to talk. I might hazard a guess that the generalization might apply to the intellectual elite in many countries.

Following dinner, Omprakash Chourasiya, who has reintroduced the classical hundred-stringed Santoor into north Indian contemporary classical music, gave me a copy of his latest cassette.

November 17:

In early morning, we drove forty kilometers to the Bhimbetka Caves. Since their discovery by a British archeologist in the 1930s, the Bhimbetka Caves have been desecrated by waves of adult delinquents. It is difficult to distinguish the remarkable Stone Age drawings from the contemporary mindless graffiti. If our era is remembered for its graffiti, that memory will not linger on.

In returning to the airport, we were informed that our flight would be delayed for four hours. Thirty minutes later, the flight was canceled, and no options were offered.

Based on a hot tip, we took a taxi to the railway station where the scheduled fourteen-hour train to Delhi was eleven hours behind schedule. Leading a baggage safari through a Sargasso Sea of humanity, we secured a taxi back to the Jehan Numa Hotel where we learned that it was fully booked.

To add insult to minimal injury, a cable was waiting for us from USIS Delhi which informed us that "ten Americans were leaving Delhi for Frankfurt on Monday, November 19 at 5:00 a.m. Your reservation is made in Moria (Maurya) Sheraton Hotel in Delhi." Now, I ask you, what possible meaning could that message have for two early risers traveling in India? One hour later, the answer surfaced. "Ten" was "Pan"; therefore, a Pan American flight was leaving for Frankfurt, but why were we expected to be on it? The answer can be found in the "Fly America" policy. Employees of the US government (including lecturers) are required to use American carriers exclusively. Since we were scheduled to speak in The Sudan (a possibility not yet confirmed), it would be necessary for us to fly from Delhi to Frankfurt to Cairo via Pan Am. Since there was not any American carrier to The Sudan, we would be allowed to take Sudan Airlines from Cairo to Khartoum.

Back at the Bhopal ranch, we attempted to charter a car and driver for a night trip to Delhi. We were dissuaded by inferior road conditions; a driver who had never made the trip; the absence of emergency accommodations; the excessive cost; and, most importantly, the Daciots in the Gwalior region.

The Daciots engage in a life of banditry. They stop every vehicle that moves, reside with impunity in the remote "Black Hills," and delight in dispatching their nocturnal victims to a premature glimpse of Nirvana.

In desperation, we found a room at the Hotel Mazur on Barasha Road in beautiful downtown Bhopal. Without describing the ambience, it should suffice to state that our new friend, the arts complex director, had resided in Bhopal for seventeen years, and he had never heard of the Hotel Mazur.

November 18 / Bhopal to Delhi:
After a sleepless night being entertained by the excessive street noise a few feet below us, we waited for a miracle to occur—reservations on a plane or train to Delhi. The miracle materialized, and we departed

for Delhi on an afternoon flight. Mr. Soi, from USIS Delhi, met us at the airport and informed us that we should leave on the earliest possible flight to Khartoum via Bahrain and Jeddah. The Frankfurt idiocy had been discarded summarily. We were informed that we would lecture in The Sudan on the New World Information Order.

November 19 / Delhi:

Since there was no word from USIS concerning our Sudan trip, we decided to take a quick taxi tour of Delhi. Our driver was a newly-shaved and clipped Sikh who was obviously taking precautions to disguise his Sikhness.

Today would have been Prime Minister Gandhi's birthday. The festivities were scheduled to begin at 5:00 p.m. By 2:00 p.m., soldiers were in evidence at every intersection. Groups of Hindu men were assembling informally. The air was oppressive.

Our Sikh driver was able to navigate to Delhi University where our son Bruce had served a decade ago as a Rotary Fellow following his graduation from Harvard. The campus is large and impressive. We completed a tour of the circumference which included the law faculty and the International Student House. In spite of the beauty of the campus, we were reminded that the university faculty is dominated by members of the Communist Party who have opposed all academic reform. The English facility of the student body is deteriorating. As the premium academic institution in India, the University of Delhi is not committed to research.

In returning to the downtown area, we drove past the Red Fort which I had visited in 1959. The open spaces which surrounded the fort are now filled with the pockmarks of urban poverty. I barely recognized the exterior of the fort.

Returning to the hotel, the Sikh taxi driver became increasingly nervous. At a taxi stand, we exchanged cars and acquired a Hindu driver. Our Sikh friend justified the trade on the grounds that he had developed a faulty tire. We continued our tour through India Gate and viewed the Rashtrapat Bhavan (Houses of Parliament) along the Rajpath (mall) where the funeral procession for Indira Gandhi had passed.

November 20 / Delhi to Bharatpur:

Learning belatedly that our departure for Khartoum had been delayed for several days, we decided to rent a car and to drive the 176 kilometers to the Keoladeo Ghana National Park at Bharatpur. The city is south of Delhi near Agra and is considered the gateway to the state of Rajistan.

Our driver, Mr. Singh, had returned to work after an absence of three weeks. During the interim, a Hindu mob killed his brother, stole or destroyed all of his family possessions, and burned his home. Obviously, Mr. Singh is a Sikh. In his possession, he had a document estimating the financial loss at $3,300. To avert future aggression, Mr. Singh has cut his hair and shaved his beard. After seven years in Delhi, his family has returned to the Punjab. Since there is no employment there, Mr. Singh will continue to drive rental cars in the nation's capital.

For one hundred miles, we followed the main artery to Agra. In 1959, I had visited the Taj Mahal, and I was disappointed that time did not permit a return trip.

In 1632 AD, the Taj Mahal and the Tomb of Akbar were constructed at the behest of Emperor Shah Jahan in memory of his spouse who died during childbirth. The main building was completed in 1643. The subsidiary buildings and the extensive gardens and ponds were not completed until 1649. More than 20,000 workers were engaged. There is a small minaret located at each corner of the mausoleum. The impact of the beauty of the Taj Mahal is indescribable. At dawn, at dusk, and at the witching hour, the Taj reflects the epitome of variable beauty.

Twenty-five years after my visit to the Taj Mahal, we turned west from Agra rather than east and entered small-farm country where the plots were painstakingly designed. Well-ordered villages, with solid adobe homes, contrasted sharply with the unkempt, unplanned chaos further north.

In mid-afternoon, we crossed into the state of Rajistan and arrived at the entrance of the Keoladeo Park, obtained the services of a park ranger named "Lamb," and booked a basic room in the virtually vacant Forest Lodge. Since the assassination, tourism has been reduced to a trickle.

Although the pain of my gout suggested a rickshaw, we undertook an extensive bird walk with Lamb.

Keoladeo is probably the finest bird sanctuary in India. As the former shooting preserve of the rulers of Bharatpur, artificial feed was never used. Keoladeo was deemed the best wild fowling ground in the world. Distinguished guests, it hurts me deeply to report, invariably recorded a daily "bag" in excess of one thousand birds. The record was 2,500. In 1903, Lord Curzon initiated the sordid bagging process.

In recent years, hunting on the twenty-nine-square-mile preserve has been prohibited. Two years ago, it was designated an Indian national park.

The area is predominantly wetlands. A large shallow lake is crisscrossed by narrow dirt dikes. The dikes can be used as foot or bicycle paths. Our guide, Lamb, has recorded 387 birds in the park, more than 300 of which are present from October through January. Although we did not see any, a few surviving members of the endangered Siberian crane species make the park their permanent home.

As the sun was setting, we boarded a flat-bottom wooden boat and poled through a series of marshy waterways. Hundreds of water birds filled the air. Their vivid colors in the setting sun in a quiet, private, scenic ambience created immediate euphoria. In addition to the varied bird life, we saw nilgar (Blue Bull), chital (Axis deer) and wild cattle. After a satisfying dinner at the lodge, we felt rejuvenated and fell into bed.

November 21 / Bharatpur to Delhi:

Before breakfast, we completed a four-hour early morning walk on a host of dike pathways. Thousands of birds shared the premises. Although the Siberian cranes were sleeping late, we were able to identify the Greater Spotted Eagle, Sirkeer Malkoha, Coppersmith Barbet, Indian Pitta, and Pied Bushchat.

At the termination of one dike, hidden in a quiet nook, was a stone bench dedicated in 1974 to former United States Ambassador Daniel Moynihan by Mr. Frank Fenton of Pittsburgh, Pennsylvania. The rationale for the designated bench never surfaced.

My wife, Patti, expressed the desire to impinge upon the privacy of an Indian python. For more than an hour, we followed Lamb as he explored every established python hostel. There were ample bicycle-like markings in the sand resulting from recent python excursions. Finally, under a shady bush, in desert-like terrain, Lamb spotted a baby python (ten to twelve feet) sleeping in the shade. The head was small, but the diameter of the body was approximately six inches. When mature, this juvenile will measure approximately twenty-five feet. He or she will be capable of hugging the essential vitality from a large deer.

Early that evening after returning to Delhi, we visited United States Ambassador Harry Barnes at Roosevelt House which is the official residence. We discussed the events following the assassination; his inundation with official visitors from the United States, including the Secretary of State and four former ambassadors to India, and his initial impressions of the performance of Rajiv Ghandi as his mother's successor. He solicited our reactions to the Indians whom we had met, USIS programming (I was not reticent), and his favorable reaction to the work of the Peace Corps in India, particularly the poultry development project.

For the first time, I learned that several foreign aid missions, representing the developed countries, have divided India into spheres of influence. Karnataka State was not included in the sphere of the United States; therefore, we did not see any USOM (US Aid program) signs in the Bangalore-Mysore region.

Harry Barnes is an effective, low-key foreign service officer whom I met in Katmandu when he was serving as Deputy Chief of Mission at the American Embassy in Nepal. During the same period, Willi Unsoeld (of K2 ascent fame), with whom I worked at Peace Corps headquarters in Washington, D.C., was directing the Peace Corps in Nepal. In a thirty-seven-year commitment with the foreign service, Harry was assigned initially as General Consul in Bombay, and subsequently as Ambassador to Rumania and Chile.

In the late 1960s, when he was Director General of the Foreign Service at the Department of State, I worked closely with Harry. Ambassador Nancy Rawls, a special friend who was our economic counselor in Nairobi, was Harry's deputy at the Department of State.

Since we had not been to the American Embassy for many years, we visited the beautiful structure which had been designed by the distinguished American architect, Edward Durrell Stone. In New York City, Stone designed the Museum of Modern Art (1937), and in Washington, D.C., the National Geographic Society headquarters building (1961) and the John F. Kennedy Center for the Performing Arts (1971). The embassy in Delhi was completed in 1954 with its unique interior water gardens and fountains.

Before returning to our hotel, we walked to the Ashoka Hotel, which had been renovated beyond recognition. The surrounding area, which was previously confined to open fields, was stuffed with American Embassy compounds and recreational facilities.

Prior to leaving New Delhi, and India, it seems fitting to cite our only trip to one of the most beautiful scenes on earth—the Vale of Kashmir.

In 1963, on the return trip to Bangkok from Washington, D.C., where my "walking" pneumonia was diagnosed, Patti met me in New Delhi. We had decided to visit Kashmir for rest and recuperation.

The quaint capital of Srinagar was exotic and engrossingly placed among the Golamarg Mountains in the Himalaya Range. After driving through the intriguing city, and the lush Vale of Kashmir along the shores of exotic Lake Dal, we arrived at our destination, a canopied white houseboat named "The Lady of Shalott." (Lord Tennyson would have been proud.) The "Lady" was berthed adjoining a grove of willow and chenar trees near the Jhelum River and the extraordinarily inviting Shalimar and Mishat Gardens on Lake Dal. With a diet of lovely lake views, and the engaging snow-capped peaks engulfing the vale, my energy level gradually returned. My enthusiasm for the scenery, the friendly people, and the scores of birds which resided near the littoral of the lake, never waned.

Partial recovery allowed a few slow-paced bicycle trips, including a five-mile spin into Srinagar. Jinnah fur caps were on full display. We were captivated by the life style and the rustic charm.

At that time, relationships between India and Pakistan regarding Kashmir were relatively stable. When I close my eyes, I can still see the enchanting "Lady of Shalott."

THE SUDAN
Bad Law Makes Hard Cases

November 22, 1984 / Delhi to Khartoum:

Arising at 4:00 a.m., we caught the 6:00 a.m. Gulf Air (Bahrain) flight to make connections for our next USIS speaking assignments in The Sudan.

With ambivalent feelings, I am leaving India. Those feelings combine respect, loathing, dismay, affection, concern, exasperation, and hopelessness. I am convinced that India will fail to cope and that India will not fail to cope. I am not anxious to return to India. If I do not return, I will not be disappointed. India has altered my perception and perspective concerning the future of the developing world. I am now aware that hope and despair arise from the same gene.

On the plane, there were more Sikhs than passengers. They were boisterous, rude and, inordinately happy. Obviously, they are the fortunate few who are escaping from the ultimate discrimination—potential violent death based on cultural and religious differences.

At Dubai, we were not allowed to disembark. The local officials must have been on a previous flight with a siren of Sikhs. At Bahrain, we were allowed off the plane to catch a connecting Saudi Air flight to Riyadh and Jeddah. The Bahrain Airport is ultra-modern, lavish, immaculate, and inviting. We browsed through the duty-free shops, admired the lofty prices, and observed what an impact sitting on oil can have for conspicuous consumption.

As we landed at Riyadh, the capital of Saudi Arabia, I had been admiring the shifting Arabian sands. Entering the arrival area, we were shunted through a separate in-transit gate. Our hand luggage was thoroughly searched by sullen, rude, and inefficient government employees. They dumped the contents of Patti's purse on the table and tore open the Buddha-head box which had been presented to us in Bhopal. When I suggested that we were international in-transit passengers, I was greeted with a surly look.

We were then required to stand in a corner for one-half hour in a remarkably beautiful, unoccupied airport. We were then herded to the departure gate where we waited for almost an hour. There was a rest room and a kiosk for soft drinks, but no other indication that Saudi Arabia is ecstatic about international passengers.

En route to Jeddah, we had luncheon, which presented exactly the same menu with which we were confronted at breakfast. At Jeddah, where we changed for another in-transit flight to Khartoum, we were herded into another corner with five other people, three of whom were airline pilots. Our passports had been confiscated at Riyadh. Miraculously, they appeared on a table at Jeddah Airport on the other side of a divider.

The pilots were excused from detention. We were joined by two bedraggled Asian travelers who had been waiting in another corner for several hours. No instructions were issued to the group. After a thirty-minute wait, I asked a belligerent guard whether it would be possible to speak with an airline agent. After another twenty minutes, I asked a passing agent whether our group might be allowed to use the facilities. He motioned to an escalator, but refused to allow us to retrieve our passports. Upstairs, we "freshened up," and I worked on my "freedom of information" lecture outline which I was scheduled to deliver in Khartoum. Patti tried the shops, but since she did not have her passport, she was not allowed to make a purchase.

When the flight to Jeddah was announced, we attempted to go downstairs to retrieve our passports. An armed guard intervened. Locating an airline agent, we were taken downstairs and placed in our familiar corner. After an elapsed time at Jeddah of three hours, our passports were returned, and we were allowed to board the Saudi Airlines plane to Khartoum. The dinner menu was exactly the same as the previous two meals, and the quality had not improved.

Subsequently, we learned that Saudi Arabia does not issue tourist visas and does not provide international in-transit status. So much for comity among nations.

Upon arrival in Khartoum, we were met at the airport by Lee Irwin, a former Peace Corps Volunteer in Ethiopia, who is employed by the United States Information Service in Khartoum.

The baggage scene at the airport was chaotic. Truckloads of the largest suitcases in captivity coupled with poorly-tied, gargantuan boxes, bicycles, mattresses, coffeepots, and other appliances, were deposited in the center of a room smaller than most kitchens. Unfortunately, all of the passengers, friends and families of the passengers, airline employees, baggage handlers, and government officials were also present. With expressive gout, exacerbated I am certain by exposure to Saudi Arabian hospitality, I crawled over hundreds of Samsons searching for our three little Davids.

Many of the Sudanese have found jobs in Jeddah and/or purchase essential items in Jeddah, which are not available in The Sudan. After ninety minutes of baggage rugby, the scrum disbanded, we found our luggage, and the Sudanese maintained their high spirits and cordiality.

Having completed our exercise for the week, we were escorted from the airport to the residence of David Shinn, the Deputy Chief of Mission of the United States Embassy in The Sudan.

While we served in Kenya, David discharged the role as a young foreign service officer in the political section of the US Embassy. Subsequently, his wife Judy and he were assigned to Tanzania. He also served as the Deputy Chief of Mission in Mauritania and Cameroon. When David and Judy learned that we were scheduled to speak in The Sudan, he offered home hospitality. We accepted with alacrity.

Upon arrival at the Shinn's, we were informed that it was Thanksgiving Day. While discharging a role overseas, it is easy to fail to recognize indigenous American holidays. Thirty members of the official US Government contingent in The Sudan were enjoying a turkey dinner. After the exemplary Saudi cuisine, I decided to confine my celebration to a Scotch and water. That did it! My knee ballooned to the size of a grapefruit. For the first time, I was painfully aware that gout can affect the knee as well as the big toe.

After a twenty-three-hour day, we crawled into bed. I was unable to raise my leg into the bed without the assistance of my spouse.

November 23 / Khartoum:

The Sudan differs appreciably from the historic stereotype. The land of the battles between British General "Chinese" Gordon and the Mahdi, and his successor the Khalifa, which led to Gordon's death in a Khartoum rebellion in 1885, has become a Muslim military dictatorship. As the largest country in Africa, ethnic Arabs control the northern two-thirds, and the southern third is controlled by darker Nilotic or Sudanic strains which practice Christianity or Animism. After Egypt had declared itself the sole colonial power, replacing Britain in 1951, The Sudan gained independence in 1956.

The land of the Nile River (the Blue and White branches merge at Khartoum) which has been captured romantically by Emil Ludwig and Alan Moorhead, has become a security-conscious, militaristic, Sunnite Muslim-controlled government of urban fortified enclaves and abject rural poverty. Travel is restricted, and generally, the Nile can only be viewed from the air.

The huge expanse which nurtured the land of the Nubia, the Anglo-Egyptian intrigues, and the camel safari, has been replaced by continuous drought, epidemic famine, escalating refugee camps, indigenous racial and religious strife, and rampaging amoebic dysentery. The storied land of dervish dancing, joyous regional music, diverse musical instrumentation, and celebrated literature and poetry has become a reactionary Islamic state enforcing an anachronistic draconian justice for infractions of dress and beverage codes.

A land of fable and myth which stirred the romantic illusions of the West, has become a graveyard of sand. The hopes of a new generation are now buried amidst poverty, greed, inequity, inadequate leadership, limited natural resources, intolerance, prejudice, dwindling food supplies, increasing numbers of refugees, and a strict moral code which defies reality.

The name Sudan suggested hope unfulfilled. In fact, The "Sudan" represents the demise of idealism.

In late 1983, President Nimeiri, a career military officer who assumed power more than a decade ago, with an arbitrary edict transformed a moderately progressive nation into a controlled Muslim state. At that time "Sharia," the Swahili and Arabic word for "law," was imposed upon an affable, apolitical, uncomplicated populace. "Sharia" incorporates into a rule of law an extensive number of Islamically-inspired prohibitions which proscribe normal human behavior. For example, the purchase, possession, use and sale of alcoholic beverages are prohibited. Violators are subject to jail sentences and flogging.

Legal sages have suggested that hard cases make bad law. The corollary is also true. Bad law begets hard cases.

For example, a Finnish businessman arrived at Khartoum (the "K" is virtually silent) Airport with the intention of engaging in normal commercial transactions in The Sudan. Reflecting Finnish practice, his luggage included three bottles of whiskey to present to his regular clients. The customs authorities inquired whether our Finnish friend had any intoxicating beverages in his possession. Reflecting another Finnish practice, a unique proclivity for honesty, our weary traveler extracted the three bottles from his luggage, placed them on the counter, and inquired about the duty to be assessed.

Naivete, thy name is Finn! Our contemporary "teller of no lies," was arrested, relegated to a jail cell, and informed that his sentence would be ninety days and thirty lashes. Since Finland is not represented in the Khartoum version of the Corps Diplomatique, the prisoner remained in his "dry" cell for a few days before the Minister of Foreign Affairs convinced the President of The Sudan that their reputation as a compassionate neighbor in the world community might be in jeopardy.

I am doubtful that our Finnish entrepreneur will return to the land of broken profit-oriented dreams or that Finnish tourism will become a prominent source of Sudanese foreign exchange.

In the cited case, quaint little Muslim idiosyncracies could have been equally well-served by confiscating the offensive elixir and sending the Finn to his clients without bearing gifts.

In the capital city, the Sudanese government is now erecting a monument, at a prominent traffic circle, which will commemorate the government's decision to relegate existing liquor supplies to the bottom of the Nile. In contrast to the impact of a historic Boston jettisoning party, I doubt that any cause will be advanced other than the sense of well-being of the agnostic Nile perch.

Without exception, the remarkably attractive, articulate, educated, caring, Sudanese people whom I met have condemned the "Sharia" edicts. They assert that unless the Sharia proscriptions are repealed, The Sudan will continue to lose credibility, investment potential, and the proceeds from tourism and other foreign exchange sources. Of greater importance, the security forces charged with enforcing the law have created a "big brother" environment which is demeaning and enervating. For the diplomatic corps in Khartoum, "Sharia" is presenting major problems of survival. Can you imagine attending seventy-five national day celebrations per annum without the benefit of something intoxicating?

When "Sharia" was promulgated, the bans did not extend to three Sudanese states (provinces) which are African (Black), Christian and/ or Animist, impoverished and ignored by the Muslim-Arab controlled central government. The rationale for the exclusion illustrates that President Nimeiri is capable of turning a pragmatic Islam cheek.

In the Southern Sudan, there is an active, powerful, effective, military-oriented dissident group, The Sudan People's Liberation Army, of 20,000 soldiers led by a former Sudanese Army officer, Colonel John Garang. Along the way, the colonel acquired a doctorate from that school of revolutionaries, the University of Iowa. With extraordinary precision, he has blown up oil barges (one thousand lives lost in the resulting fire), destroyed convoys, and created a security problem for the Southern Sudan excluding the major city of Juba.

The southern dissident forces were able to kill three, and maim ten, non-American employees of Chevron in the southern producing oil fields. As a result, Chevron has suspended a one billion dollar oil exploration and extraction operation. President Nimeiri, honoring his social service commitment, has questioned the Chevron concern about "only three lives." Until improved security measures have been devised,

Chevron will discontinue the operation. In the meantime, southern Christian refugees continue to pour into Uganda, Kenya, and Ethiopia.

Back at the fort, President Nimeiri has been flirting with Adnan Khashoggi, a Saudi financier who appears to own half of Saudi Arabia, Blue Nile resorts in The Sudan, the Utah Jazz professional basketball team, and other vital public-oriented interests. For a reputed $400 million, Khashoggi has agreed to develop The Sudan's oil resources while retaining a fifty percent interest. Several Sundanese officials have suggested, not in jest, that Khashoggi has, in reality, purchased The Sudan. The latitude of a powerful national leader, without democratic restraints, is becoming a fact of life in many important countries.

Security problems in the Khartoum region are equally acute. Colonel Qaddafi's hired thugs, financed by Libyan oil revenue, have staged several abortive coups directed at President Nimeiri and the American Embassy. In each case, the plans have been thwarted by the requisite intelligence information being received in timely fashion.

Security is now a preoccupation for senior American officials serving overseas. In The Sudan, a multi-million dollar American compound will be constructed to house all staff members in the United States mission.

Following World War II, the Russians decreed that their overseas representatives would reside in Russian "ghettos." Because of Cuban and Libyan worldwide terrorist activities, Americans who represent the antithesis of a controlled state will now be forced to follow the Russian bear down the path of overseas isolation from local cultures.

In Khartoum the American Ambassador's expensive Chevrolet incorporates the heavy armor of a tank. The Deputy Chief of Mission has an official car with double safety windows and a reinforced frame. Principal US Embassy employees travel with accompanying backup security cars, and armed guards patrol constantly at every home where Americans reside. In addition, decisions concerning official and personal travel are based on security criteria.

After a few short years of increased security-consciousness, Americans with sound international sentiments will become relative reactionaries. They will resent famine aid to Ethiopia because it will be alleged that Ethiopia is utilizing its own internal financial resources to subvert United States and other developed country interests.

Within the past week, a bomb has exploded outside the US Embassy in Bogota. Ten American diplomats and their families have been evacuated. The bombing has been attributed to drug lords who recently threatened to kill five Americans for every Columbian extradited to the United States on drug-related charges.

Recently, the US Department of State praised the Italian government for the successful intelligence efforts which uncovered a terrorist plot against the US Embassy in Rome. In the previous section dealing with India, I cited the bomb threat to the USIS facility in Bombay.

In every country, local security forces are incapable of protecting American lives. It is politically infeasible, and probably financially impractical, to contemplate sending US military units to protect Americans assigned overseas. To curtail or disband American operations in a number of increasingly sensitive overseas locations would also be counterproductive. Protecting vital American foreign economic interests and American lives deserve priority attention; however, the selected targets, and the extent of security coverage, must bear close scrutiny.

The answer clearly emerges. We do not need to emulate the Russians in hiding our overseas representatives from the world outside. A global information program must be launched, utilizing all of the media, to pin the tail of guilt on the Russian donkey.

At the same time, the Central Intelligence Agency must be downsized and focused. The legitimate overseas intelligence-gathering function must be assigned to a newly-created agency reflecting the requisite checks and balances. Third World leaders must be informed repeatedly that there is a vital distinction between flawed freedom and uncontrolled tyranny. The former must be nurtured.

November 24 / Omdurman:

Last night, we crossed the Nile River into Omdurman from where the Mahdi launched his final successful attack against the starving General Gordon, and his few remaining supporters, at the Khartoum Palace.

Our mission was to observe the Dervish dancers. Once per week, the dancers assemble at a bleak desert mosque, called Hamad El Nie, to demonstrate their religious commitment to a predominantly foreign, picture-taking circle of potential admirers.

The Dervish cult represents an amalgam of North Sudanese Moslem sects who believe in the supernatural power of their deceased leaders. While dancing, they move their bodies in paroxysms of inspiration to support their religious convictions.

The music is basic, in fact, simple. The increasing pace of a drum beat induces a motley array of men and boys, in Jellabuya-white robes to stomp about with arms emulating a standing broad-jumper. The priests who are clad in quilt-patch robes to differentiate them from the ranks provide the requisite inspiration.

Only the priests spin a bit to conjure up words of wisdom from the dead. The festivities cease promptly at sunset to allow the devotees to face East and to complete a lengthy session of prayer.

This morning, we returned to Omdurman to visit the Suk, the principal market. The gold, ivory, cloth and ebony products appear to assuage the cavernous, materialistic appetite of the typical Western tourist. Even the local residents discharge the role as consumers.

With my gout arrested, but not incarcerated, I confined my purchases to a heavy ebony cane, with an ivory handle, which will insure a modicum of mobility in The Sudan and a modicum of conversation in the United States. In truth, the purchase represents an affectation. I do not really need the cane. I object to the use of ivory, and the folks at home will not manifest any interest.

With my new cane as a putative prop, I stood in the shadows of the Suk watching the passing parade of "farangs" with their incessant, acquisitive-oriented prattle; the Moslem wives, in purdah, with their veiled faces; the elderly, bearded men riding patient donkeys; the small children already exposed to the value of the Sudanese pound, and the Sudanese Arab traders who could probably sell the Torah to a Saudi Prince.

Since the early 1920s, when Sudanese university students rebelled against their Egyptian faculty masters, student dissidents have been extremely active in The Sudan. Their complaints have always been external to the university. Political causes have been emphasized to the exclusion of examinations, parietal rules, or the joys of hanging university leaders in effigy.

Recently, the dissident tradition exploded at the southern regional university in Juba. The Arab-Muslim northerners are convinced that the Christian or Animist Black southerners have "just emerged from the trees." The faculty at Juba has been predominantly northern. The southern Black students rebelled against the ostensibly prejudiced, authoritarian Arab faculty; the lack of government support from Khartoum, and the paucity of employment opportunities upon graduation.

To emphasize their displeasure, the students took their grievances to the streets rather than confining the rebellion to the campus. Traditionally, Sudanese officials have been remarkably permissive when student opposition has been restricted to the university premises; however, once the students are "in the streets," the protesters have been arrested summarily, and the university has been closed. With the closing of Juba, there are now only three viable regional universities and the central University of Khartoum.

After playing tennis (gimp and all) at the Nile riverside retreat where Ambassador Hume Horan and his wife Nancy are eligible to relax, I took a quick dip in the small frigid pool.

November 25 / Khartoum:

I arose early to prepare an outline for a lecture on "Freedom of Information." After meeting the Undersecretary of Information and Culture, with the USIS Public Information Officer as escort, and completing the required tour of the photography labs, I presented my talk to approximately fifty senior members of the ministry staff. The level of English facility was encouraging; however, none of the women attendees was willing to ask a question or venture an opinion. Although I made some progress in pinpointing the threats to media freedom from a controlling governmental system, the staff members were preoccupied with their perception of the need for an improved "balance" to the news about the third world countries reported in the West. Obviously, the issue relates to the parties who insure that "balance." If the government controls the news that flows to the West, lack of credibility will produce greater imbalance.

Following the lecture, I met Minister Ali Shummo, an impressive civil servant who received Master's degrees from the Maxwell School at Syracuse University and from the University of Indiana.

Late that afternoon, my wife and I attended the tenth anniversary celebration of the founding of the Graduate College at the University of Khartoum and the graduation exercises for doctoral candidates. In a peaceful stupor, I listened to the familiar words of art and the resulting cheers as loved ones received the coveted diplomas. A few universal human reactions appear to be genuine.

At an American Embassy dinner, which was arranged in our honor, we met the head of the Council of Higher Education (read Minister of Education); the director of the Institute of Music and Drama, who wrote The Sudan section of the Grove Dictionary, and whom I surprised by my interest in percussion including the indigenous "gugu" drum which is carved from a log; the director of the Corporation for Radio and Television, and the chair of the Foreign Relations Committee of the National Assembly (Parliament). The Sudanese leaders were remarkably outspoken in describing the deficiencies of elected officials and the limitations of Sharia.

November 26:

After meetings with the Director of Information and the Director of North and South America (imagine) of the Ministry of Foreign Affairs, I conducted a seminar at America House (directed by the United States Information Agency) for working members of the media and government information officers. My topic was "The Media and the Government." Since many of the participants were employed by government, my task was formidable. Freedom of the press is an unusual concept in most countries of the world.

At an embassy sponsored luncheon, we met the director of the University Press who is also a playwright. He had just completed a play for children which is based on a fable concerning a prince and an extraordinary camel who talked and danced. As long as the camel was ridden with a saddle, the immediate world reacted peacefully. If the camel were to be ridden without a saddle, dire events would ensue. The prince made fun of the caveat; jumped on the camel's unsaddled back, and the camel pranced off into the desert. Neither of our heroes was ever seen again. The moral, I assume: if you ride without a saddle, have a definitive oasis in mind.

November 27:

Beginning to feel a minor surge of energy, I met the director of the Council of Higher Education Grants Committee, who controls the purse strings; hence, the destiny, of Sudanese higher education. Without sufficient openings for university graduates, and with the need to devise a curriculum geared to an explosion in technology, higher education in The Sudan is discharging an unenviable role.

While I was involved with higher education, Patti toured a refugee camp for those from rural areas who were immobilized by severe famine conditions. She also delivered an address at Ahfad College on "The Emerging Role of Women in the 1980s." In the evening, she visited the Women's Development Center and met with the Women's Studies Group at the University of Khartoum.

I completed a taping at the Voice of America which will be translated into Arabic. The questions emphasized the New World Information Order which has emanated from Third World leadership and which is attempting to lessen the "tyranny" (monopoly) of the Western media. I was also asked to comment on my general reactions to The Sudan. I was willing to respond to all of the questions with the exception of the rationale for Morocco's decision to withdraw from the Organization for African Unity. I believe that I am a generalist, but there are many limitations.

Before leaving Khartoum, we were notified that the USIS lecture program in Cyprus had been postponed. Since we were scheduled to leave for Cyprus tomorrow, we decided to spend the interim period in Kenya where we had served from 1966 to 1969.

On our last evening in The Sudan, we took David and Judy Shinn to dinner at the Hilton Hotel in Khartoum. David and Judy have been exceptional hosts, and we shall treasure their hospitality and their friendship.

At age forty-four, David is discharging his third Foreign Service assignment as a Deputy Chief of Mission. He has risen rapidly in the foreign service ranks. If he is not promoted to the Senior Service, for which there are few openings, within the next eighteen months, he will be retired from the foreign service. There are more than two hundred senior Department of State employees in a comparable position. Only thirty will be promoted.

David Shinn is an effective foreign service officer. He is bright, thorough, creative, and caring. As an African expert, he is fluent in Swahili, Arabic, and French. (In subsequent years, he served as American Ambassador to Burkino Faso and Ethiopia and as Coordinator for United States aid to Somalia during the emergency. David was promoted to the Senior Service.)

KENYA
Eden and Profound Changes

November 28, 1984 / Khartoum to Juba to Nairobi:

In early morning, we boarded a bulging Sudanese Air vessel for the trip to Nairobi via Juba. We thought of the Nairobi area as our "second home." Most of the passengers were destined for Juba. Clearing customs at the frame-hut airport, we reboarded for the trip to Nairobi. After an absence of twelve years, I was looking forward to renewing my love affair with Kenya. In 1975, Patti had visited George Adamson's lion experiment station in northeastern Kenya. She was returning after a gap of nine years.

At the Kenyatta airport, I was struck by the juxtaposition of profound change and tradition. In contrast to The Sudan, the airport was modern. It reminded me of Munich and the trappings of efficiency. At the same time, the brief incoming view of the hand "knuckles" of the Ngong Hills overlooking the Rift Valley, the courtesy and attractive features of the Kikuyu customs officials, and the omnipresence of the Swahili language conveyed vivid reminders of things past.

Although I was never motivated to maintain a personal journal prior to 1981, a chronicle of our 1966-1969 residency in Kenya, when I served as American Ambassador, would now prove invaluable. I am intimidated by the self-imposed requirement to capture the essence of our second home after a gap of many years. My emotions are raw; my feelings are deep; my impressions are mixed, and the modifications are acute.

In February, 1969, after submitting my resignation, President Nixon provided less than one month for us to leave Kenya. As a political appointee, I was aware that we were subject to summary replacement, but I assumed that my successor could be nominated quickly. Six months elapsed before Robinson McIlvaine arrived as my replacement. Rob was a career foreign service officer. When we returned in 1972, we visited the American Embassy for a courtesy call. Rob informed us that the home of the Deputy Chief of Mission was available for a short time, and with gratitude we accepted the invitation.

During our 1972 visit to Nairobi, I contacted Eric Khasakhala, a friend who was a member of the parliament and Assistant Secretary of Commerce in the late 1960s. We also had brief reunions with AJL Okuku, Tom Mboya's brother, who was running a travel service in Nairobi; Dr. Karanja who was in charge of the University of Nairobi; Attorney General Charles Njonjo; and Narain Singh, Editor of the *Nairobi Post*, who still expressed concern about our rapid departure from Nairobi in 1969.

We arranged a brief safari to the island of Lamu, reflecting Arabian traditions, on the Kenyan coast. While waiting for the ferry at Kilifi, we heard on the radio that Senator George McGovern had nominated Sargent Shriver as his vice presidential running mate on the Democratic ticket. We were optimistic that the slate would be able to compete with the Nixon-Agnew duo. We also made a return trip to the arid, but beautiful, National Park at Samburu, north of Mount Kenya, where the Gerenuk and Reticulated giraffe play.

While Patti and the children departed to climb "the Mountains of the Moon" (in the Ruwenzori Mountains in Western Uganda), I departed for London and a few days as a visiting fellow at St. Catharine's College at Cambridge University.

Today, thanks to the courtesy of the United States Information Service, we were met at the airport by a driver with a car. The trip into town, contiguous to the border of Nairobi National Park, reminded us of the many happy early morning hours devoted to the birds and wild animals of the park: lion, cheetah, leopard, and baboon, and a plethora of birds ranging from the Secretary Bird to the Rufous-Crowned Roller and the Yellow Bishop.

In addition to the flora and the fauna, Nairobi National Park presents disparate memories. After his California defeat, in preparation for the 1968 presidential campaign, Richard Nixon came to Kenya for a general briefing. He stayed with us at the embassy residence for a few days. He knew the name of every Kenyan Minister. It was obvious that he was in final preparation for a rigorous political campaign. En route to the airport at the time of his departure, I drove him through Nairobi National Park in a Land Rover. He had worked every waking minute, and I assumed that he would appreciate a few moments in an extraordinary natural setting. I was wrong. Mr. Nixon concentrated on making notes on his omnipresent, legal-sized, lined yellow pad. He did not look up to observe the passing scene which included lion, zebra, waterbucks, and gazelles. He was uniquely focused. At that time, I was concerned about his preoccupation with single issues and his unwillingness to observe the world around him.

Subsequently, Vice President Hubert Humphrey also spent a few days in Nairobi before he returned to the United States for the 1968 presidential campaign. The Vice President, and his wife Muriel, captivated the government officials and the populace. He led a parade in downtown Nairobi. He was exuberant and obviously enjoyed "leading the band." Vice President Tom Mboya, and hundreds of Kenyan dignitaries, joined the parade. I mention the parade as an indication of Humphrey's style. Everywhere he went, he seemed to provoke a warm, positive response.

At an open air forum, an exceptionally large crowd gathered to hear the Vice President speak. Following my brief introduction, he informed the crowd that "the Ambassador can introduce me on any occasion." I regret that I did not have that privilege.

In his remarks, lengthy as always, and extemporaneous, he succeeded in conveying his commitment to civil rights and to Africa. He believed in the future of independent African countries. He was confident that the United States cared. He was one of the few officials who was able to communicate, even during the Vietnam War, that sense of commitment. When he met with the Kenyan leaders, he was able to make the case for regional donor aid from the principal Western countries to Eastern Africa.

En route to the airport, prior to their departure from Kenya, the Humphreys were ecstatic about the animals that appeared, as if on signal, in Nairobi National Park. I am not suggesting that an awareness of nature is a prerequisite for service as President of the United States, but it is certainly not a liability.

Nairobi National Park also resuscitated memories of returning to Nairobi from Mombasa at the India Ocean coast. During the Vietnam War, Mombasa served as an excellent port for visiting US civilian and Navy ships. We made several trips to welcome Peace Corps Volunteers who were assigned to the coastal region. Since I was also accredited to the Seychelles Islands, which were located 1,500 miles east of Kenya in the Indian Ocean, Mombasa was our point of departure. We had fond memories of seeing the beautiful Sable Antelope in the Shimba Hills and spending a few weekends at Dhani Beach, a lovely, unspoiled, sandy strip lined with palm trees, which was located a few miles south of Mombasa.

After the reveries associated with Nairobi National Park, we passed through a new, modern, urban complex. We were deposited at the Hilton Hotel which, in 1967, was only a figment of Hans Winkler's imagination. Hans was a friend who built the hotel and served as long-term manager.

Basking in privacy, and the first tap drinking water since leaving our home in Rhode Island, we opted "to take in the town." Since we had missed lunch, I suggested that we partake of a cheeseburger (a unique Kikuyu dish) at the New Stanley Hotel. The New Stanley had served as a watering hole for the colonial crowd and continued to discharge that function for independent Kenya.

During my three-year stint as Ambassador in Kenya, most luncheons were official. Occasionally, I would walk from the office to the New Stanley Grill for a cheeseburger. It provided an opportunity for me to collect my thoughts before returning to the office, to absorb the "local color," to watch the jet set strut at the adjoining Thorn Tree open-air café, and to pay a brief tribute to the fast food culture of my homeland.

Alas, in the intervening years, Jack Block had sold the hotel and the cuisine had deteriorated. To illustrate the quality of service, Patti and I waited for forty minutes for our cremated, hard-bun repast.

I had forgotten the inventiveness, and occasional chicanery, of the majority and controlling central Kenyan Kikuyu tribe. As the best educated and most powerful tribe in Kenya, they have mastered all of the tricks to euchre the unsuspecting.

In 1966, on the day following our initial arrival in Nairobi, I was stopped twice on the sidewalk. First, an elderly British expatriate woman hailed me with the news that she recognized me from my photograph in the morning newspaper and from the airport arrival press conference. I had conducted my press conference in Swahili. For that reason, my new British friend informed me that "I had sold out my national heritage." She opined that "one never speaks the local language with the locals." Before I could muster a response, she disappeared into the glorious sunshine.

The second confrontation was more noteworthy and involves a young, attractive Kikuyu who stopped me with a gracious smile. He informed me that he was employed at the Protocol Office of the Ministry of Foreign Affairs, and that he had attended my airport press conference. After complimenting me on the presentation, he asked whether I would be willing to grant a fifty shilling loan ($4.00 at the time) for the payment of an urgent bill. He informed me that since the banks were closed, he would not have access to the requisite funds until the following day.

Although I was on guard, the request seemed plausible. I was unwilling to risk offending a staff member at the ministry or to inform him that I did not recognize him from the press conference. I complied with the request. You guessed it! I never heard from the bloke again.

Today, we were stopped by a charming Kikuyu gentleman, with a superb smile, who stated that he was a customs official from the airport, that he recognized us and would we . . . (hold it buster, my memory of a previous encounter was clear). We thanked him for his kindness and continued down the street. The following day all of our personal possessions were confiscated by the customs authorities. Oh well, live and learn!

The building in which the offices of the American Embassy were located during my term of service has deteriorated badly. The adjoining parade grounds are surrounded by tall, modern government buildings; the pace has quickened; yet, Nairobi is still "ours."

The air is cleaner than most other major cities (5,600 feet and minimal air pollution). The flowers are larger, more diverse, and more beautiful (sunshine, high altitude, adequate rain, and effective care). The people are extremely friendly and courteous, and the urban core continues to represent an understandable and controllable magnitude.

Walking on the streets of Nairobi is fun. The passing scene is both educational and colorful. Much of the British-style architecture has been preserved. Even shopping was a pleasure.

With the exception of "airport art," which presents poorly-carved wild animals for the nondiscriminating tourist, most of the goods for sale are relevant, designed or painted with precision and skill, and represent something about the environment which may prove memorable. The objects for sale include low-priced British paperbacks, both fiction and nonfiction; current magazines from around the world; colorful paintings of flora and fauna; indigenous tribal profiles; wooden sculptured pieces which capture the heritage and spirit of East Africa; clothes which are pragmatic, colorful, attractive, and blend with the environment; jewelry which combines precious stones with impressive mountings; fruits which are exotic, distinctive, and delicious; fresh vegetables; meat and fish from local sources which are fresh and appetizing, and assorted trinkets which are unusual and worth a second look.

Nairobi and Kenya have changed. Since Uhuru (independence) in 1964, the changes are not all positive. The annual population growth is a frightening four percent. The promise of free primary education has not been realized. Poaching in the national parks is a way of life. Venal politicians instigate abortive coups. Consistent famine in northern Kenya constitutes a national emergency. Because of incipient crime, foreign exchange from tourism is peaking. The quiet, natural, picturesque Kenya of the colonial days is difficult to emulate. When discovered, it is costly and in short supply.

Driving on the deteriorating highways is life-threatening. There is also the increasing risk that the land which the White residents possess will be expropriated in the name of enlightened post-colonialism.

In spite of emerging problems, permanent residency in Kenya could be attractive. If the cost of real estate were not prohibitive, and if I could afford to visit Kenya every year, I would treat it as a second home. The quality of life for the expatriate is infinitely superior to most other nations. The essential ingredients for a remarkable existence are present in generous supply: love of life; warm, generous people; an ideal climate; remarkable scenery; variable surroundings; an exemplary natural environment; clean air and water; a change of season; an inviting harvest; and in the world of ideas, access to the written and spoken word and to stimulating friendships. Returning to Kenya is a special treat, but the warning signs are acute. Unless population growth is arrested, and corruption is controlled, the die is cast.

With few exceptions, the Asian (Indian) leaders in Nairobi have disappeared. In 1969, virtually every retail shop was owned and operated by Asians, and they dominated the service-oriented functions. In politics, Asians rose to the senior ranks. For example, our good friend, Fitz De Sousa, was Deputy Speaker of the Parliament. Although the Asians were generally resented by the Black Kenyan majority, a viable accommodation had been forged between the two ethnic communities.

Today, the number of Asian shop owners is minuscule. The outstanding professionals, such as the photographer John Karmali, have been forced to sell their shops to the Black Kenyans. Most of the relatively affluent Asians have emigrated to England; the middle class to India, and the few lower-middle class Asians have remained as subaltern civil servants, owners, or employees at inconsequential retail establishments, or have moved to provincial locations.

On the streets of Nairobi, we witnessed a new generation of callow, White, underemployed, overeducated, affluent, expatriate or transient youths who have discovered "the bush." The arrogance is overt. It is intriguing that the new generation of immature "jet-setters" has accepted the same dress style and demeanor as their predecessors.

I had assumed that the new crop of youngsters would be wearing the "in" Levis rather than the khaki safari shirt (for male and female) and the tight khaki shorts (for male and female) of the previous generation. It would be easy to deprecate the new breed of "White hunter" when the wearer of the garb has never heard of a "White hunter" and has never spent a night in the bush. On the other hand, it is preferable for the profligate to deposit their unearned western currency in Kenya where a small percentage of the loot might support the environment.

After a dozen years of disuse, my facility in Swahili is slowly returning. It is disconcerting that essential vocabulary has been lost, and that the verb tenses appear arcane. Unless a foreign language is learned at an early age, facility can disappear. On the other hand, even though our return to Kenya was unplanned, I should be able to conduct a normal conversation without extensive review. If I could only retain the "inputs" to which I have been exposed in a lifetime, I might qualify as an educated person.

A miracle has occurred. Prior to returning to Kenya, Patti and I agreed that if the option materialized, we would prefer to stay at the Lake Naivasha cottage owned by Doria Block. We would make the cottage our base for short automobile safaris in the central region, and when the Cyprus lecture series was finalized, we would be able to depart quickly.

This evening, as we were strolling through the lobby of the hotel, Doria Block appeared. She was searching for an art exhibition, and we chatted in the lounge. Last year, as a former President of Lincoln Center in New York City, I had been able to secure a last-minute ticket for her to attend a performance of the Metropolitan Opera. After a lengthy residence in London, Doria returned to Nairobi last week. She suggested that we stay at the Lake Naivasha Cottage for our last few days in Kenya. She plans to join us for the weekend. We are anticipating an extraordinary experience.

November 29 / Nairobi to Naivasha:

This morning we rented a Toyota jeep, secured new reservations for our trip to Cyprus, arranged a few important Nairobi appointments prior to our anticipated departure, sent a cable to Cyprus, and headed for Nirvana (alias Lake Naivasha).

En route to the Rift Valley, we stopped at Westlands, a suburban shopping center which Patti used to patronize ("The Green Grocers"). I recognized an attractive Kenyan woman who arrived with three small children. It was Lillian Mungai who worked at the American Embassy during our stint in Nairobi. Following our departure from Kenya, she married a Kikuyu physician, Njoroge Mungai, who was Minister of Defense during my term and who was extremely close to president Kenyatta. Dr. Mungai is now engaged in private practice.

After purchasing essential groceries, we began the happy one-hour trip to Naivasha. The drive along the ridge of the Central Highlands, the homeland of the Kikuyus, evoked memories of speeches given (Rift Valley Academy); of birding safaris completed with the leading Kenyan ornithologist, John Williams, and with the famous American ornithologist, Roger Tory Peterson, and of the uniquely beautiful Rift Valley.

A new highway has been constructed above the old road. The former road meandered down the escarpment past a tiny pink church which was constructed by Italian prisoners during World War II. The new first view of the Rift is not as dramatic as the old, but the panorama of Lake Naivasha, Longonot and Suswa Mountains, and the Rift Valley per se is still overpowering.

Without difficulty, we located the road which circumnavigates the lake. After ten kilometers driving along the southern shore, we arrived at the lakeside cottage which Jack and Doria built on their Longonot farm.

In the late 1960s, Patti and I had dinner at the Blocks' home in Muthaiga, a Nairobi suburb where the American Embassy residence was located. We became friends, and the relationship blossomed over the years.

Jack Block was born in South Africa and came to Nairobi prior to World War II. He and his brother, "Tubby," married sisters, and with an entrepreneurial flair, they invested in and ran a number of ventures including hotels. Along the way, they acquired a 3,500 acre farm at Naivasha which provided the hotels with dairy products and vegetables. Two years after Kenyan independence, they were forced to sell all of the farm except for 100 acres along the lake. The hotels included the Norfolk (of Robert Ruark's *Something of Value* fame) and the New Stanley in Nairobi and principal hotels at the coast in Mombasa and in the Rift Valley.

Jack was "the genius" and Tubby was the implementer. Jack met, and was liked by, everyone. He and Doria, who was also born in South

Africa, traveled extensively in Europe and in North and South America.

Eighteen months ago, Jack was trout fishing in Chilean mountain streams. Evidently, he experienced an epileptic seizure, provoked by the frigid water, and he drowned. Doria has inherited their home in Nairobi and the Lake Naivasha cottage. She is nurturing her long-term interests and expertise in art, music, and the theater.

The Naivasha cottage is basic. There are three bedrooms, one in a small separate unit; a small living room with an essential fireplace; an eight-foot square windowless dining room; and a long, covered front porch which overlooks a spacious lawn with mature Acacia trees partially obscuring an exquisite view of the lake.

The Lake Naivasha cottage is my favorite spot on earth (with the possible exception of the western view over the lake from the porch of our old shack at South Lake in Ontario, Canada).

Lake Naivasha has a circumference of sixty miles. It is the only non-alkaline lake remaining in the Rift Valley. It is filled with fish (delicious Tilapia), hippopotami (several hundred), beautiful papyrus marshes, and lovely vistas of the Rift Valley and Mount Longonot (9,100 feet). The air is sweet, the breeze is soft and invigorating, the sun shines every day, and frequent rains maintain the lush, verdant surroundings. The evenings are cool enough for sweaters and a root fire in the fireplace. The equator sun, coupled with an elevation in excess of 5,000 feet, fosters tepid days which do not sap essential energy.

The foliage is tropical. The flowers are large, profuse, and colorful.

On the first morning, I was seated at a small, round, outside table, wearing a sweater, writing in the journal (infrequently), looking every sixty seconds at the rippling lake fifty feet away, and watching the remarkable number of bird species.

The birds—the glory of Lake Naivasha! Cormorants, gulls, ducks, jacanas, darters, snipes, fish eagles, pelicans, flamingoes, terns, grebes, storks, ibis, herons, crakes, and plovers have converted the shores into a private sanctuary for water species. The land species are competitive: starlings (Superb, that is), grenadiers, shrikes, bulbuls, woodpeckers, flycatchers, weavers, firefinches, boubous, warblers, and cisticolas (Winding, that is).

After a rewarding day, and postprandial tea, served by our friend David who constitutes the permanent house staff, I took a short walk before falling into a soft bed covered with an exotic safari-like mosquito net and an essential blanket.

November 30:

Awakened by the screams of the African Fish Eagles and the squawks of the Glossy Ibis, we had breakfast on the porch before beginning the trip around the lake.

The dirt road was deeply rutted. After stopping every few minutes to observe the scenery, the foliage, and the birds, we bounced to the Elsamere Conservation Center which was the occasional former roost for Joy Adamson.

Joy was a comely British expatriate who became the premium painter of Kenyan flowers, particularly exotic wild species. Her earlier colorful paintings accentuated fish, animals, and tribesmen of Kenya in authentic dress. Until she began the Elsa series (*Born Free*, etc.), she was known as an accomplished artist.

Elsa and her cubs initiated a new era for Joy which developed an international cult of anthropomorphic lion, cheetah, and leopard devotees who became more concerned with the playful mannerisms of selected wild animals than with the conservation or preservation of those animals. The movies, and the related subjective treatment, provided little support for Kenyan wildlife and a great deal for tourist excursion owners. Thousands of low-budget tourists wanted to see a cheetah behave like Uncle Joel.

Joy's final mate, George, was as eccentric as Joy, but a bit more stable. He patronized lions in the remote arid region of northeastern Kenya. George and Joy were estranged, and he eschewed Joy's modern pad at Elsamere. George succeeded in returning several semi-domesticated lions to their natural habitat where they had difficulty interacting with the local populace and recapturing their previous lifestyle.

Whose contributions will be remembered? While George and his conservation efforts remain underfunded and constitute a desert mirage, Joy's work lives on through an international trust and a conservation center at Naivasha which serves as a convenient location for "scholars." Every afternoon, the tour bus coterie make the pilgrimage from Nairobi to Elsamere to pay for the privilege of visiting the Joy Adamson Memorial Room. A British expatriate warden and his wife sell Joy trinkets including notepaper with animal and flower drawings which were not painted by Joy. Joy's life was creative and productive, but the remnants reflect the least common denominator.

Heading south from lake Naivasha on a virtually impassable, washboard, pitted road, we crossed the Mau Escarpment on the southwestern edge of the Rift Valley. We enjoyed the arid, stimulating views of the Loita Plains which lead to the lion country in the Masai Mara National Reserve and to the Serengeti National Park in northwestern Tanzania.

Returning to the lake, we stopped for a picnic lunch on the north shore road. Black and White Colobus monkeys gamboled in the acacia. For miles there was not any habitation. We were amazed when a British expatriate in a Land Rover stopped to inquire whether we were experiencing car trouble. In Kenya, on the open road, flat tires and overheated engines occur frequently.

In the sixties, Patti and I had spent the evening with Jack Hopcroft and his wife on the northern shore of the lake. Spotting a small sign near the road, we drove ten kilometers toward the shore when the driver of a large truck shouted at us in what we perceived to be a rude fashion. With rusty Swahili, we learned that we had a flat tire. Three farm hands assisted in changing the tire, and we continued to the Hopcroft compound.

During our residency in Kenya, the Hopcroft's son, David, an agricultural doctoral degree recipient from my alma mater, Cornell University, was monitoring the habits of wild animals through small transmitters implanted in the skin. David is no longer in residence. His father is deceased. After visiting the cottage where we stayed, we enjoyed the beautiful stand of papyrus on the shore, and returned to our Camelot cottage in the driving rain.

When we lived in Kenya, we generally observed wild animals in the national parks. The tourist groups were not oppressive. It was possible to sit quietly watching a pride of lions without listening to a visiting buffoon.

With the current noisy crowds of tourists, visiting many of the national parks in Kenya is roughly comparable to walking through an urban zoo. As a result, it is now preferable to traverse formidable, isolated roads, in remote areas, with the expectation of seeing an occasional (probably less than exotic) animal in a natural habitat. Following this approach, we have had the privilege of seeing Black-faced vervets, baboons, giraffe, wart hogs, Thompson's and Grant's gazelle, common waterbuck, impala, duikers, and hippopotami. Before leaving Kenya, we may see a few of the "big five," but our memories of lion, elephant, leopard, rhinoceros, and African buffalo, may not be refreshed.

December 1 / Naivasha to Aberdere National Park to Naivasha:

This morning, we left early for the Aberdere Mountains via the Kinangop, the remarkable temperate climate plateau west of the mountains which nurtured the British expatriate "happy valley" crowd. Featuring a lavish lifestyle, lovely stone homes, and the violence of Mau Mau insurgency which led to Kenyan independence, the Kinangop was the embodiment of the British White settler. Since independence, the farms have been subdivided and subdivided again. The resulting scale is inadequate for efficient farming. The well-scraped roads have been replaced by mud monstrosities which provoke broken axles. The exquisite bordering hedges have disappeared.

What remains? Beautiful scenery, an indigenous people enjoying their heritage, and a population explosion which will destroy the environment.

Before reaching the Kinangop, we stopped at the US Peace Corps Training Center located on the eastern plateau overlooking Lake Naivasha. To obtain directions, we hailed a young woman who appeared to be a Peace Corps type. She was a volunteer trainee awaiting permanent assignment in Kenya.

In 1961, as Special Assistant to the director, in Washington, D.C., I recruited many of the Peace Corps Representatives who established initial Peace Corps programs in a number of countries. Subsequently, I established the Peace Corps program in Thailand and served as the Peace Corps Representative for two years. Returning to Washington, D.C. as Associate Director, I was responsible for selection, training, and volunteer support.

When I was directing Peace Corps training, we relied upon US-based university programs which stressed language and cultural exposure.

Now, after a brief indoctrination in the United States, the volunteers are assigned to an in-country training site before being dispatched to a permanent post in that country. The approach is sound, and less costly. However, trainees who are unable to cope must be returned to the United States. The training site at Naivasha was impressive. As usual, the Peace Corps Volunteers appeared to be a credit to their country.

From the farmlands of the North Kinangop, we took the Ministry of Forestry road through the foothills of the Aberderes and mountain subsistence villages, back to the Kinangop and the road to Ol Kalou which was the situs of "happy valley" social activities. After a picnic in a copse of eucalyptus trees, we were fortified to enter Aberdere National Park.

Elephant spoor inundated the narrow, winding road. At every bend, we expected to be confronted by a pachyderm. Our substitute rewards were a francolin and the rustic western entrance to the park in a heavy rainstorm.

In the late sixties, the first director of the Peace Corps in Kenya, Robert Poole, his wife Lee, and our two families had made a trip to the Aberderes in a Land Rover. Using the eastern entrance, we spent a few days tenting. The flora and fauna were spectacular. On this occasion, we were only able to drive a few kilometers before the deep, soggy, treacherous potholes intervened. The terrain was lush, and the dark clouds and the wind produced an eerie quality. Lions have been reintroduced in the Aberderes, and a few have become man-eaters. However, on this occasion, we did not see any of the "big five."

Returning to the cottage, we stopped at the Lake Naivasha Hotel to inquire about access to Crescent Island. Two young Kenyans offered to show us a hippo and her progeny. We started off merrily across the swamp. My guide was a huckster who had enjoyed minimal exposure to nature. Patti's companion was merely a huckster. After fifteen minutes of walking, Patti's guide inundated several acres with his alcoholic breath. He also insisted that she establish an endowment for his six children whom he was confident would matriculate at Harvard. My guide confined his requests to my walking shoes, binoculars, and the requisite cash to purchase a number of expensive books. He did introduce me to a cormorant rookery; a bishop (the bird family) and a few other water birds. Our parting with the guides, prefaced by another request for sufficient cash to purchase a Cadillac, was not characterized by mutual trust.

December 2:

After several hours of bouncing on corrugated dirt roads, it was a pleasure to place our feet on terra firma and to enjoy the familiar delights of the cottage. Once again, I am seated at my favorite writing spot overlooking the lake. At this moment, a beautiful African Fish Eagle is sunning the interior of his brown and grey wings. A cormorant is watching the fish eagle. Two mousebirds are playing hide and seek. A weaver has just entered its pendular, inventive nest. A giant tortoise has moved (slowly) into view, and a Black-headed Oriole has begun his liquid song from ten feet away. A flotilla of silent White Pelicans has just flown by with their undulating wings responding to the leader's beat; changing course in unison, and fishing by inserting their beaks underwater accompanied by Olympic-precision swimming.

Joan Root joined us for luncheon. She is Doria Block's nearest neighbor on the lake. In the sixties, we visited Joan and Alan to see their menagerie of wild animals and birds. At that time, they were raising a beautiful, virtually extinct Bongo. Subsequently, they nurtured thirty more which were released in the national parks. As a result of their efforts, the Bongo in Kenya has made a temporary recovery.

For seventeen years, Alan and Joan Root photographed and produced animal and bird documentaries. They live in the Lake Naivasha house which was constructed at the turn of the century by E.S. Grogan, the author of *Capetown to Cairo* who, a century ago, walked the length of the continent. The plot has become a small wildlife refuge with reedbuck, duiker, and gazelles which have been raised and released.

My ornithology mentors are disappearing. Leslie Brown, the leading East African expert on birds of prey, is dead. The modicum that I learned about raptors was through the courtesy, persistence, and written record of Mr. Brown.

John Williams, the author of the only reliable East African field guide for birds, was forced to leave Kenya after depositing fees for professional services in a foreign bank account. To survive, many expatriates engaged in the practice, but John must have generated a bit of animosity in officialdom. John was a mild, caring, wonderful human being who represented the antithesis of the "criminal type."

Most of the outstanding bird watchers I have known do not suffer from a lack of certitude. Scratch a consummate bird watcher, and you unleash an expert who is never wrong. Of course, Roger Tory Peterson, who visited us in Nairobi in 1968, and whom I introduced to Kenyan birds at Lake Naivasha, is never wrong.

He is one of a kind. Most of the leading ornithologists, if you will excuse the certitude, are fallible. Very few bird watchers see or hear a bird without shouting the name of the alleged species instantaneously. To hazard a contrary opinion would be unthinkable and certainly unsporting. There is only one problem. Back in the confines of my den, with definitive bird guides readily available, the certitude of the experts becomes suspect. Solitary bird walks do represent a positive approach even though essential expertise is lacking.

December 3 / Naivasha to Elmenteita to Lake Baringo:

Arriving at the Lake Elmenteita sign on the Nairobi-Nakuru road, we took the "worse road in Kenya" along the eastern shore of alkaline, isolated Lake Elmenteita. Hundreds of Greater Flamingoes were roosting in the alkaline flats at the eastern end of the lake. From a distance of five hundred yards (there are no roads or habitation closer to the lake) the birds looked like a soft, pink cloud covering the surface.

The landscape was appealing. The short rains had converted the generally arid bush into a verdant, wild pasture. Herds of zebra and Thompson's Gazelle ran or grazed in the distance. If we had not met Lord and Lady Delamere, we would not have been exposed to the area.

More than fifteen kilometers from the main road, we passed a gate marked "Soysambu Estates." We hailed a small truck, and the driver was the manager of Soysambu. We were informed that Lord Delamere died in 1979. He was one of the "happy valley" crowd who used to dance on the tabletops at the Norfolk Hotel in Nairobi. Some of the participants emptied their pistols while performing the feat. Lady Delamere is in a Nairobi hospital in the terminal stages of a debilitating disease. The estate has been inherited by a son, Lord Chumley.

While resident in Kenya, Patti and I spent a night at the Delamere Estate. The view of the lake was breathtaking. The size of the ranch approached Texas standards. The swimming pool rivaled a marble Roman bath. On this occasion, we bypassed the ranch, noted the stately riding horses, and headed for an unmarked crossroads which the estate manager informed us would lead to the shore of the lake.

After a few kilometers, we reached the soda flats. Turning the car around, and making certain that the terra was firma, we enjoyed the inevitable picnic lunch, using the hood of the car as a table, and started walking across the flats.

In the midday equatorial sun, the alkaline flats were alive with fire, and the shimmering, brackish water in the distance emitted fumes which distorted the image. A solitary Thompson's Gazelle walked slowly away. The gory remains of several species of plains game were evidence of unrequited thirst or the nocturnal attacks of leopards.

The whiter the soda mud, the further our feet sank. Only by returning to firmer ground were we able to reach a higher point where the eastern end of the lake was visible. The hordes of Greater Flamingoes were barely visible.

In the absence of any sign of life, we completed the return trek to the car. The landscape was eerie and fascinating. There was not any sound. Only a few flowers and shrubs on the shore conveyed the presence of life. Thoroughly parched, and enervated by the dry heat, we completed the lake circuit and headed for Lake Nakuru.

In spite of the fact that Nakuru is a relatively large, important central city in Kenya, there were no road signs. We did not detour to the lake, which is also replete with flamingoes, but headed west towards Eldoret. We climbed quickly to the Mau Escarpment where the British settlers raised cattle, sheep, wheat, and sugarcane. Except for proximity to Nairobi, it is inexplicable why the White settlers fought for the Kinangop rather than concentrating on the lovely plains between Nakuru and Eldoret. The Aberdere foothills served as a unique staging ground and Mau Mau retreat for their sorties into the Kinangop.

After the inevitable detour, we hit the new tarmac highway north to Lake Baringo. The road just happens to be near President Daniel Arap Moi's ancestral home.

Arriving at the Lake Baringo Lodge, Patti enjoyed a swim in the small pool. I took (you guessed it) a short bird walk. I was able to "spot" the Spotted Eagle Owl. After dinner, Patti joined me for the walk to the owl's roost. At the lakeshore, the hippos were cavorting in the reeds.

December 4 / Baringo to Naivasha:

The morning walk featured the rare Verraux's Eagle, two species of hornbill, the Cliff Chat, and assorted Rock Hyrax. The flies were persistent. The heat was oppressive. Standing in one spot incited a mild form of torture.

As we were checking out, the resident ornithologist, Terri Stephenson, appeared. Terry is an Englishman who has been in Kenya for seven years, the last four at the newly-constructed Baringo Lodge where he has fostered a bird-oriented environment and clientele.

Terri won the November annual Kenyan bird safari which enhanced his reputation. In the absence of John Williams, Terri is now the most distinguished ornithologist in Kenya. In the space of twenty-four hours, his partner and he identified 304 species of birds of which 10% were identified by song. Alan Root won second prize.

For the first time in the bird safari, all forms of transportation could be utilized. By air, Terri visited Nakuru, Naivasha, and the coast near Mombasa. He spent the early evening hours at Tsavo watching the migrants fly by in the light from the lodge. The predawn hours were spent shining flashlights into abandoned weaver's nests to catch the small songbirds of the bush country.

The airplane cum flashlight bird safari seems ridiculous. It would be preferable to devote successive dawn to dusk days as a real test of ornithological skill.

After several partially helpful answers to "Bwana Leakey iko wapi?" (where does Mr. Leakey live?), we found Jonathan in a small dingy lab near an inaccessible house.

Jonathan's father, Louis, discovered some of our earliest progenitors at Olduvai Gorge in Tanzania and near Lake Rudolf in Kenya Turkana country. When we lived in Kenya, we met Louis and his wife, Mary. Before leaving Kenya in 1969, we enjoyed a bit of Kikuyu cuisine—a meat-filled pumpkin—which Louis Leakey had prepared personally. Louis was a showman who attracted young pseudo-scientific female apprentices. As a scientist, his nonscientific approach and sporadic publishing of his findings discouraged a large percentage of the paleontological community. The human bones which Leakey discovered have revised the estimate of the duration of man's roots; yet, the suspect methodology has minimized the scientific impact of his discoveries.

Following Leakey's death, his spouse, Mary, who never went to college, continued Louis's research. Her scientific approach and findings were professionally sound. Without the requisite academic qualifications, most of the scientific community tended to treat Mary as they had treated her husband.

The three Leakey sons went their separate ways. More than twenty years ago, Jonathan became a hermit at relatively inaccessible Lake Baringo where he milked the venom from poisonous snakes. The venom was sold commercially.

The second brother, the only post-independence White elected to the Kenyan Parliament, had a winning manner, no ostensible interest in archeology, and two functioning kidneys, one of which he donated to save the life of his brother, Richard.

Without adequate collegiate or scientific training, Richard became interested in archeology. He discovered the remains of ancient homo sapiens which rivaled the digs of his parents. He became the director of the Kenya Museum and a successful international fund-raiser. He is the third member of the family to earn international recognition. In recent years, under the presidency of Daniel Arap Moi, Richard has founded an opposition political party; served as the Minister of Wildlife; and, most recently, he has attempted to reform a manifestly corrupt civil service.

Twenty years ago, we had visited Lake Hannington (named after a European Catholic Bishop). At that time, a Land Rover was essential. We camped overnight, saw a few Lesser Flamingoes on the semi-alkaline lake, and observed the maji moto (hot springs).

A new road has been constructed from the equally new national tarmac highway to the reserve entrance. Twenty years of protection has created a haven for thousands of Lesser Flamingoes (the Greater are larger, have a pink not a red bill, and the plumage is not as red); a refuge for other water birds, and a retreat for the majestic Greater Kudu.

In 1969, I was convinced that East African wild animals were doomed. Because of adequate rain, the closing of the Tanzanian border which forced the Kenya government to open up Baringo and Nakuru to tourism, improved national park management, and the sustained financial help of international wildlife groups, the national parks and reserves have been given a temporary reprieve. Inevitably, the population explosion, corruption, poaching, and uncontrolled tourism will reverse the positive trend. In the meantime, Lake Bogoria (nee Hannington) is a pleasant surprise.

On the return trip to Naivasha, we spent a few hours at Nakuru National Park. The park has been transformed. Recent generous rains have assisted, but the bulk of the credit can be bestowed on the Kenya Ministry of Tourism and Wildlife. The protected southern and western shores have been extended. A few years ago, an attractive lodge was built on the southern heights with a lovely view of the lake and the adjoining savannah. The herds of bushbuck, wart hogs, impala, tommie's, grant's, zebra and baboon are impressive. The road system has been improved. Most importantly, from my impartial point of view, the birdlife is remarkable. Flamingoes, ducks, plovers, terns, and stilts abound. In the surrounding hills, the song birds are thriving. The open country scenery above the lake is among the most engaging in Kenya. Park fees are standardized throughout the country: thirty shillings for an adult, twenty shillings for an automobile, and five shillings for a child.

Leaving via the southern gate of the park, in the inevitable rain, we enjoyed the isolated twenty kilometer dirt road to the main Nairobi highway. As we approached Lake Elmenteita at sunset, we were reintroduced to one of the most engrossing scenic treats. The setting sun filtered through sporadic storm clouds over the glistening lake and the arid, eerie, diverse, hilly, exotically beautiful Rift Valley—the cradle of mankind.

In Kenya, the combination of climate, scenery, clouds, sun, rain, dust, elevation, and people create unforgettable moments. The setting sun, even in urban America, can provide a few moments of joy. In Kenya, it is a constant blessing without disguise.

December 5: Naivasha

After a midday nap, we mounted our Japanese steed for the short journey to Hell's Gate, a small national reserve southeast of Lake Naivasha. In the vicinity are the 10,000-foot Mount Longonot, which our family climbed with the USAID Director, Carol Hinman, and his family, and Mount Suswa, a lesser peak, which we climbed with the British High Commissioner, Sir Ted Peck, and Lady Peck.

The entrance to Hell's Gate is through the Kenya Light and Power Company facility. The company retains ultimate ownership. The public enjoys a right-of-way. The road—and I realize I am repeating myself—is the worst in Kenya.

The reserve features a long sheer cliff, and some minor cliffs, which provide refuge for Klipspringers, Rock Hyrax, Mottled Swifts, and a rare pair of Lammergeiers (Bearded Vultures). On this occasion, only the swifts and the hyrax appeared. The rolling, arid, bush country was remarkably diverse. Because of adequate rain, we spotted relatively calm herds of kongoni, gazelle, and an elusive family of Silver-Backed Jackals. Augur Buzzards were assembling in full dress, and the larks, pipits, weavers, starlings, sunbirds, and kites kept us fully occupied.

Very few tourists have seen Hell's Gate or a few of the lakes which we have described. We are rediscovering Kenya and savoring exposure to "our" scenery, wildlife, birds, flora, and local inhabitants. A Kenyan private safari can be bliss. A group excursion can be sheer pain.

December 6:

On Joan Root's invitation, we took a long walk on her grounds. In the absence of restraining fences, the hippos keep the spacious lawn nicely mowed. They tend to miss the sections near the flower beds, but their eyesight is suspect. Reedbuck, duiker, and dikdik scampered from every glade, and the water birds along the two hundred yard waterfront were omnipresent.

Joan and Alan acquired the old house, and one hundred acres, for the grand sum of 4,000 Kenyan pounds more than twenty years ago. Since they were not able to afford the asking price, they rented for a year, and the owner then sold at a reduced price. Today, the choice plot would probably sell for one million Kenyan pounds.

Upon returning to Doria's cottage, David gave us a guided tour of the farm. The truck gardens are huge, cultivated by a score of resident farmers, and include every vegetable and fruit known to personkind. At the lake, two adult hippos were basking in the morning sun. They were standing in three feet of water twenty feet from shore, and the powerful grunts suggested that closer observation was not in order. Several African children, who had not previously seen hippos at close range, were entranced with their discovery that large wild animals are in the water as well as on the land.

In mid afternoon, we returned to Crescent Island, an extensive, moon-shaped spit of land which Roger Tory Peterson and I had visited years ago.

The Lake Naivasha Hotel now rents boats which allow guests to view a small portion of the island. We decided to attempt to find the land access. After driving through the spacious, acacia-covered Sanctuary Horse Farm, we reached the narrow causeway to the island.

Recently, the extensive farms, the main house, and rights to the sanctuary were sold to an African. He immediately sold the property to a third party who is raising herds of sheep which impinge on the land formerly enjoyed by wild animals and birds.

During an hour's walk, we were constantly in the midst of herds of wildebeest, antelope, a few zebra, and waterbuck. The ground was thick with plovers. The beautiful stands of acacia were loaded with waterbirds. Several years ago, John Williams identified more than 300 species of birds on Crescent Island.

After tea on the lawn of the Lake Naivasha Hotel, which we shared with friendly Superb Starlings and belligerent Marabou Storks, we headed for the town of Naivasha. Because the main east-west truck traffic in Africa passes through Naivasha en route from Mombasa to the Congo, a quaint British-style farming village has become a congested, noisy, dirty, unfriendly pit stop for unhappy, embittered truck drivers who deposit their wages at the local houses of ill-repute and implant and take with them the seeds for an epidemic of social diseases.

This morning, Joan Root had discovered an eight-foot python in her squirrel cage. The snake had devoured an entire family of squirrels. Joan had grabbed the python behind the neck, avoiding the vicious bite, and threw the culprit into a gunnysack. When we arrived at her home, she removed the python from the sack and allowed it to wind around her chest and arms. She held the back of its head while it attempted repeatedly to strike. After she replaced one of my least favorite wild things in its temporary home, Joan's arms were red and deeply marked from the squeezing pressure exerted by the snake. Having felt that pressure, I am now aware that a twelve-foot python in India could squeeze the stuffing out of an adult deer. Joan plans to return the python to the bush.

We then made friends with a self-assured civet and watched Joan nuzzle a caracal, the most ferocious representative of the wildcat family in East Africa. The caracal sleeps on Joan's bed and must be carefully restrained to preserve the free-running duikers and reedbuck on the property. With pointed ears and a sinister look, the caracal did not appear to be the prototype of a house pet.

Deciding to make friends, I approached the caracal. When I was four feet away, the cat snarled. With a quick leap, it took a swipe at my leg. The claws pierced my trousers which persuaded me to limit my affectionate overtures.

In 1966, Frank Minot, a good friend and the first resident president of the African Wildlife Leadership Foundation, introduced us to the wonders of African wildlife. As my son, Bruce, and I sat with Frank in a tent in Amboseli Game Reserve at the foot of Mount Kilimanjaro listening to a lion roar, Frank told us about seeing the torn shoulder of a mature leopard. He said that the musculature was unbelievably powerful. He had realized for the first time that a wild member of the cat family possessed remarkable strength and agility.

My brief encounter with the little caracal demonstrated forcefully the truth of Frank's assertion. The speed of the leap was extraordinary. Coupled with a nasty disposition, a wildcat of any size is a formidable opponent.

Our next encounter was with "Chickie," an African porcupine. After exposure to the porcupines in Canada, I expected to see an attractive little animal with a lovely coat and several two-inch quills which are to be eschewed.

Out came Chickie, from one of two adjoining holes which were large enough for a truck. Her head was the size of a hereford, and the quills were more than a foot long. As she ambled toward her food dish, I realized that African wildlife portrays a dimension that is difficult for an unexposed westerner to comprehend. Many species in Kenya are larger, quicker, more colorful, and more interesting than their counterparts in temperate climes.

The remaining members of Joan's "living free" menagerie include discards, rejects, and orphans whom Joan has nursed to maturity. In contrast to a zoo, most of the animals roam free in a large plot which has been fenced to protect them from the outside world. The denizens include an Aardvark that has a quixotic mate who fills in the holes after she digs successfully for termites, a Leopard Tortoise recovering from a broken back, a huge bullfrog, a slither of snakes, an Oribi, and the previous cast of freewheeling characters.

Joan's house represents a page from the Africana of the British colonial settler: high ceilings; antique wood; original animal paintings; mementos from the bush; dated, comfortable furniture; and vistas of the beautiful surrounding natural habitat. I would not want the responsibility of caring for the score of Africans who take care of the hundreds of animals, but I admire the lore, love, and dedication of an anachronistic White settler named Joan Root.

Joan's father-in-law who lives with her is over eighty. He is a former meat processing expert and an avid listener to the BBC and VOA.

Based on a recent broadcast, he informed us that there was a serious poison gas leak at the Union Carbide plant in Bhopal, India which has caused the death of more than 8,000 inhabitants of the city. More than 200,000 people in the city of 800,000 inhaled the fumes. The tally of deaths continues to mount.

Since we had just come from Bhopal, we are hopeful that our new friends were spared. American leadership of Union Carbide has been accused of gross negligence. Six Indian employees have been arrested. With the Indira Gandhi assassination and the Bhopal disaster, India is suffering.

After ten days in Kenya, the Deputy Chief of Mission at the American Embassy in Nairobi has informed us that the USIA lecture tour in Cyprus has been canceled. The Turkish-Cypriot discussions at the United Nations headquarters in New York City have necessitated the attendance of the senior Cypriot leadership. I understand the gravity of the UN discussions, but I regret that the speaking tour issues could not have been resolved at an earlier date. Oh well, there is consolation. If we had been informed earlier, we would not have enjoyed the privilege of returning to Kenya.

December 7: Naivasha to Nairobi

After a leisurely breakfast, and an emotional moment paying homage to the ambience, we departed for Nairobi via the old Rift Valley route. Traversing the narrow, pocked road up the precipitous escarpment, the nostalgia was present but in short supply. Intersat domes now dominate a beautiful stretch of the valley. Small wooden frame houses restrict the formerly limitless view of the open spaces which were teeming with plains game.

On the escarpment, the little Christian church still blends in beautifully with its environment. There are pews for only ten devotees.

Taking the Limuru Road, we approached Nairobi through some of the most inviting country in Kenya. Tall, manicured green hedges hide former British estates from the road. The houses are constructed of grey stone, in Tudor style. The gardens are tropically luxurious. The tea and coffee plantations, coupled with the flowering trees and shrubs (jacaranda, flame, bougainvillea) portray the essence of the milieu for which the British and the Mau Mau fought.

During the past fifteen years, the African settlement of Banana Hill (a Nairobi suburb) has become a muddy blight. The population explosion is evident in every village, but the colonial "estate" facade is relatively untouched. Tourist foreign exchange dollars increase the coffers of the politicians. A tithe for the average Kenyan has not been allocated.

Approaching Muthaiga, a northern residential area of Nairobi where we lived in the American Embassy Residence, we passed a new complex devoted to the United Nations. More than two hundred international civil servants are provided with office space under the auspices of the UN Environmental Development Agency and other UN affiliates.

In Muthaiga, we stopped at the residence of the American Ambassador. In striking contrast to the new Middle-Eastern oil-oriented diplomats who have built, or are building, significant mansions, the American Ambassador still lives in an attractive white, stucco house which appears to be going to seed. The incumbent, Ambassador Gerald Thomas, is a former US Navy Admiral. Since he was out of the country, we decided to pay a call on our former cook, John Shillingi.

John is now grey, still personable, and a friend. He is scared to death of the incumbent "Black Ambassador." The military approach must be a shock. John's reaction illustrates the difficulty which Kenyan Africans experience in adjusting to American Blacks who are assigned to senior positions in Kenya.

John was afraid to have us step inside the residence. We did have the opportunity to pay our respects to John, the gardener, who has been a member of the staff since a year before we arrived in Kenya in 1966. Kitangi, Kewa, Peter, and the driver, Bernard Hinga, have all departed for greener pastures. John wanted us to convey special best wishes to our younger son, Scott, with whom he enjoyed a close relationship.

We also spent a few minutes with our neighbor across the street, Fitz De Souza. Although he no longer serves as Deputy Speaker, he is practicing law. Several of the homes of our diplomatic friends and neighbors are flourishing.

Luncheon with Sir Michael Blundell and his wife, Geri, was interesting and disturbing. We met the Blundells at their lovely estate at Subukia in the Aberdere foothills. In pre-independence Kenya, he served as Minister of Agriculture and as Governor. His fair, and politically enlightened, treatment of the Africans is documented in an autobiography entitled *So Rough a Wind*.

After independence, Sir Michael served as director of a major private corporation while continuing to operate the garden and estate at Subukia. His unique expertise with wild flowers has been captured with the first volume of an exquisite book of photographs.

Eight years ago, at age 73, the Blundells sold their Subukia home and moved to a small tract north of Muthaiga where Michael can still exercise his "green thumb." Two years ago, Geri died of a postoperative heart attack. Michael continues to travel, to write, to advise (informally) the President of Kenya, and to enjoy the fruits of an active life.

Michael Blundell expresses the fervent hope that Kenya will survive in a meaningful manner. He believes that he, and a few other White citizens, facilitated the transition to Black rule. With few exceptions, White citizens have remained in Kenya since independence without retribution. Sir Michael offers a minimal positive evaluation of President Daniel Arap Moi because of his success in holding the country together following the death of President Jomo Kenyatta. At the same time, corruption is being practiced at a high level, and an heir apparent to the presidency has not been identified.

When we served in Kenya, Daniel Arap Moi was Vice President. As a representative of the small Kalenjin tribe, he served as a peacemaker between the powerful Kikuyu and Luo political factions which represent the two largest ethnic groups. As a former school teacher, Moi was a warm, friendly person who was needed in his critical role.

The incumbent Vice President Mwai Kibaki, who was in the cabinet twenty years ago, has undergone brain surgery. Although he recovered, he has been unable to discharge his previous work ethic.

In the late 1960s, Bruce McKenzie, the only White in the Kenyatta cabinet, was an effective Minister of Agriculture and a close advisor to the president. In recent years, McKenzie became involved in a number of private deals which impaired his reputation. While flying over the Rift Valley in a light aircraft, a bomb placed inside the plane exploded killing McKenzie and the pilot. The culprits were never apprehended.

The other person who might have qualified as president was Charles Njonjo, who served as Attorney General. Njonjo was brilliant and a superb politician. For a generation, presidents Kenyatta and Moi relied upon his advice.

Recently, it was alleged that Njonjo was active in a conspiracy against President Moi which was supported by an unspecified foreign power. It was also suggested that Njonjo should be the next president. President Moi responded to these rumors by conducting "tribunal" hearings which were inconclusive; however, Njonjo's political career was ruined, and his passport has been revoked.

I paid a visit to the Deputy Chief of Mission, George Trail, at the newly-constructed American Embassy. With the most modern communications equipment in Africa, coupled with a completely computerized system, more than two hundred employees provide African continental, East African regional, and Kenya country services.

To illustrate the political changes in Africa in the last two decades, George Trail's most recent assignment was in South Africa; he is married to a South African, and he is an expert in military affairs. With the Ambassador a former Navy Admiral and the DCM a military affairs expert, the changes in the nature of American representation are profound.

From 1967-1969, our Deputy Chief of Mission was Wen Coote, a career foreign service officer with extensive service in Africa and a lengthy stint in London as the African expert at the American Embassy. Wen had close contacts with the African leadership in Kenya, and he enjoyed Africans. His advice was extremely useful. For more than two years, it was a pleasure to work closely with him. Wen was a former Wesleyan University athlete. In Nairobi, we enjoyed frequent bouts of squash and tennis. In the mid 1970s, Wen died from cancer at a relatively early age.

December 8:

Our return to Nairobi National Park was rewarding. The park constitutes the "neck of a funnel" which is fenced on three sides with Embakasi International Airport on the northern side. The City of Nairobi and Langata Road, which leads to Karen (Von Blixen and *Out of Africa*) and the "knuckled" Ngong Hills adjoin the other fenced borders.

In dry periods, the wild animals gravitate to the "neck of the funnel." As a result, Nairobi National Park is richly endowed with the major species except for the African Elephant which cannot be sustained by the limited land area.

The environment of the park is remarkably diverse, ranging from open plains to lush, forested hills. In a gentle rain, during the course of two hours, we saw twiga (giraffe); five rhino; all of the plains antelope except eland; baboon, Vervets, and a variety of birds of prey. The most rewarding moment featured two young lionesses running through the bush in search of their evening meal.

Although this short, confined trip to Kenya has not produced leopard, cheetah, or eland, we are convinced that the wildlife of East

Africa has a reasonable chance for survival. Nairobi National Park may not transcend the population and tourist explosion, coupled with indigenous corruption, but there is sufficient international interest in the perpetuation of a unique natural resource to insure continuity of support.

At the village of Karen, we visited with the artist, Mary Minot. Her husband Frank, with whom I discussed the muscular power of a leopard, left a New England poultry business to settle permanently in Kenya. In 1966, as President of the African Wildlife Leadership Conference, Frank introduced a series of successful programs to train indigenous wildlife administrators and rangers.

December 9 / Nairobi to Tsavo:

For three hectic hours, we drove the death-trap highway which connects Nairobi with the vital port of Mombasa. Fifteen years ago, the two-lane tarmac highway was treacherous. Today, it is a nightmare. Hundreds of antiquated, poorly-maintained, overloaded trucks travel in both directions. The innumerable, deep potholes, and the absence of shoulders, create an aura of mayhem. From Nairobi to Mtito Andei, halfway to Mombasa, there were five overturned trucks which had been involved in recent serious accidents. At one point, there was a traffic jam of more than one hundred trucks waiting for the nonexistent tow truck to clear the debris away from an overturned oil van. As we passed, we noticed that oil covered the road. Without fire or police services, it was extraordinary that a conflagration, or a rebellion, had not occurred.

Last week, seven American tourists, in a safari bus, lost their lives in an accident on this highway, the only east-west highway in Kenya. Kenya represents a facade of modernity without the superstructure or essential services to support modern transportation.

At Mtito Andei, we drove the thirty kilometers east on an inadequate dirt road to the Athi River. Leaving the car on the west bank of the river, we were rafted across the Athi to the Tsavo Tent Tsafaris. ("Tsafaris" is an obvious affectation.)

The tent safari concept was created by Glen Cotter (Cotter's Camp) in the mid 1960s. Basic living in the bush is accompanied by the sounds and smells of an old-time safari. An open-sided shed, with a thatched roof, serves as a shell for a tent which can be zipped down as a partial defense against scorpions, and hypothetically, mosquitoes.

In theory, the approach is grand. In practice, it represents a less than memorable experience. The current management is represented by a young, inexperienced British couple. Sanitary conditions were frightening. The food was deplorable. The noise of small children was grating. With only a single small lantern, I was unable to read or write.

The occasion was rescued by a two-hour Land Rover expedition. With a guide who knew the dirt roads in Tsavo East National Park, we stood on the backseat exposed to the elements. Through the open roof, we enjoyed some of the most glorious scenery in eastern Kenya. There were crocodiles in the swift, muddy, Athi River; bushbuck; dikdik; and baboons galore; and an encouraging assortment of hornbills, weavers, eagles, francolin, and rollers.

On the ridge above the river, we observed miles of unspoiled bush shimmering in the setting sun. The Baobab trees, which appear to be growing with the roots up, were green with unaccustomed leaves. The wild flowers were plentiful, and we reveled in the glory of the Kenyan "bush."

December 10 / Tsavo to Amboseli:

After re-crossing the Athi River, we began the River Circuit to the main highway. After three kilometers, we were forced to turn back because the dirt "path" was washed out. Since it had been in that condition for weeks, we experienced another poignant example of poor management.

Following an alternate, and inevitably longer route, we entered Tsavo West National Park and drove the thirty-eight kilometers to Kilaguni Lodge. In Tsavo Park, the overpopulation of elephants has ruined the original tree cover. The resulting barren waste supports only limited wildlife.

At the lodge we enjoyed a cup of coffee and watched the wildlife at the water hole fifty yards away. With our field glasses, we observed a herd of handsome oryx and a number of Ground Hornbills.

Armed with picnic lunches, and two essential bottles of water, we began the alleged seventy-eight kilometer trip to Amboseli Game

Reserve. Halfway, we were greeted by a thunderstorm. Within minutes, we were inundated with flash floods and dangerous, wet cotton soil.

Through a modicum of skill, and a generous dose of luck, I was able to keep on the road until we were confronted by a large, leaderless herd of Masai cattle. Two callow herdsman were observing the situation. Of necessity, I attempted to go around the herd. We slid into the river-like gutter. Masai youngsters responded with gales of laughter. With extraordinary good fortune, I was able to back up on the solid land above the road and to generate sufficient traction to carry the gutter.

After several near mirings, we arrived at the Buffalo Amboseli Lodge which we discovered was not affiliated with the game reserve. The lodge was a disaster. Unless a full luncheon was purchased, a cup of soup could not be ordered. The service was deplorable. The clientele was noisy. We fled like Cheetahs.

In the mud, we followed a sign for Serena Lodge. We passed another signed marked "Amboseli Lodge." We proceeded for another thirty kilometers. Realizing that the western foothills of Mount Kilimanjaro were receding, we retraced the route to Amboseli Lodge.

The northern entrance to the park was abandoned. After another ten kilometers of deep water-filled potholes, we reached our target. The one sign to Serena, which was also Amboseli Lodge, had been turned in the wrong direction. We drove 180 rather than thirty-eight kilometers.

After securing a room, we were rewarded with several majestic tembo (elephant)and a quick swim in a frigid pool. German tour groups were omnipresent.

The Masai are learning quickly. With the scores of tour buses on the dirt roads between the parks, the Masai have recognized that there are easier ways to make a shilling than herding cattle. The tall, lonely, ochre-robed, regal figures have disappeared. The current generation of young Masai stand in the middle of the road defying the motorists to pass. If you stop to protect their limbs, hordes join them from the bush. The rationale is to receive a bit of compensation for the privilege of taking their photographs.

The most memorable event headlined a bevy of young, topless, Masai maidens, in colorful skirts, who formed a phalanx in the middle of the road. Normally, Masai women do not appear bare-breasted, at least in the middle of the roads. The infamous tourist, in the omnipresent tour bus, has brought another quaint Western custom to East Africa.

The young Masai are disappointing. Ignoring tribal customs, they beg for shillings and resemble the professionally-trained juvenile beggars of India. They are not cute, endearing or rustic.

December 11 / Amboseli to Nairobi:

Awakened at 5:00 a.m. by our friendly German neighbors, we consumed a dry roll and departed on the road to Namanga at the Tanzanian border. We were advised to take the route because, in the event of an emergency, there would be more traffic. In theory, the rationale was sound. In practice, there was not any traffic.

Amboseli is nestled at the northern base of Mount Kilimanjaro which is located in Tanzania. Although the summit is generally obscured by clouds, when the sun emerges, the view is spectacular. A snow-covered peak at the Equator is difficult to emulate.

In February, 1969, a few weeks prior to our permanent departure from Kenya, my wife, Patti; our daughter Sherry; our son, Scott and I began the climb of Mount Kilimanjaro from the Tanzanian access. Patti, and our older son, Bruce, had made the trek a year earlier.

With a number of porters carrying the baggage and provisions, we completed the round-trip climb to Kibo, the 19,340 foot summit, in five days. On the ascent, we spent three nights at different basic huts. On the third day, we arrived at the "saddle" at 16,890 feet and walked for most of the day over the large plateau between Mawenzi Peak and our destination at Uhuru Peak. Wild flowers were abundant. At 14,000 feet, we were greeted by horned frogs, skinks, and butterflies. At that elevation, there were not any flies or mosquitos. At 9,000 feet, the squirrels and lizards had departed.

After a few hours sleep in the third hut at 15,690 feet, we rolled out of our sleeping bags at 12:30 a.m. and began the final ascent. At 7 a.m., after several enforced breaks because of lack of oxygen, we reached the top. We were welcomed by brilliant sunshine accentuating snow-filled glaciers. Following a quick view of the extraordinary scene, we started the return trip down the scree, including an occasional lengthy slide. In three hours, we were at the third hut. In six more hours, we were at the second hut where we spent the night. At seven a.m., with the evidence of tropical jungle returning, we passed the first hut in four hours. In three and one-half additional hours, we were at our starting point, the Marangu Hotel.

The lengthy, leisurely climb of Mount Kilimanjaro allowed us to observe the flora and fauna at different altitudes. The changing scenery was inspiring. Although the last few hours of the ascent presented a significant breathing challenge for a former inveterate pipe smoker, the five day excursion represents a singular family accomplishment.

Amboseli is an extremely small reserve which depends upon a fragile lake to attract the game from the normally dry surrounding plains. In the past, the shallow lake was large, and the game was plentiful, particularly lion and elephant. Because the government of Kenya has been unwilling to control the Masai cattle, goats and sheep in the reserve, the extraordinary tract is becoming an arid waste. The Masai herds have decimated the limited vegetation. The lake has shriveled to a small pond. With ample "short rains" in the foothills adjoining the park, which are privately owned hunting tracts, the wild animals are excluding the arid park from their normal range.

The once beautiful Amboseli has become a race track for tour buses and a desert for Masai herds. Sighting a few elephants at the lodge, as they head for the shrinking marsh, is scarcely reassuring. In the absence of mineral resources, Kenya is wasting its premium natural resource, the wild animals.

In 1969, upon completing a three year residency in Kenya, I was fearful that corruption, poaching, inadequate management, and poor training, would curtail the attraction of the Kenyan national parks within fifteen years. The trends are probably insurmountable, but the inevitability of disaster has been deferred.

Not a shilling appears to have been spent recently on park roads. I have not seen a park employee except at the gates, and many of the gates are closed. Even when receipts are provided, there is no assurance that the revenue will leave the guard's pocket. Signs are nonexistent. Essential services are severely limited. No brochures or maps are distributed. Not a single road scraper was active. The research groups dedicated to conservation are generally private and are located in

Europe or in the United States. Generally, those groups are engaged in uncoordinated, repetitive, esoteric research.

If income generated by the parks is not being devoted to the parks, Kenya's lifeblood is threatened. The former profusion of wildlife is being reduced. The remaining critters have been relegated to a shrinking, unattractive series of arid zoos.

Our final brush with Amboseli was a near disaster. On the road to Namanga, a series of downpours precipitated another quagmire. For sixty-five kilometers we did not see another vehicle. We were fortunate to get through. At Namanga and Kajiado, there were no service stations, rest rooms, or other amenities.

Because of general tourist disinterest, Kenya birdlife is still replete. In some non-park areas, such as Naivasha, wild animals can still be observed in a semi-natural habitat; however, Peter Beard's *End of the Game* prognostication is becoming a reality.

Speaking of Peter Beard, I had luncheon recently with Peter at Les Pleiades in New York City. As usual, Peter was alarmingly frank and quixotic. Peter's acute dislikes were placed front and center. They include all publishers; the "do-gooders" in the field of conservation who want to preserve the wild game species rather than the habitat in which they must survive; American tourists, and Kenyan covetousness.

Born with a "silver spoon" and educated at Yale, Peter has become an excellent photographer, a man without a country, an aberrational character, and a deeply committed human being.

December 12 / Nairobi to Brussels:

While President Daniel Arap Moi was addressing loyalists at the stadium in Nairobi on the 21st anniversary of Jamhuri Day (Independence), we fled to the airport.

Daniel Arap Moi, the son of a Kalenjin herdsman, was born in 1925. He was raised in the northern section of the Rift Valley. The Kalenjin are a smaller tribe which has never possessed power in the tribal configuration. Because he represented a nonthreatening tribe, and was a school teacher who did not appear to manifest political ambition, at Independence, President Kenyatta appointed Moi Vice President. The rationale was for Moi to serve as a buffer between the powerful and ambitious Luo and Kikuyu factions.

During my term in Kenya, Moi and I became friends. As relative youngsters, Moi was 41, I was 37, and we met frequently. At that time, Daniel Arap Moi was likable, accessible, interested, responsive, and honest. He discharged the role as peacemaker in the Kenyatta cabinet and represented the president at ceremonial functions.

Following Kenyatta's death, the Kiikuyu wanted to maintain control. With a weak Kalenjin as an interim president, a smooth transition was guaranteed. In 1978, Moi became President of Kenya.

Because of the quest for power involving Mungai, the omnipresent Njonjo, and occasionally Kibaki, the interim nature of Moi's presidency was extended. Without charisma, relevant training or education, tribal support or leadership skills, Daniel Arap Moi was attacked repeatedly by influential tribal leaders. In defense, he took umbrage and developed a hard exterior. By accident, he survived as president.

In August, 1982, there was an abortive Air Force coup in Kenya. Significant elements of the Air Force community were supported by left-oriented University of Nairobi students. The looting of Asian-owned and operated stores was extensive. Nairobi Airport and the principal radio stations were controlled by the rebels for more than nine hours.

The rebels alleged that President Moi was tolerating corruption; that he was maintaining power through the intimidation of his political opponents, and that he was incapable of solving the deteriorating economic situation.

It is patently clear that President Moi had cracked down on the dissident press; that Editor George Githi was fired by his London-based, business-oriented board for the Nairobi daily newspaper, the *Standard*, because of an anti-Moi editorial, and that Oginga Odinga and his opposition Luo political party had been relegated to political oblivion.

In Kenyan national politics, these manifestations of power were not unusual. In the late 1960s, President Kenyatta forced the passage of the Detention Act, which facilitated the incarceration of the same culprit, Oginga Odinga; declared KANU the only legal political party; had constant freedom of press altercations with George Githi, who was then at the *Daily Nation*, and responded forcefully to left-wing disaffection at the University of Nairobi.

In the summer of 1969, a few months following our departure from Nairobi, Tom Mboya was assassinated. During our residency,

Tom served as the Minister of Economic Development. He also coordinated the strategic planning function for the government of Kenya.

Mboya was a leader of the Luo tribe which was predominate in the area adjoining Lake Victoria. The Luo represented the second largest tribe in Kenya. Mboya was the only Luo in the cabinet.

The dominant Kikuyu, for which Jomo Kenyatta served as leader, considered the Luo their natural enemies. Given Mboya's brilliance, his following, and his leadership potential, he represented a major threat to Kikuyu control.

During a period of three years, I met Tom Mboya frequently. He displayed a generous dose of hubris, but if you relied on substance, and represented power (even as an ambassador), Mboya was responsive and friendly.

Tom Mboya had a vision for Kenya, and for East Africa, which was based on pragmatic economic development including cottage industries and cooperative efforts with Tanzania and Uganda. Because he was articulate and informed, Kenyatta sent him, reluctantly, to virtually every international conference. Although Mboya did not evidence any personal political ambition, his Luo following and non-Luo support among the educated was immense.

Minister of Defense Mungai and Attorney General Njonjo convinced President Kenyatta that Mboya represented a long-term political menace to Kikuyu domination. Kenyatta was beginning to display the initial pangs of senility. The seeds of distrust bore fruit. Mboya was increasingly isolated from the corridors of power.

Because of Kenyatta's awareness of Mboya's unique contributions; his personal fondness for Mboya; Moi's semi-independent status as Vice President, and Mboya's ostensible lack of political ambition, I was convinced that Mboya was not personally in danger. I was wrong. Mboya was assassinated. It was assumed that Kikuyu interests were responsible. The culprits were never identified. One potential successor to President Kenyatta had been eliminated.

In 1982, the coup failed. Order was quickly restored. Casualties were limited. Political stability prevailed. The standard of living was relatively high. Kenya was still a haven in the general chaos of sub-Saharan Africa. At the same time, Kenya was a single-party state.

President Moi had restricted essential freedoms. The requisite reforms were unlikely to be introduced.

If we had departed on schedule for the USIA speaking tour in Cyprus, my reactions to a short Kenyan visit would have been inordinately sanguine. After Tsavo, Amboseli, and Nairobi, my views are more balanced. Much of the Kenya which I remembered has disappeared. Kenya has become more reality than reverie.

April 21, 1986 / Nairobi:

Before leaving on the current African trip, we saw Meryl Streep and Robert Redford in *Out of Africa*. The photography was exquisite and evoked vivid memories of the flora, fauna, and people that captured our minds and hearts. The direction was tight and intelligent. With few exceptions, the plot followed the relevant Isak Dinesen textual sources.

The vintage pre-World War II British expatriate class was depicted with sensitivity. The essential humanity of a spoiled elite transcended the overt cancer of depravity, lust, and racial discrimination.

Robert Redford was clearly an American portraying a Britisher, but his acting ability overcame that deficiency. Meryl Streep not only played the character of Karen, she *was* Karen Von Blixen. As the story unfolded, I realized that I was seeing Meryl, and Karen, react to limited options in a beautiful, complex, inequitable world. Through Ms. Streep's sensitive interpretation, the characteristics which made the Whites in Kenya eccentric, the Black Africans endearing, and the country beautiful, came alive.

In spite of President Moi's tirade for home consumption which alleged that the movie glorified the White settlers, African Kenyans flocked to see *Out of Africa*. It is true that the Africans in real life were seldom treated as fairly; the leading characters were never as attractive or virtuous, and the ambience was never as inviting. *Out of Africa* satisfies my intrinsic subjectivity about Kenya.

Following my assignment as President of Lincoln Center, I assisted in the founding, and served as president, of Equity for Africa. The nonprofit organization was created to support small-scale private enterprise in Sub-Saharan Africa. At a time when Black Africa generated only limited interest in the United States, I was able to raise $1.2 million dollars from US corporations, individuals, and foundations to support the basic mission.

Twenty-two projects were launched in eight African countries with low interest loans, not grants. The Equity for Africa Staff was restricted to the president and one secretary. Virtually all of the funds were devoted directly to project support. The Board of Directors was distinguished and included President Obasanjo from Nigeria, President Kaunda from Zambia, and Senator Kassenbach from Kansas. Most of the loans were repaid. The proceeds were recycled into additional private projects in Africa. My wife, Patti, and I monitored the African projects. We relied upon part-time, unpaid consultants in the African countries involved to provide limited technical assistance.

Subsequent to monitoring several private projects in Zambia, where Equity for Africa supported eight projects, following a two-year absence, we returned to Kenya.

After attempting to resurrect our Kiswahili (language) facility at the Nairobi Airport, we went directly to Doria Block's beautiful Muthaiga home. During the filming of *Out of Africa*, Robert Redford had rented the home. From all reports, he was delighted with his surroundings.

We headed for the swimming pool, embraced the lovely terraced garden, started the inevitable "bird list," and arranged appointments for our limited stay in Nairobi.

In walking through the Muthaiga residential district, we were struck by several overt changes: increased security—police dogs and armed guards, high fences and walls, alarm systems, and periodic vans and patrols; the press of people, and the trappings of Middle-Eastern oil. It is difficult to believe that Kenya has sufficient diplomatic traffic to warrant the construction of new, ugly, ostentatious, extremely costly palaces for ambassadors representing Kuwait, Oman, Saudi Arabia and other oil fields.

Muthaiga still depicts unique suburban beauty. The British-style stone homes were built to enhance the landscape. The spacious gardens, anchored with flame and thorn trees, abound with large, colorful tropical flowers and shrubs—bougainvillea, hibiscus, poinsettias, bird of paradise, and flowering vines. The wide, grassy borders of each street set off the homes with grace and distinction.

In contrast, downtown Nairobi has lost most of its charm. The daily traffic is undisciplined, frenetic and frightening. Towering office buildings, devoid of style, restrict the air and blot out the sun. Walking is difficult and dangerous. The sordid hucksters of tourism dominate the urban landscape. The infirm and the destitute appear to inherit the capital city. In twenty years, the quaint allure of Nairobi has disappeared.

April 22:

In 1964, Bill Attwood was the first American ambassador appointed to newly-independent Kenya. Bill served in Nairobi until six months before my arrival in 1966. Previously, Ambassador Attwood was editor of *Look* magazine, and President Kennedy appointed him Ambassador to Guinea.

Bill Attwood wrote a book entitled *The Reds and the Blacks* (without apologies to Stendahl) which revealed confidential information to which he had been privy in his role as Ambassador to Kenya. Unfortunately, shortly after my arrival in Nairobi, the book was released.

When the Kenyan leadership became familiar with the contents of the book, I was ostracized by the ministers in the Kenyan government and by senior members of the extensive diplomatic corps. It was suggested that I be declared persona non grata. The memoirs incorporated, verbatim, sensitive conversations with President Jomo Kenyatta and other senior government officials.

The British Secrets Act prohibited publication of sensitive classified security information for a period of twenty-five years following overseas service. Each US Ambassador signed a comparable ten-year restriction prior to his or her overseas assignment. For a ten-year period, an American ambassador was precluded from writing or speaking about confidential matters, particularly involving a head of state.

As a journalist, it is assumed that Bill Attwood felt that his "freedom of press" rights took precedence over the document regarding confidentiality which he signed at the Department of State.

My assignment in Kenya became tenuous. In the absence of requested guidance from the Department of State, I called a press conference in Nairobi. I informed the representatives of the media that I was taking a voluntary oath that I would not write about, or talk about, information to which I was exposed as Ambassador for a period of five years following my departure from Kenya. I wanted the Kenyans to be aware explicitly of my oath of secrecy. The approach was effective. The Kenyans were willing to accept my good-faith declaration. Within a period of several months, normal relationships were restored.

Two years later, based on my performance as American Ambassador to Kenya, I was selected as a recipient of the Arthur Flemming Award as "one of ten outstanding young men (prior to affirmative action) in the Federal Service." This was the first time that a representative of the Department of State had been designated for the award. The nomination was submitted by the Department of State.

April 24:

Patti and I had luncheon with the Parfets at their exquisite estate on Tchui (giraffe) Road in Muthaiga. In 1953, Cort sold his successful confectionery business to General Foods and moved to Europe. In Paris, he married Claude and launched a chewing gum business which scooped the incipient chlorophyll market.

In 1965, he emigrated to Kenya. While Bill Attwood was American Ambassador, Mr. Parfet acquired a ten square mile plot of land near Nanyuki in Kikuyu country at the foot of Mount Kenya. Soliciting the personal assistance of Minister of Agriculture, Bruce McKenzie, Parfet obtained the requisite exemptions from Africanization. With beautiful Charlerois cattle on the major spread, he built a high fence around one-fourth of his property which was converted into a private game reserve. In the intervening years, he has assembled and/or bred forty lions, twenty-three White Rhino, eighteen Black Rhino, and the full range of antelope including eland.

Recently, Cort Parfet was granted an audience with President Moi. The land surrounding his ranch had been given, in small plots, to local Africans. The new residents were accessing, for irrigation, the small river which flows through the Parfet ranch. Parfet's source of water has been severely restricted. President Moi designated the river a national resource which precludes the local shamba owners from diverting the river.

April 26 / Nhahururu:

At Nakuru, we discovered that the sole road to northern Kenya was marked "to the War Cemetery." Driving through the Kinangop, we passed subdivided and re-subdivided British farms which are not of sufficient size to sustain the new generation of farmers.

In 1966, we devoted out first free weekend to a drive to Thompson's Falls. The falls are located about one hour's drive northwest of Nairobi. At that time, the well-kempt lodge overlooking the impressive falls included a beautiful British-style garden. Today, the clientele is exclusively African, which is their right, but the lodge has become a dilapidated hovel. The former gardens have become a series of small camping sites which rent for less than two dollars per day. The town of Thompson's Falls, which was previously a playground for British expatriates, is now called Nyahururu.

Twenty-seven kilometers east, on the new tarmac road to Nyeri in the Central Highlands north of Nairobi, we arrived at Sharp's dirt road and the second crossing of the equator within an hour. Our destination was Kufuma Carpets, a Kikuyu women's artisan project managed by Joy Mayers.

As we approached Joy's home, the long rains presented the first downpour of the season. Within two minutes, the road became deep mud, and we slithered our way to the Kufuma entrance. At the last hill before habitation, we were hopelessly grounded. Within seconds a Land Rover arrived, and we were towed to safety.

Roy Mayers was born near Brisbane, Australia. He joined his father in Kisumu, Kenya on Lake Victoria in 1926 to assist with the first sugar estate in Kenya. After innumerable bouts with malaria, and disenchantment with the humid, tropical, Lake Victoria climate, he left for the Kenyan highlands to marry the attractive Joy and to raise sheep. His ranching skills did not convert to shillings. He was not a success as a farmer with cattle in Masai country, with vegetables, or with sheep.

Fifteen years ago, he decided to manage a tea estate in Nandi.

The clever and efficient Joy converted twelve acres of scrub into a beautiful landscaped, productive tea plantation.

Three years ago, after creating permanent gardening jobs for fifteen Africans, Joy was informed that her assignment was being Africanized summarily. The Mayers moved to their present location and developed the Kufuma carpet enterprise which has been nurtured by Joy's daughter. Since Roy is now incapacitated with severe emphysema, Joy and her daughter run the carpet operation.

Kufuma means "woven together." At the "factory," thirty-five African weavers are making natural sheep's wool carpets on cedar looms. Joy prepares the designs which are derived from traditional Ethiopian models. It is curious that the tribes of Kenya did not develop comparable techniques; however, cattle, not sheep, have prevailed.

Pile and flat weave carpets ranging in size from one-half to five meters, and handwoven to precise pre-order, are marketed in Kenya. A woman weaver is paid twelve cents for completion of a small area of carpet and is compensated when the carpet on which she is working has been completed. Since each employee also maintains a farm plot, and raises a family averaging seven children, she prepares the carpet sections at her own pace. As a result of this relaxed approach, Joy does not know precisely when an order will be completed or how many hours will be required for the finished product.

For the second time, Joy's venture was Africanized. She was told that she would have the option of acquiring Kufuma Carpets, in her own name, but when the bids were opened, a Kikuyu schoolteacher from Thika was declared victorious. Within days of the change of ownership, the bright young Kikuyu whom Joy had trained to manage the venture was perceived as a threat by the new owner and was discharged. As a concept, Africanization has merit. In practice, time and expertise are required to complete a meaningful transition. This pattern is being repeated throughout former colonial Africa. The prognosis is not encouraging. The Mayers have decided to spend their remaining years in Australia.

After a marvelous roast lamb luncheon, we were grateful for another Land Rover pull to the tarmac. A bent wheelbase delayed our departure from Nyahururu. The essential repair was completed by a young Wakamba who was an auto mechanics student at the nearest

Polytech. He was employed by the gas station but just happened to be in the area. If the condition had not been spotted, a serious accident might have ensued.

For two hours we drove through exceptionally heavy rain. The "Dudus" (locust-like insects) were attracted to our headlights in droves and inundated our windshield. The cars and trucks failed to dim their high beams (as a matter of principle, I assume). Pedestrians were walking without flashlights on the totally darkened roads. There were veritable floods on each side of the road, and the potholes were filled with water. When we arrived at the Naivasha cabin, my hands were shaking. Driving in Kenya can be pleasurable. Unfortunately, the proper conditions only exist on December 12th of every other year.

April 27 / Naivasha:

In late afternoon, two adult Hippopotami emerged from the lake. Until sunset, we watched the Hippos watching us with their highly developed periscopes which Joan Root calls "the tip of the iceberg."

It would be inappropriate to complete another short trip to Kenya without recognizing a virtually insoluble problem—a four percent annual population increase.

Since our departure from Nairobi in 1969, the population of the country has doubled. It is scheduled to double again before the end of the century.

Two years ago, President Moi displayed exceptional courage in proclaiming that no Kenyan family should include more than four children. Within months the Pope arrived and in one speech undermined the incipient population control policy introduced by President Moi.

In East Africa, the most effective indigenous population control effort has been implemented by the Mandaleo ya Wanawaki women's movement which has been led by Jane Kiano, wife of the former Kenyan Minister of Labor, and financed by Pathfinder. After stunning initial success in educating East African women concerning birth control methods, grassroots opposition demonstrations have been arranged, and the educational program is now in jeopardy.

Many Black Africans are convinced that birth control measures were devised by the White man to maintain White supremacy. Of equal importance, the men of many Kenyan tribes are committed to the notion that the larger the family, the more breadwinners there will be to support a secure old age for the father. In addition, rapid strides in controlling drought and famine may reduce the natural curbs for population growth.

Kenya is choking with people, and the noose is growing tighter. No external development program can cope with the population explosion. It is remarkable that coitus cannot be practiced without destroying the environment in which people live. Unless birth control becomes a reality, Kenya's prospects for a meaningful future are limited. Unfortunately, both the Pope and President Reagan are opposed to reform.

April 28 / Nairobi:

After leaving Naivasha, we drove to the Ngong Hills which overlook the Rift Valley and can be seen distinctly from Nairobi. In *Out of Africa* the views of the Rift Valley from the Ngong Hills are exquisite. The small village of Ngong, at the foot of the hills, has become a depressing African slum. As the entry to the Ngong "circuit," the town does not offer any attraction.

At Karen, we stopped to visit Karen von Blixen's home, which has been designated a unit of the Kenya Museum. In response to attacks from African leaders, the Museum Director, Richard Leakey, defended the decision on the grounds that the *Out of Africa* legend is an essential component of Kenya's history.

Since the Karen Museum was closed, we were only able to see the exterior, which is "settler basic" but attractive. To date, the donations to the interior collection have been confined to a few simple pieces of furniture. The remarkable original collection of furniture and paintings has been expropriated by unknown parties.

Returning to Nairobi, we experienced a ninety-minute traffic jam on Uhuru Highway (the main artery) at 6:30 p.m. While dressing for dinner, there was a power outage. While the outage continued, we attended a dinner as special guests. Candlelight was the order of the day. The expatriate guests informed me that Equity for Africa "will fail because Black Africans will steal you blind in the absence of constant supervision." It should be stated that previous expatriate monitoring of developed country projects has not been notably successful.

October 19 / Return trip to Kenya from the United States:

I have been invited to participate in a Nairobi conference which is sponsored by the Aga Khan Foundation. The conference is devoted to the "Enabling Environment" for private development in Black Africa. More than one hundred delegates representing US and European profit-making and not-for-profit organizations with self-help projects in Sub-Saharan Africa have been invited to attend.

On a Sunday morning, the streets of Nairobi were practically deserted. I strolled past Cotts House, the situs of the former American Embassy, and visited the New Stanley Hotel book store. Returning to my room at the Intercontinental Hotel, via Kenyatta Avenue, I admired the jacarandas in bloom and savored the memories of a less complex era. West on Koinange Street (named after a former Minister of State who was a personal friend), and south to Uhuru Highway, brought me to Central Park and Uhuru Park where the Superb Starlings and sunbirds prompted a yearning for Lake Naivasha.

Proceeding north on Harambee Avenue past the parliament buildings, I continued my walk to the president's office (where I presented my credentials a generation ago); Jogoo House (where Vice President Moi had his office), and City Hall (which was the situs for most of the diplomatic receptions).

The walk solicited nostalgic place recognition, memories of friends and associates, and the strange sensation of being unknown to those who now discharge comparable roles.

October 20:

Today was Kenyatta Day. The contrasts with the celebrations in the 1960s were startling. Kenyatta Day commemorates the arrest and detention of Mzee Jomo Kenyatta, in solitary confinement at Lodwar in the remote Northern Frontier, prior to Kenyan Independence.

In 1966, the veneration for the "George Washington" of Kenya was unlimited. Jubilant crowds filled the streets of Nairobi to honor "Mzee." As the open-roofed Mercedes limo passed by, thousands of wananchi (citizens) cheered, ululated (the women), and laughed as the revered, charismatic, trusted, founding father and effective leader waved the omnipresent, wooden-handled, fly whisk through the open roof. Charisma created the electrifying presence; however, leadership cemented the permanent bond with the people. Kenyatta could be tyrannical; however, compared to other early independent African leaders, with the possible exception of Tanzania's Julius Nyerere (known as "Mwalimu," the teacher), he was more honest, more committed to democracy, and more concerned about his countrymen and his country's future. Including Mwalimu, Kenyatta had the most acute national vision, the most rational prescription for development, and the unique ability to mobilize the former colonial White rulers as partners in post-independence change.

In October 1966, upon arriving in Nairobi, I presented my credentials to President Jomo Kenyatta at State House. During my tenure, I visited the president regularly at his Nairobi office. On several occasions, we met at his Gatundu rural home in the heart of Kikuyu country, one hour north of the capital.

At the time of our initial meeting, Mzee ("wise old man") was in his early eighties. He was a commanding charismatic presence who sported a distinguished white beard, displayed penetrating eyes, an erect carriage, and wielded the fly whisk with dispatch (which illustrated tribal identification and which enhanced the electrifying appearance). He wore glasses only for reading, walked with a brisk and authoritative stride, and his attractive third or fourth wife, Mama Ngina, who was in her early thirties, was a constant presence. Following Kenyatta's demise, Mama Ngina became the epitome of corruption.

Based on several years' residency in London, Kenyatta's English facility was exemplary. He was intrigued with my efforts to use Swahili. Each time we met, he would begin the conversation in Swahili to test my progress.

With me, he was invariably kind and considerate. In 1967, when my elderly father and mother visited Nairobi, President Kenyatta arranged, without my advance knowledge, for my father and me to meet him at Gatundu. Kenyatta was a father figure and a dominating presence.

On this Kenyatta Day, with Daniel Arap Moi as president, the hundreds of citizens walking to the celebration at Uhuru Park were sullen, unhappy, and clearly required to attend. On two occasions, President Moi passed by on Kenyatta Avenue and near the parliament buildings. At each corner, where a score of people waited for his limousine to pass, Moi would raise his white stick (a la Kenyatta) through the open roof provoking only a polite guttural recognition from the disinterested citizens.

At Uhuru Park, one hundred thousand people sat on tiers facing the grandstand. As the jeeps, youth corps members, and military units passed in review, to the beat of a British-trained but uninspiring marching band, the audience responded with polite clapping. Without enthusiasm, the choirs sang. Without verve, the tribal dancers performed. The magic of prior years was gone.

As President Moi read his prepared text, clapping interrupted his presentation only once. He did not smile, and the audience was not responsive.

Twenty years after my arrival in Kenya, the country is inundated with corruption. The decay appears to be a factor at every level of government in every functional area. Moi is becoming exceedingly rich, and the wealth is becoming visible.

After less than ten years as president, democratic institutions have been sullied; elections have been curtailed or postponed; political opposition has been eliminated or immobilized; the attorney general, Charles Njonjo, has been discredited; and the heir apparent, Mwai Kibaki, has been subjected to disparagement. Moi's advisors are increasingly Kalenjin. He is generally inaccessible. Although a few critics consider him benevolent, most agree that he is becoming authoritarian.

When Jomo Kenyatta died in 1977, Kenya might have been exposed to internal revolution without the calming presence of Daniel Arap Moi. Now, President Moi is generating sustained opposition.

October 21:

While serving as the first Director of VISTA (Volunteers in Service to America) in Washington, D.C., in the early summer of 1966, I was informed that my name had been submitted to President Lyndon Johnson as a potential ambassador.

In July, 1966, Joseph Palmer, the Assistant Secretary of State for African Affairs, asked me to visit his office. He informed me that I was to be nominated as American Ambassador to Kenya. Subsequent meetings with Chester Crockett, the Deputy Assistant Secretary for African Affairs, and Undersecretary of State George Ball, made me realize that I was not dreaming.

At an August 8th interview with President Johnson at the White House, we discussed our initial meeting in November, 1964, at his Perdanales Ranch in Texas when I was establishing the VISTA program. Five senior members of the President's Task Force on Poverty (VISTA was an affiliate of the Office of Economic Opportunity), including Sargent Shriver, flew to the San Marcos Ranch to discuss the launching of the poverty program.

In 1966, President Johnson asked me several basic questions about Kenya and requested a status report on my Swahili lessons. I was impressed that he was interested in my qualifications. After thirty minutes, he informed me that Secretary of State Rusk would submit my nomination to the Senate Foreign Relations Committee for further consideration.

On August 13th, the nomination was mentioned in the *Washington Post*, accompanied by a favorable editorial reference. On September 15th, I appeared before the Senate Foreign Relations Committee, chaired by Senator William Fulbright. I will never forget the initial question: "Aren't you a bit young to serve as an Ambassador?" (I was 37 years old.) The only appropriate answer was the truth: "Yes, sir." The Senator was aware that I had not made a donation to a political campaign, that I had voted consistently as a Democrat, and that I had been employed as a civil servant at the Peace Corps.

On October 4th, I was sworn in at the Department of State by Ambassador Averill Harriman, the Under-Secretary of State for Political Affairs.

In August, 1966, following my nomination as Ambassador, I was informed that I was expected to complete a four-week counter-insurgency course. Then, in contrast to now, that subject was academic. The course would have been of marginal value. After requesting reconsideration, I was granted permission to enroll in a special four-week Swahili course at the Foreign Service Institute.

Every morning, five days per week, I drove from our home in

Bethesda, Maryland, to Roslyn, Virginia, to meet my instructor, John Thiuri, a Kenyan. Six hours per day were devoted to the task plus reviewing the tapes at home. After four weeks of that regimen, I was near the breaking point. I was beginning to dream in Swahili, and the commitment paid dividends.

On October 31, 1966, upon our arrival at the old Embakasi Airport in Nairobi, I conducted my initial press conference in Swahili. My extemporaneous opening (previously prepared with painstaking care) was well-received. When I attempted to answer questions, I found that my expertise was not generally adequate to meet the professional challenge.

For the first year in Kenya, I continued Swahili instruction with a personal tutor, Mohamed Mahuruma from Mombasa, for approximately five hours per week. As a result of the improving facility, I was able to rely upon Swahili in a number of speeches, usually "up-country": the Thika Community Center, the dedication of the Mariani Health Center, the arrival of Peace Corps Volunteer contingents; the Rift Valley Academy graduation, the dedication of the Union Carbide plant in Nakuru, and the dedication of two roads in Kajiado. When I was admitted as an elder in the Abaluhya Tribe in Kisii, I delivered a brief speech in Swahili.

Near the end of our assignment in Kenya, it became increasingly clear that many Whites were uncomfortable when I spoke in Swahili, and that urban Black Africans preferred to demonstrate their superior English facility. As a result, I limited my Swahili efforts to "up-country" efforts and to reliance upon an occasional Swahili aphorism, e.g. "Chembe na chembe mkate huwa" (Little by little we make progress).

Back at the "Enabling Environment" Conference, it was transparent that the rationale for the meeting was erroneous. In theory, the excuse was to convene representatives from three vital sectors which were important in Black African development: African governments, African and international private business, and African and international private, nonprofit development-oriented groups.

In fact, the group did not include an international businessperson of stature, none from Africa, and only a few third-tier business representatives from the United States and Canada. There were no chiefs of state or senior ministers. The most senior representation was from the nonprofit contingent in the United States: the President of the Rockefeller Foundation; the President of the Rockefeller Brothers Fund; and the presidents or executive directors of Interaction, Technoserve, and Africare, and senior delegates from the Ford Foundation, the Council on Foundations, the Industrial Council on Development, and, of course, the remarkably influential Equity for Africa. The leaders who must be educated to developmental priorities and expectations were not in attendance. Salient priorities for economic and social progress were not identified.

October 22:

In the government of Kenya, the politicians are controlling private external sources of funding, including private projects. The activities of the myriad international and binational nonprofit organizations with offices in Kenya have not been coordinated. In this environment, it would be inappropriate for Equity for Africa to consider funding projects. Several other Black African countries represent priority needs.

In Kenya, the partial solutions are controls on corruption; coordination of donor efforts; reduction of the abuses of capitalism; diversified food crops; a generation without coups and with honest elections, and a generous dose of good fortune. The prognosis is not encouraging. Discussions with officials of the Ford Foundation, USAID country and regional staff, and Kenyan officials concerned with economic development confirmed this conclusion.

If all African major ventures reflected sound management, and a successful record, small-scale private enterprise would still represent a pressing need. Unless the evolution of private ventures is encouraged, the requisite incentive, leadership, pluralism, competition, and nurturing of local institutions will be limited.

Only grassroots private development can rescue Black Africa. Without effective population controls, which is unlikely in the absence of endorsement by the United States, even small-scale enterprise will be unable to meet the challenge.

After the conference adjourned, I stopped at Alan Bobbe's restaurant to pay my respects to the elderly proprietor who has run the establishment, featuring excellent French cuisine, for more than thirty years.

As I departed, I saw former Attorney General Charles Njonjo who was dining with his wife and friends. He was warm and friendly, kidded about his intent to visit us in Rhode Island "as soon as they returned his passport," and reminisced a bit about our friendship in the late 1960s. He is still svelte, dapper, articulate, informed, and totally incongruous in the Black African context.

Earlier in the week, I had called State House and left a message with President Moi's executive secretary that I would welcome the opportunity to see the president for a brief, purely personal, non-substantive meeting. At 10:40 p.m. this evening, the executive secretary called me at the hotel to inform me that the president would be able to see me next Friday at 8:00 a.m. at the State House in Nairobi. What a remarkable call at a remarkable time of day!

October 31:

After several days discharging Equity for Africa affairs in Dar es Salaam, Tanzania, I returned to Nairobi to meet President Moi en route to my next Equity for Africa commitments in Cote d'Ivoire and Senegal.

After a short wait at State House, I was ushered into President Moi's private office. Following a gap of seventeen years, the president was relaxed, friendly, and positive about our reunion. He is relatively trim and still flashes a ready smile. With the exception of the gray, curly hair, almost a score of years has treated Rais Mzee (the Venerable President) fairly.

After a few exchanges in Swahili, the president said that "Kenya is not what you read in the media" (i.e., graft and corruption). He stated that he was planning a visit to the United States in the near future. In response to my description of the progress of Equity for Africa, he endorsed the objectives and urged me "to undertake projects in the Rift Valley granary" (the area of his Kalenjin tribal roots). "Kenya is doing very well," he said, "but I am worried about the instability of some of our neighbors."

Since Moi was leaving immediately for a rural visit, I took the initiative in terminating the session quickly. He encouraged me to "pay him a visit" each time I returned to Kenya. President Moi may be ignoring corruption, but he can certainly behave in a 'benevolent' manner, and he is still concerned about Kenya's development and international reputation. When positive memories are long-term, it is difficult to make a rational judgment about a human being.

Following the appointment with President Moi, I walked through the University of Nairobi campus and the grounds of the Norfolk Hotel. The former is well-planned, attractive, and beautifully groomed. The library is bulging with books and students. The guest lecturers are impressive. The students are actually attending classes.

The latter is one of the most attractive hotels in captivity with early twentieth century architecture, high ceilings, and two aviaries which feature Ross's Turaco. The Delamere Room is a staid contemporary of the ambience which induced Lord Delamere to dance on the dining room tables. While we resided in Kenya, we avoided the Norfolk Hotel because of the British expatriate stereotype. Now it would be appropriate to patronize the Norfolk to avoid the sterile, modern watering holes with inferior cuisine and busloads of tourists.

August 1, 1989 / Nairobi:

After a three-year absence, I have returned to Nairobi from London. The unique combination of climate, scenery, flora and fauna, and people still constitute a remarkable attraction. The Moi regime, wildlife poaching, greed, poverty, unemployment, and the omnipresent pressure of population growth are still acute realities; however, the entrancing ambience, with shrinking dimensions, continues to flourish.

In the interim, Toby Block has sold the Norfolk and New Stanley hotels. The chain that purchased the Norfolk caters to package tours. The grounds, English-style courtyard, and dining room are now bulging with loud, gauche, inebriated tourists representing caricatures of the safari crowd of earlier generations. A power "outage" (a bit of modernity) has curtailed Nairobi telephone service.

In visiting a few of the commercial art galleries, I was amazed that Robin Anderson, a local artist of renown, is devoting her considerable talent to Masai-batik, "modernistic" themes which can only be described as aberrational. I am delighted that we have been able to retain several of her remarkably sensitive, genuine, stimulating paintings from her earlier "impressionistic" period.

Rowland Ward continues to stock the lovely Lalique-like, animal-etched, crystal, cocktail glasses which we have admired, and used, for more than twenty years.

Given the increasing civil rights strictures of the Moi regime, the level of political opposition has been curtailed; however, an evening walk, which is still appropriate in Nairobi, to the university, accentuated eager student faces, and the usual signs of harmless student dissidence.

Richard Leakey, who served as Director of the Museum, has been appointed Minister of Tourism and National Parks. With the exceptions of Bruce McKenzie and Richard Leakey, no other White has served in the Kenyan cabinet.

Richard's initial policy decisions were to encircle all of the national parks with high security fences and to burn several million dollars worth of stored elephant ivory tusks.

The fence proposal has not been implemented. President Moi authorized the burning of the ivory. It is not difficult to disagree with both proposals.

Several of the Kenya national parks are even larger than the King Ranch in Texas. Poachers could easily cut the fence wire. Because anti-poaching personnel would become even less vigilant, the practice would probably increase. Of greater importance, the animal migration of plains game would be severely interrupted. If natural migrations are threatened, the parks would become even more sterile.

Regarding ivory, I believe that the destruction of existing supplies will increase the world price and the incidence of poaching. A worldwide ban is unlikely given Japanese and Chinese aphrodisiac proclivities. South Africa and Zimbabwe will refuse to implement the ban because those countries control poaching successfully, engage in selective cropping to limit the size of the elephant herds, and rely upon the generated revenue.

President Moi lit the torch which destroyed the ivory trove in Nairobi. That public relations gesture will not generate the spark to control the poachers or to diminish the Asian quest for sexual potency.

August 22:

Returning to Nairobi from Mozambique and Swaziland where we were exploring the Equity for Africa potential, I was reminded of the Kenyan rigidity regarding travel to South Africa in the sixties. As an Ambassador, I could not travel to South Africa, and return to Kenya, with a diplomatic passport. Since the passport would have been stamped with a South African ingress and egress date, the Kenya immigration authorities might have interposed an objection to my return. At the very least, it would have become a media event.

During that period, several westerners were engaging in the subterfuge of obtaining a second passport for use to and from South Africa. I considered that practice duplicity. It would have been useful to have visited South Africa for educational purposes, but the current trip to the airport was my first experience in that country.

After checking in at the Nairobi hotel, we attended a luncheon hosted by Doria Block which included Lee Harrigan as a guest. Lee's father, Lord Harrington, prosecuted unsuccessfully the self-confessed wife murderer who was featured in the Kenyan novel and subsequent movie based on fact, *White Mischief*. Lee read the entire transcript of the trial and corroborated the impression that the alleged killer was guilty.

Subsequent to the luncheon, we accompanied Lee to the extraordinary former British colonial mansion which he rents at Kiambu. The mansion, located at a suburb north of Nairobi, overlooks a natural fifty-foot waterfall and incorporates an unbelievably attractive garden. The estate is rented for a pittance from an African coffee estate proprietor who is not interested in the mansion.

August 24 / Naivasha:

At Naivasha, we made a pilgrimage to the unoccupied lakefront property of Alan and Joan Root. In Joan's absence to direct the fortunes of the audiovisual natural history series, most of the wild animals have disappeared. The birds are still present and the hippos continue to use the front lawn for forage. The old-style settler house, the first constructed on Lake Naivasha, is intriguing even when unoccupied.

In today's Nairobi newspapers, several senior government ministers applauded Kenya's ability to feed, clothe, house, and partially educate the gigantic, increasing population. Not one minister hinted that the increase may produce counterproductive conditions. For example, there are currently one million jobs in Kenya. For the current school-age generation, seven million additional jobs must be created in the next decade.

August 25 / Nakuru:

As mentioned previously, Nakuru National Park is one of the few Kenyan environments which is improving. Since our last visit, the rhino population has increased, the Lesser and Greater Flamingoes have thrived, and the flora has blossomed.

With the exception of the overloaded safari buses churning up the dust to allow the occupants to become the first in the chow line at the lodge, the number of tourists is reasonable, and poaching is partially contained.

Hundreds of thousands of flamingoes feed on the alkaline water. An amazing number of other water birds are making Nakuru their home. The acacias at the northern end of the park are statuesque, and the billowing grass at the southern end provides excellent cover for the increasing number of plains animals. With a modicum of effort, the more frequented national parks could follow suit.

August 26 / Eserian Farm:

Leaving Naivasha, we took the familiar route over the Kinangop, the "happy valley" land, to Nhahururu, nee Thompson's Falls. From Nhahururu, we followed the paved road to Nyeri and to Eserian Farms.

In the Masai dialect, Eserian means a "place of peace." J. F. Carnegie, a Scotsman who selected the name, chose wisely. Located at 7,000 feet in the northern foothills of the Aberdere Mountains, Mr. Carnegie created a farming empire including the original house replete with a clock tower and two impressive stone houses. The current seven-acre plot is leased by John and Jane Carver.

The Carvers have converted the larger of the structures into a guesthouse with three bedrooms. The veranda presents a view of a small pond through stately acacias. There is a pleasant garden adjoining the guesthouse. The seven-acre plot is surrounded by thirty-eight additional acres of forest where elephant and buffalo are prevalent. The adjoining areas are predominantly national forests.

The elephants are a recent addition. In 1978, poaching in Samburu National Park, sanctioned illegally by senior representatives of the Kenyan government, forced several hundred elephants into the farmlands near the Aberderes where elephants had never lived previously. The African farmers had their shambas devastated by the herds and several lives were lost.

Rather than dealing with the root problem, poaching in Samburu, the government enlisted the support of game wardens in small aircraft, with amplified police sirens, to drive the elephants from the small farms.

The ruse did not work. The elephants returned. Several still remain in the forests surrounding the Eserian Farm. The saga of the Samburu elephants has been portrayed in an excellent *National Geographic* video.

For thirty-five years, John Carver managed a large cattle farm in the Masai Mara in southwestern Kenya. Subsequently, he managed Elsamere, the Joy Adamson inspired museum at Lake Naivasha. After a short stint as a game warden at the "Ark" resort near the Aberderes, John leased Eserian for two years. The lease has been extended for an additional five years.

Jane Carver left England for Kenya when she was eighteen. A superb tennis player was converted into a farmer's wife.

John and Jane Carver are wonderful people. John represents the best of the White colonial farmer and big game hunter genre. He is sensitive and knowledgeable regarding nature with an emphasis on flora. Jane is attractive, an excellent ornithologist, and possesses a rare sense of humor.

The night before our arrival, Leslie Stahl and her family were guests at Eserian Farm. According to the Carvers, the national television news commentator was charming.

On the first afternoon, I walked in gentle rain. Since I had not been informed that the elephants had departed temporarily, I expected to hear a trumpet call at every bend.

The birdlife at Eserian is incredible. Although only 230 species have been recorded, including the efforts of an ornithological group from the British Museum, some relatively rare species are represented: the African Hawk Eagle, the African Snipe, the Little Mountain Thrush, and several shrikes. The trees and flowers were varied and superb. Although an occasional Turkana farmer or preoccupied cow crossed my path, my sense of well-being was only enhanced.

August 28 / Eserian Farm to Prettejohn Ranch:

From Eserian Farm, on the main route south to Nyeri, we passed the entrance to the Mount Kenya Safari Club and a grand view of snow-capped Mount Kenya at the equator. Both the extraordinary mountain and the Safari Club reminded us of our friend, Bill Holden.

In 1967, Patti and I met Bill Holden at the Mount Kenya Safari Club near the town of Nanyuki. The club was remarkably private and attractive. The ranch-style cottages, separate from the hotel, provided stunning views of Mount Kenya. The cuisine was excellent. The amenities, including birdwatching, were unparalleled. At that time, we also met Bill's wife, Ardis Gaines, who used the screen name Brenda Marshall. Through Bill, we were introduced to a number of entertainment dignitaries including the movie star, Jack Hawkins.

We saw Bill Holden frequently. He was warm, friendly, and committed to conservation.

At a tract adjoining the Safari Club, Bill contributed a significant plot of land for a game farm which was conceived to breed eland as a commercial source of meat. Initially, the concept appeared to work; however, conservationists deprecated the scheme because it converted the innocent field of wildlife management into unacceptable commercial exploitation. In truth, the creator of the game farm was neither a hero nor a villain. When eland meat failed to stimulate a significant market, Bill Holden was considered the latter by a number of conservationists.

Increasingly, the entrepreneurs affiliated with Bill were perceived by the leadership of the Kenyan government as capitalist exploiters. Bill gradually withdrew from the fray, except for his devotion to the Mount Kenya Safari Club. He committed generous portions of his time and fortune to the Wuvulu conservation project in the South Pacific which was conceived by Jacques Cousteau. The project involved the creation of a bird sanctuary and primate center near Papua, New Guinea.

During our residency in Kenya, Bill Holden never traded on our friendship or asked for assistance with government of Kenya contacts.

Following our departure from Kenya, Bill and I maintained a sporadic correspondence through his residence in Palm Springs. In spite of his motion picture success, he was a private person who disdained the frivolities of Hollywood. In his later years, he derived satisfaction from his role in *Network* and in a 1981 movie filmed in the Australian outback. He was also romantically linked with the actress Stephanie Powers who shared his interests in Kenya and in conservation.

At age 63, Bill Holden died. The UPI obituary devoted one sentence to his conservation commitments. I shall remember Bill for his grasp of international affairs, his dedication to the preservation of our natural heritage, his charm, and his essential human decency.

After leaving the Mount Kenya area, we passed Cort Parfet's Texas-sized Solio Ranch. Cort allows guests at "the Ark," which is affiliated with the Aberdere's Country Club, to visit his private game reserve for a limited period each morning.

In order to retain his ownership of the gigantic ranch, Cort has been obligated to reward scads of officials for the privilege. Now, in spite of President Moi's agreement, the government is attempting to partition Solio into a number of smaller parcels.

Kenya, Zimbabwe, and South Africa are the only remaining Sub-Saharan African countries where Whites can own extensive tracts of land. In Zimbabwe, President Mugabe is changing that condition through squatters and violence. In Kenya, bureaucratic pressure has been applied with reasonable compensation. Expropriation has not become a reality. Given the population explosion and the Kikuyu thirst for land, President Moi may resort to less subtle measures.

At the Aberdeen Country Club, we were met by Michael Prettejohn's driver who took us in a Land Rover over a single lane, hilly, scrubby track to the Prettejohn's 750,000-acre spread which adjoins Solio.

During the Mau Mau insurrection, Michael Prettejohn was second in command in a covert, quick-strike British military unit which was assigned to the Aberdere Mountains, the heart of the rebellion. Subsequently, he inherited a large tract from his father and acquired the present "smaller" ranch from a relative. Until 1976, when all hunting was banned in Kenya, except on designated tracts, Michael made his living as a big-game hunter.

In recent years, Michael has invested heavily in the Galana Ranch which he and an American investor have developed in an arid wasteland adjoining Tsavo National Park near the Kenya coast. Thousands of acres of semi-desert land have been converted to ranches for cattle. More than four hundred jobs have been created. The cattle breeding research at Galana has become world-renowned.

President Moi has manifested increasing interest in Galana. Through a series of pseudo-legal interventions over a period of two years, the Galana management has been immobilized. The government of Kenya has refused to allow Galana to sell cattle. It is unknown when the final decision will be made concerning the future of the ranch. At issue is the amount of compensation which the owners will receive for divestment by unilateral government action. If the compensation is less than eight million US dollars, the amount of the current investment, expropriation will be the result.

Michael Prettejohn is convinced that no compensation will be awarded. If that occurs, the amount of foreign capital invested in Kenya will be curtailed appreciably. Kenya will join Zimbabwe in the quest for exclusive Black land ownership.

Although Prettejohn has realized considerable wealth, mostly in realty, I do not feel that the government of Kenya would be justified in imposing expropriation. The abuses of former White colonials, and current foreign developers, are clever and covert. The results are extremely profitable. In response, expropriation is not the answer. Taxation and other controls would present reasonable alternatives.

When Michael Prettejohn divorced his first wife, she committed suicide. The second wife, Jane, is dressage-oriented, and has displayed a head for business. To supplement their income, Jane sells trinkets at the Aberdere Gift Shop and accepts boarders at the Bandas which are located at a lake created by the ranch dam.

The Bandas comprise several separate units each with a duplex of bedrooms. A distinct unit houses a kitchen and dining room. A near-by hovel, approximately six feet by eight feet, without windows, provides a home for an African family including several watoto (progeny).

We were the only guests at the Bandas; however, at least a score of noisy Africans, of all ages; a herd of horses; and assemblies of sheep and goats were omnipresent during our one-day visit. Four hours of that day were devoted to a luncheon at the ranch house before we were transported to a Banda four miles away.

In late afternoon, we took a game walk with Bwana Prettejohn's former tracker. After an hour following his soft step through semi-arid country, we returned to base without having seen a four-legged critter except for cattle in the distance.

August 29 / Prettejohn Ranch to Nairobi:

This morning, I took a very early bird walk. The water birds at the small lake were active. As I was watching a Paradise Flycatcher in the thick bushes, a herd of imaginary African Buffalo stampeded toward me. I turned to make a last, pitiful defense. As the dust quickly cleared, I realized that approximately thirty horses were being directed to their breakfast grounds by a few of our new African friends.

Upon returning to the ranch house, which was built in 1928 and is the most inviting settler ranch I have visited, Michael informed me that two of Jane's young friends needed a ride to Nairobi. In the bush there is no option. Two young men sat in the backseat of our compact car for more than two hours. While Patti nursed a sore throat, I nursed a slow burn following payment of an exorbitant bill for less than a full day of up-country bliss.

August 30 / Leaving Kenya:

As we arrived in France to visit our younger son and his family in Bourron Marlotte, we did not realize that we had returned to our "second home" for the last time. Completion of our work with Equity for Africa, and a sustained bout with cancer, intervened.

In 1998, the bombing of the American Embassies in Nairobi and Dar-es Salaam provided a personal shock. After three years residency in Kenya, innumerable visits to Tanzania, and a number of stints overseas, I identified in a very personal way with foreign service personnel both American and local.

In Nairobi in the 1960s in a downtown office building, we were concerned with security. US Marines were present at the entrance to the building which was shared with other tenants. To enter the embassy offices, identification procedures were rigorous, and security issues were a regular senior staff topic.

On the other hand, it was my conviction that the US Department of State had not devised a comprehensive anti-terrorist program. USSR covert activities were stressed. For an African post, most of the security procedures were limited.

Many years following my departure from Nairobi, the new embassy building was constructed without fanfare. The latest security measures were incorporated. In 1998, the new embassy was partially destroyed by a powerful truck bomb. There were 250 deaths. The incumbent US Ambassador alleged that she had requested funds for modernized security measures which were refused by the Department of State. The Department responded that the Ambassador's pleas were buried in at least two annual budgets submitted by the embassy.

When the United States government evacuates ten injured citizens of the United States who were employees of the embassy and leaves more than 1,000 injured Kenyan citizens, including embassy employees, without adequate medical attention in Nairobi, the priorities are clear. The United States is losing critical goodwill abroad.

Kenya was, and remains, a remarkable country. Unless the United States advocates population control, Kenya will become a lovely memory.

NIGER
The Agadez Cross

December 21, 1987 / Paris to Niamey, Niger:

In November, my wife Patti departed for Niamey, Niger, to discharge a consultative assignment with VOCA (Volunteers in Overseas Cooperative Assistance) at the National Museum. After a month's separation, she greeted me upon my arrival at Niamey Airport.

At the Grand Hotel, where we would reside, we went to the terrace for a "Coka." I had the pleasure of meeting a half dozen of the Nigerien talent with whom Patti was working at the Museum arts and craft cooperative.

As a "dependent," I felt like Cary Grant in *I Was a Male War Bride*; however, the Chavue Souris (fruit bats) flying overhead, and the muddy Niger River below, were vivid reminders that Europe was far away.

December 22 / Niamey:

How do you capture the essence of a national culture? As a tourist in an arid, Moslem, landlocked, impoverished, west African country, is it possible to reflect the stimulations and frustrations of a developing country without resorting to stereotype?

With six million people, ninety-five percent of whom are affiliated with the Sunnite Branch of Islam, and a large percentage of the rest are Christians residing in Niamey, Niger (named after the River) was the "last stop" for the French West African colonial empire.

Until the discovery of uranium, Niger represented 400,000 square miles of waterless Sahara sand dunes; a particularly green southwestern strip hugging the Niger River, and a bit of vegetation near Lake Chad on the southeastern border.

Since the arrival of the French in 1899, the limited natural resources and development potential handicapped colonial exploitation. The facade of French language facility, confined generally to the capital city, is one of the few remnants of the colonial period. Niger was granted independence in August, 1960 (early for Sub-Saharan Africa).

In ninety-percent of Niger, the Fulani nomads, the same cultural stock who are prevalent in Cameroon, reside. The Tuaregs are found in the arid northern region. The Hausas, who reside in the south and who constitute one-half of the population, have provided the principal language. With seven national tribal languages, and a plethora of smaller itinerant tribes, the concept of nationhood is secondary.

In the southwestern corner of Niger, where Nigeria, Benin, Burkina Faso and Mali meet, the life-sustaining Niger River nurtured the semi-fertile environment for the evolution of the major city, Niamey. With 450,000 inhabitants crowding the banks of the swift-flowing, endlessly fascinating river, the capital has become the modern statement of a nation and the market place for a barter economy. Hausa, Jerma and Tuareg tribes interact effectively with the Islam faith as the adhesive. In this metropolitan oasis, the sand blows twelve months per year, and six months may elapse without rain.

The Niger River dominates the attention span and the landscape. The Pont Kennedy (the inevitable JFK impact in Black Africa) connects the urban area of the city with the newly-constructed University of Niamey and the so-called suburbs. An island, midway across the bridge, serves as a bathroom; laundry; truck garden plot for rice and vegetables; haven for kingfishers, egrets, and herons; and reminder that life becomes problematic when the Niger River floods or when the rains cease.

From the Grand Hotel terrace, located at the summit of one of the stark cornices on the right bank, we watched the swift, decorated pirogues convey rice farmers, fishermen, and fellow travelers on their appointed rounds.

The capital city, in the government-oriented core, features modern, sand-colored, French-style buildings appropriate for the ecology. Reflecting the prior predominance of uranium, the most attractive buildings are still devoted to mining interests. The same phenomenon is true on the university campus.

Within a blink, the ultimate in poverty prevails. Beggars are omnipresent. Garbage is uncollected. Unpaved streets emerge from all directions. Dust partially masks the reality of unemployment, disease, overpopulation, and ennui.

December 23:

At the Musée, where the artisan cooperative has located its shops, the potential for additional employment is represented. On the most attractive plot in the city, a far-sighted French bureaucrat carved out a tract for the National Museum which incorporates a zoo, aquarium, boutique, and education center. A score of small, attractive, indigenous structures attempt to tell the story of a nation—ethnic diversity, tribal pride, historic continuity, artisan skills, mineral resources, and eternal hope. The museum complex is open to the public without charge. It is administered with the loose efficiency which prompted the derivation of the word "genius."

The artists affiliated with the cooperative are silversmiths, sculptors, weavers, leathersmiths, and potters. Working in the open at narrow looms or in dirt-floored huts, more than two hundred artisans ply their trades.

As a VOCA volunteer for two months, Patti is committed to the proposition that systematic scheduling, design diversity, a marketing strategy, a semblance of organized development, and a generous dose of encouragement will create an attractive product line. In four short weeks, she has earned the respect of her coworkers coupled with the gratitude of the cooperative and museum leadership.

The American Ambassador, Richard Bogosian, a career foreign service officer who has served in Niamey for three and one-half years, hosted a holiday reception at the residence. A makeshift chorus sang Christmas carols, while two hundred Americans, Koreans, and

Europeans, without a Nigerien in sight, drank heavily and complained about the weather, the food, the limited recreational options, and the local citizens. The conversation was a vivid reminder of why Peace Corps was founded twenty-six years ago.

The Peace Corps staff who were present acted like employees of USAID. They were preoccupied with housing allowances, salary scales, the plight of "singles" in Niamey, and the essentiality of frequent vacations.

There are many major challenges to be undertaken in Niger. In my opinion, the American mission is wasting scarce personnel and financial resources without any tangible substantive impact. Speaking the French language without earning the respect of host country nationals does not reflect enlightened American representation.

December 24:

At the University of Niamey, most of the buildings are newly-constructed. Limited rainfall makes the structures appear to be foreign legion fortresses in the middle of the Sahara. The roads are sand, and it is totally incongruous to see a College of Pedagogy in the middle of a desert.

The French West African Regional School of Minerals and Mines is the most impressive building and offers the only discipline or profession which incorporates a regional dimension. It is not surprising that private corporate entities, coveting uranium, have underwritten the costs of the regional program.

From the university, we walked back over the JFK bridge. The painted piroques were unloading fruits and vegetables for the local market. Young men were washing clothes, and themselves, in the river. Ladies were bashing the clothes of hotel guests against the rocks. A few muzzled, desert-worn camels with their staggering loads, rested in partial shade. Pedestrian and vehicular traffic ambled in both directions across the life-line bridge.

Without the Niger River, the country would represent a desert waste. With the river, Niger grows some food; educates a few; provides employment for a minority; serves as home for too many; and carries the germs which attack, but fail to curtail, the population increase.

Prior to dinner, we went to the home of Jean Pierre and Mary

Kaba. Patti had met them on a short river trip. Subsequently, she asked Jean Pierre, a photographer and film producer from Senegal, to prepare some photographs for a museum cooperative brochure.

Mary is an American, born in Germany, who teaches French linguistics at the University of Niamey. She also speaks several local dialects including Hausa.

Jean Pierre speaks limited English. The couple met in Niamey seven years ago. They have three sons. They are kind, likable, competent people who will probably not be fully accepted in America or Africa.

December 31:

With further exploration of Niamey, a more complicated city unfolded. Patti and I completed a lengthy tour which included the old French quarter, cooperative truck gardens, the industrial complex (beer and chemicals which were spawned by uranium discoveries), and the riverside drive. With the exception of the inevitable "Coka," there are not any business interests from the United States in evidence.

In 1926, the French colonial authorities transferred the capital from Zinder to Niamey. There was no planning involved in the expansion of the city. With the exception of the broad street which houses the museum and several ministries, urban blight is predominant.

The majestic and totally inappropriate French Embassy and residence of the American Ambassador are located a considerable distance from the downtown area in the old French quarter. Since the French were the colonial power for two generations, there is a plausible excuse for the display of affluence. In contrast, the United States, with limited interests, development programs, tourists, corporate involvement, or official representation supports a veritable mansion for the ambassador. The ambassador's residence incorporates a commanding view of the river. Across the street, a large US Embassy building has been constructed. A mammoth USAID building has been erected next door which houses the inconsequential development program. A large swimming pool and recreational complex is being constructed for employees of the American Mission.

The complex also includes horse stables and dressage and jumping areas for the expatriate community. Two kilometers beyond, the most impoverished villages in the region are located. Each day, the masses must pass the trappings of luxury in the search for daily employment.

In contrast, the Peace Corps has leased an appropriate office near the Grand Market. It would appear that a quarter of a century of demonstrated performance of another form of representation has provoked little interest from the official American community in many countries. The post exchange and commissary mentality still prevail.

We visited SCORE, the only grocery in town, to purchase food and water for our projected up-country trip. There were two hundred people (one-third customers and two-thirds gawkers who enjoyed fondling the merchandise) in a room the size of a typical convenience store in the United States.

The fruits and vegetables were in deplorable condition. The choices were severely limited. Two sullen, lethargic, poorly-trained checkers were making a feeble attempt to cope with the increasing clog of patrons. As Patti waited in an ostensible line, I watched at least two dozen people, mostly women, push in front of others. The American queue is an endangered species.

At the commercial bank and at the airport the same behavior pattern prevailed. Lines do not form. Tempers do not flare.

David Levin, a former Peace Corps Volunteer who is the Deputy Director of the Peace Corps in Niger, is interested in the development of small-scale private enterprise and has agreed to identify a few entrepreneurial agricultural projects which might warrant Equity for Africa financing.

Patti and I "dressed up" (for me a clean white shirt) for New Year's Eve and enjoyed a mediocre dinner at the Galweye Hotel. A bevy of French expatriate children surfaced with loud voices intact. After our usual holiday carousing, we retired at 10:00 p.m. Unfortunately, we missed the annual Times Square excuse for a New Year's celebration.

January 1, 1988 / Niamey to Agadez:

With Salifou as our driver, we rented a car and drove 1,023 kilometers, relying upon our halting French facility, from Niamey to Agadez in the arid north central region. The trip required twelve hours.

Heading east, north of the Niger River, we were in reasonable proximity to "W" National Park, named after the bends in the river. No wild game was sighted. As we passed the first of eleven police and internal customs checkpoints, the military guard on duty was identified as Salifou's father.

At Dogoudoutchi (think of the high school basketball cheers), Salifou claimed his home town and pointed out a rural truck-farming plot which is run by his brothers. Since Salifou has ten children in Niamey, the plot may prove inadequate.

At Birni, in Konni Province, at the border, we saw signs of comparative Nigerian market affluence, and turned north away from the main road to Zinder. The narrow road on which we had been traveling hugs the Nigerian border and enjoys sufficient rainfall to support a modicum of farming, including peanuts, which is a cash crop in Niger. From Birni to Tahoua the green belt gradually disappears and is replaced by barren Tuareg sand brick villages; donkeys; goats; legions of emaciated children; the absence of water and color; and a sand-filled sky which obscures both the sun and the moon. The beehive-shaped grain silos, built by the Tuaregs, are attractive and ingenious. An occasional bore hole yields a small reservoir which serves all purposes including home base for an occasional fish.

At Tahoua, we passed two more checkpoints. At one security gate, a policeman inquired about my profession. After more than an hour of explanation, he still allowed us to proceed on our journey.

We then turned northeast on an excellent paved road which was constructed to serve the uranium mines at Arlit. A convoy of thirteen trucks loaded with ore was heading south to Niamey. As usual, the general population is untouched by natural resources which provide wealth for a few.

Arlit is located about three hundred kilometers north of Agadez. The paved road does not provide access to the attractive Air Mountains, which represent legitimate tourist potential. Currently, only young, hardy camping types with extensive leisure, and strong intestinal tracts, are able to enjoy the scenic beauty.

Approaching Agadez, we lost a muffler which Salifou repaired with dispatch; ran out of gas for which Salifou had a spare five-gallon can; admired the increasing number of grazing camels; cited the patience and skill of the Tuareg nomads who survive without water of other visible means of support, and watched the changing colors of the moonlike, desiccated surface. Arriving at Agadez, we were reminded that Libya and Algeria were located across the Sahara, and that Tripoli and Tunis would be the next permanent settlements to the north.

Agadez—city of mystery and intrigue. Since the fifteenth century, it has been a depot on the trans-Saharan caravan routes; one of the last bastions of the Foreign Legion; the southern gateway to the Sahara, and the traditional headquarters of a powerful sultan.

In contrast to what we imagined, Agadez is a city with one paved street which serves the uranium ore traffic—sand in your eyes, sand in your shoes, beggars, small nude children with open sores and flies engulfing their eyes and mouths, aggressive hawkers pressing their artisan wares, and more sand.

Without overt amenities, the city features two fascinating markets, a link with history, kind and friendly people, and artisan products which reflect ingenuity and diligence.

January 2 / Agadez:

Today, we traveled twenty-six kilometers north of Agadez, through expansive desert, to an oasis which is the situs of a Tuareg village and a women's basket-weaving cooperative. For seven years, under the auspices of the central development agency and the German government, the nomadic Tuareg tribe has been converted into a stable, productive, truck-gardening community. The Germans have departed, but the seeds of a new way of life remain—bore holes, irrigated patches of vegetables and wheat, basic subsistence, and children who possess a reasonable chance for healthy survival.

The ten-year old boy leading the camel that activates the contraption conveying water from the bore hole into the irrigation pipe will probably never attend school. In Niger, free education is provided, but few young people are able to attend. In this community, there is a regional school ten kilometers away which represents nirvana for the few fortunate students involved.

In a Tuareg village, the men control the market, the wealth, leisure time, and attention. The women do the work, including tilling the fields; therefore, the cooperative represents a sea-change in gender status. While some women make attractive baskets, a few with leather bases, for sale in the Agadez and Niamey markets, others tend individual five-foot square irrigated plots. On one plot they grow wheat for sale. On another, they grow lettuce, red peppers, cabbage, and corn for their own consumption. The surplus is sold in the open market. The income is distributed by the women responsible for the plots.

Christina, a young German, unaffiliated, home economics student from Cologne, provides minimal advice to the cooperative. She depicts the ultimate in effective volunteerism. She is low-key, persuasive, patient, competent, and effective. Christina makes periodic pilgrimages to Agadez to heal assorted ailments and to gain essential perspective.

At another Tuareg village, we dodged the goats, small children, and offal, to see the products of a women's weaving cooperative. The work was inferior, reflecting the absence of Christina's expertise; however, it was rewarding to view the superb house-building skills of the Tuaregs. Cane from the Doum Palm is used for both houses and baskets. The results are waterproof, durable, and attractive. For baskets, the young Doum Palm shoots are used. Since extraction may kill the tree, environmental authorities are conducting a study. The results may not be available for an eon.

In the oasis, I enjoyed my first birding success in Niger. The green havens have attracted barbets and sunbirds.

For our village safari we were fortunate to obtain the services of a bright, unemployed mechanic, who served as an interpreter. Since he worked in neighboring Ghana for six years, his English facility was exemplary. Except for the accident of birth, with expertise in French, English, Hausa, Tuareg, and several other major dialects, he could make a fortune with a specialized agency of the United Nations.

Several centuries ago, Agadez was reputedly as large as Tunis. It served as the metropole for major camel routes. The Great Mosque, with its spiky, clay minaret, is still a haven for the devout. The former Sultan's Palace, currently the Hotel de L'Air (remember the mountain range), served as our home away from home. In spite of its heritage, the hotel rooms were as small and basic as comparable establishments in rural Thailand; however, it should be noted that we were staying at the leading Nigerien Hotel outside of Niamey. A communal toilet was shared by the patrons of the bar, dining room, sleeping rooms, the staff, and the public at large. A cold water drip provided the shower. A bare floor, single overhead neon light, one small towel for two guests, no hooks or hangers, no chairs or tables, a board (almost) for a bed, and constant noise from every possible source were the features of our room.

A door banged all night. The mosquitos and flies enjoyed alternating bombing runs. A dozen chickens were strangled in the adjoining court at 5:00 a.m., for the noon repast we assume. Our fellow guests appeared to have emerged from six months in the desert without an oasis.

A French woman, Brigitte Butel, has lived in Agadez for seven years. Formerly, she was a tourist agent. Now, she is employed by a Catholic Mission as an advisor to artisan cooperatives. She is informed and respected. She introduced us to the camel market and the iron and silver artisans. We enjoyed a steak (the species was unknown) dinner as the only guests at a Moslem restaurant.

The Agadez crosses, from a variety of districts, which can be worn as pendants, represent a profitable artisan's line in iron and silver.

At the camel market, Patti had a field day making friends with the occasional blue-eyed camel (according to local custom, the blue-eyed sub-species is hard of hearing) and the goats and donkeys.

Back at the hotel, we strolled across the sandy main street to an Italian (imagine) ice cream parlor. Patti sampled a tasteless, sourball-sized scoop, of an undetectable flavor, which cost the equivalent of $1.00.

For one day the sights and smells of Agadez are educational. After two days, illness and ennui intervene. After seven years, Brigitte faces a formidable challenge.

January 3 / Agadez to Niamey:

The return trip to Niamey required thirteen hours. After breakfast at the hotel, hot tea and a plain piece of stale bread, our food intake for the day was confined to a "Coka," a banana, a piece of fruitcake which I brought to Patti from the United States, and a glass of tepid water.

We ran out of gas, and another five-gallon can saved the day. The engine overheated and severed the main steel part which holds the fan belt in place. Fortunately, on a Sunday afternoon, the driver was able to coax the car one hundred kilometers to his sandy hometown. At a neighborhood garage, he was able to solder the part, and we continued the journey in two hours. Without the driver's expertise, we would have spent the entire Sabbath on a sand dune.

At the garage, Patti took a snooze. I left the car to demonstrate relaxed friendship in the presence of waves of interested citizens who requested cadeau (gifts); attempted to sell local "goodies," and gawked and gesticulated at the silly "farangs."

After a dozen checkpoints, with temperatures in excess of 100°F, we fell into the tub, and then the sack, at the increasingly luxurious Grand Hotel in Niamey.

January 4 / Niamey:

The explorer, James Richardson, reported that the omnipotent Sultan of Zinder made several fortunes selling slaves to Arab traders. Initially, he confined his slave-hunting raids (razzias) to infidels (kafirs). Greed convinced the Sultan to expand his market to include Muslims who disobeyed or displeased him.

When the final chapters concerning the slave trade are written, a modicum of the blame for the dastardly practice must be shared by indigenous Black Africans, Arabs, ship captains, and mercantile middlemen, as well as the eventual slave owners.

Before leaving negative reporting, "the Tree of Death" should be described.

In the Tenere region, northeast of Agadez, the reigning Sultan tore out the hearts of his offending victims and hung the bodies by their heels on the "Tree of Death" for the enjoyment of the vulture brigade. The remnants of "The Tree" are prominently displayed at the Museum in Niamey as the ultimate tribute to man's inhumanity.

We walked across the first span of the Pont Kennedy to the bucolic island which we admired from our hotel. Relying upon the elevated boundaries of flooded rice paddies, we passed an oasis filled with Doum palms and followed the main channel of the Niger River to the terminal southern point of the island. A few curious farmers waved. For the first time in Niger, we were not approached by hawkers, gawkers, or beggars.

Large white water lilies surrounded the rice paddies. The birdlife was fascinating—warblers, cisticolas, rollers, plovers and shrikes. Pirogues with young fishermen floated by, and farmers cutting rice from smaller pirogues acknowledged our presence. In the distance, the ministry buildings and the Grand Hotel accentuated the quest for modernity.

January 5:

After a score of years of living, working and traveling in lesser-developed countries, I have been exposed to an infinite variety of maladies. Life in the Third World requires some perspective in coping with illness and disease; however, I am confident that Niger deserves special notation.

Proximity to the Sahara brings sand into the Nigerien existence. It not only obscures the sun and moon on the clearest day, but it also makes breathing difficult and hazardous. Respiratory illnesses are omnipresent. Since arriving in Niger, I have experienced constant chest congestion, blocked nasal passages, coughs, colds, and drips. When the lack of cleanliness associated with daily life, including the preparation of meals, is coupled with limited sources of potable water, open sewers, and insects, the plot sickens.

As we complete the Niger saga, in spite of the daily preventive pill, my gout has returned. Diarrhea is a fixture. The mattresses, or lack thereof, have provoked back pain. My muscles and ligaments are sore, and a constant cold has become a way of life.

I do not wish to overreact. A traveler must assume the risks in order to enjoy the benefits. Inconveniences to which we are exposed are usually only different rather than deadly. At the same time, it was necessary for me to get this issue off my chest (wrong metaphor). In any event, at a ripe old age, I should expect my share of physical ailments. World travel is safer than taking a walk in a major city in the developed world.

We rented a forty-foot, canvas-covered, pirogue. Sporting a number of poles for seats, we headed downstream on the Niger River. With visions of Mungo Park, Gordon Laing, Rene Caillie (who was a better Arab impersonator than Lawrence of Arabia), and Henry Barth, dancing in our heads, we poled into the main current. With the unanticipated assistance of a small outboard motor, we went five miles downstream and returned to our launching pad under the Kennedy Bridge in two restful, educational hours.

Several small islands served as temporary refuge for large flocks of water birds. Along the banks of the river, weavers, warblers, and canaries eked out a living. The environment suggested hippos and crocodiles; however, our river boatman informed us that they frequent the river 200 kilometers upstream near the Mali border.

The strong current was flowing southeast, and a sand-filled wind was blowing northwest. The confrontation caused a series of eddies.

Because of the severe annual floods, settlements along the river are sparse. Small motors were lifting water for irrigation. Cattle, goats, and homo sapiens utilize the river for most natural functions. An occasional hand-hewn pirogue served the needs of a solitary fisherman. The sand dunes in the distance were forceful reminders that the river scenes were atypical.

In returning along the northern shore, we passed the stately, unoccupied Presidential Palace (which was the situs of the shooting of a group of tourists); the palaces of the French and American Ambassadors, and the ubiquity of the slums.

The cool breeze, the lulling sound of the miniature motor, the gentle roll of the pirogue, and the vivid scenes from a novel vantage point presented an essential change of pace.

The President of the Museum Cooperative Association, Mr. Garba, invited us to dinner at his suburban home near the University. Mr. Garba is a comparatively wealthy man; yet, the invitation was extraordinary and a tribute to Patti's ability to relate. As a thoughtful gesture to accommodate our limited French facility, Garba included a Belgian tire salesman who deprecates Niger and whose uninformed prejudices yielded comic relief.

I would estimate that Garba is in his early forties. He is a devout Moslem who has three young, attractive wives and ten children (five of each gender). He anticipates that the ultimate number of progeny will approximate twenty. As we arrived, two of the wives and two of their daughters were presented briefly and then relegated to the kitchen. The third wife had just served one of her essential purposes and was recovering from childbirth at the country house en route to Zinder.

The five sons were allowed to interact with the guests throughout the evening. They were well-dressed in Hausa two-pieced pajamas. They were polite and interested in the conversation.

Hausa Muslim wives do not enjoy legal rights. They can be divorced at will, command no rights to progeny, and their possessions belong ultimately to the husband.

As we entered the small home with small rooms (ten feet by ten feet), we passed through the sand floor entry, barren of furniture or light. In the open-roofed dining room, the simple table was stuffed with food. Four basic chairs were available for the diners. From the Garba family, only the man of the house was eligible to eat with the guests.

In a bucket, filled with large chunks of ice, placed on the ground, we were offered the choice of bottled water or French wine, both purchased for the occasion. Since Moslems do not drink alcoholic beverages, Garba left the table, drove to an unknown destination, and returned with a corkscrew. Patti and I had a sip of wine and our Belgian confrere drank one and one-half bottles with the anticipated result.

The first course was a salad composed of lettuce (beware) and onion. Garba consumed several gigantic servings. Next came guinea fowl, much tastier than the local chicken. Garba had six large pieces. Then we were served mutton chops, wrapped in plain brown paper, as was the fowl. The mutton was excellent, and "pili-pili" powder enhanced the flavor. Garba enjoyed a half dozen chops. With the meal, we were served sliced fried potatoes topped with a delicious cheese concoction. For dessert, we were offered watermelon, papaya, and pamplemouse (grapefruit). Garba had a half-dozen of each. Following each course, the remains were dispatched to the adjoining unlighted open-air kitchen which received a slight glow from the sand-obscured moon. Two wives and ten children finished the remaining food.

There were not any condiments, napkins, tablecloths, etc. We were served with, and ate with, a spoon. We were never introduced to the bathroom facilities. Our boorish fellow guest went "out to see Africa" on the sand floor of the adjoining room. In the dining room there were not any pictures, personal possessions, glassware, tables, or lamps (except for the table on which the servings were placed). Throughout the meal, Garba played with three huge, rough-cutting knives (I assume one for each spouse).

Following the meal, Patti entertained two of the boys with a coloring set which she had brought as a gift. I followed Garba into an adjoining room which was his bedroom. Total chaos prevailed. The furniture was confined to a simple, cluttered bed, a bookshelf with one book (a leather-bound Koran), and one trunk and several suitcases on the sand floor. Dirty clothes were strewn in every direction. With great pride, Garba displayed at least twenty elaborately designed prayer gowns which were clean, ironed, and safely ensconced in the suitcases and trunk.

Garba plugged a lengthy extension cord into the only electrical socket in the house. The cord extended through the dining room and into the kitchen where it emanated from a television set. Twelve eager faces were glued to the screen as *Different Strokes* or a comparable program was presented. All of the viewers stood in the dark.

At this point, Garba went quietly into his bedroom, shut the door, and there was not any sound for thirty minutes. At 10:00 p.m., Patti and I suggested in raised voices that it might be time to return to our hotel. Garba emerged in a white, unadorned daily robe. Without seeing the wives, to express our gratitude, we were driven back to town.

The home I have just described represents affluence in Niger. The ingredients of the meal were superb. The cooking was excellent. It was a special privilege to view a Hausa family in action. The cultural differences were profound.

As we left Garba's home, we commented on the local music which we had heard during dinner. Garba suggested that we stop at the provenance, an open plot of ground lit by a floodlight. Two hundred Hausas were assembled in a large circle.

The music was provided by an amplified guitar and three drummers. As a percussionist, I was fascinated that the drums were halves of Calabash gourds, placed in the sand, and beaten with whisks of cane which served as drumsticks. The beat was lively. The drum rudiments reflected skill. The guitar lead played basic chords. No other musical instruments were involved.

Elderly Hausa women in their finest long dresses formed lines of four to six and displayed their tribal dancing ability as they approached the combo. The few male dancers displayed superior expertise. The working-class audience, including a few artisans from the Museum Cooperative, showed their appreciation by placing coins on the foreheads, and then in the hands, of the favored dancers.

The dancers, musicians, and audience made us feel at home. They were genuinely pleased to have outsiders attend their tribally-inspired dancing.

The evening was special The sentiments were sincere. We felt indebted to Garba for his friendship, confidence, hospitality, and generosity.

January 6:

From 1982 through 1985, William R. Casey served as President Reagan's Ambassador to Niger. At the time of his appointment, he was a private mining consultant in Paris with primary interest in uranium. As a Denver resident, his political clout is unknown; however, he contributed to Reagan's campaign. Since uranium was a significant Nigerien export, it follows that Casey was eminently well-qualified for the ambassadorial assignment in Niamey.

Casey compiled a positive record as a conscientious and committed Chief of Mission. Since leaving the foreign service, he has founded a small venture capital firm, Birni N'Konni, which is based in Denver and which has generated business in a few West African Francophile countries. Currently, he is peddling a private potato growing and marketing scheme to Niger and Mali.

William Casey appeared at the Grand Hotel terrace when Patti and I were having the inevitable "Coka" as a substitute for lunch. In a brief discussion, I learned that he is attempting to arrange an appointment with the new President of Niger, Ali Seibou, who runs a pseudo-military dictatorship. The agenda will be restricted to securing tax exoneration for his potato caper.

Because Patti was able to focus exclusively on the immediate artisan's plight in Niger, she generated a positive attitude and made significant progress. In contrast, because I was responsible for evaluating small-loan project potential in several countries including

Niger, my reaction to the economic development reality rather than to the people, is generally less than positive.

In Niger, I have been frustrated. The noisome acquired traits of the urban, sophisticated Nigeriens; the loathsome official representatives of foreign countries; the unthinking tourists and the inadequacies of the religious ethic are the major roadblocks to development. At the same time, the latent skills and obvious potential of the indigenous people are encouraging.

Although it is doubtful that I will ever return to Niger, I shall remember the Nigerien people with affection.

URUGUAY
Launching a University

March 12, 1992 / Miami, Florida, to Rio to Montevideo, Uruguay:

Upon completing interviews for the presidency of the American University of Paris, I flew from Paris to meet Patti at the Raleigh-Durham, North Carolina airport. We boarded an immediate flight to Miami where I savored an hour's nap before boarding the Varig flight to Rio de Janeiro.

After flying all night, we arrived at the Rio Airport to meet Dr. and Mrs. Richard Epply, who will join us in discharging the International Executive Service Corps university project assignment in Montevideo. Dick is a retired marine biologist from the Scripps Institution of the University of California. After a pit stop in Buenos Aires, and twenty-four hours in airplanes, it was reassuring to place my feet on terra firma.

With the exception of two days in Buenos Aires and two days in Lima, Peru, on a Peace Corps assignment in 1964, I have never spent any time in South America. In fact, if you add two days in Bogota, Columbia, also on Peace Corps business, and a short stop in Panama, my Latin American experience has been revealed (excluding Mexico).

In contrast to most international airports, the Aeropuerto

Internacional de Carrasco represents acceptable size and reminded us of a few distinctive airports in Africa.

We were met by Captain Eitel Ravena, a retired naval officer, who serves as the president of the commission appointed by the President of Uruguay to implement the presidential decision to create the Instituto Superior San Fernando de Maldonado (a potential university). Adhemar Louis Pigni, an agricultural engineer and former Captain in the Navy, who served as Uruguayan Naval Attache in Paris, and who is the only full-time employee of the Institute, joined the welcoming party.

On the Rambla, a beautiful drive adjoining the Rio de La Plata, the confluence of three rivers which becomes the Atlantic Ocean at Punte del Este, we saw the homes of the affluent in Carrasco and the luxury apartments of the moderately wealthy which adjoin the playas (beaches). Although the water is polluted, there were hundreds of bathers and sun worshipers on an abnormally hot day in the South American autumn.

At the Parque Hotel and Casino, which is located on the beach, we received the first week's assignment from a representative of the International Executive Service Corps. Unfortunately, from our jet-lagged perspective, the assignment begins tomorrow.

A generation ago, the Parque Hotel must have been a premium spot. Now, it is owned by the City of Montevideo, which realizes the profits from the casino and has allowed the hotel to deteriorate into a dirty, dark, unattractive shell.

The room to which we were taken did not seem like an appropriate home for a one-month stay. The single bed, just slightly larger than a twin, with a sagging mattress and filthy bedspread, dominated the exceptionally small room. It had not been painted for a generation. On a 90°F plus day, the air conditioner was inoperable. The window, which faced the extremely noisy Rambla, could not be shut completely. The small refrigerator was not functioning. There was no rug on the floor, no dresser, and the closet was a three-foot-square portable unit with a broken door and no hangers. If there were hangers, only three or four could have hung in the available space. There were not any chairs, tables, or a desk. The lighting was confined to a single, exposed, overhead forty-watt bulb and a very small table lamp placed on the floor.

After opening the door to the hallway for air, the shutters banged and the traffic from the thoroughfare grew louder. The shouts of the guests surrounding the inner courtyard were constant. On the ground floor, sounds of construction completed the scene.

Venturing into the bathroom, I was greeted by chunks of broken tile on the floor, a leaking commode, a decrepit shower with only a slight cold drip at maximum volume, no washcloth, a single small towel, and no drinking glasses.

In the hallway, I investigated the closet which serves as the linen and towel repository. Empty liquor bottles and grimy dishes provided a feeding ground for scurrying insects, and dirty towels and linens were strewn on the floor.

The hotel kitchen was unbelievably dirty. There were not any customers in the dining room. The coffee shop, which adjoins the casino, furnished a napping area for four inebriated gamblers. In the dining room, there were not any outside windows, the lighting was dim, the tablecloths had been used frequently, and the menu was exceptionally limited.

I asked the surly room clerk whether an alternate room might be available. We were shown another disaster area with the same insurmountable conditions.

Taking the initiative, we rented a room for the night at the upscale Victoria Plaza Hotel at Independence Plaza. The room was even smaller than the Parque abomination, but the premises were clean. We were unable to open the window. The air conditioning unit would not cool the room, but the linens were clean and the bathroom was adequate.

After being informed before leaving the USA that we would be staying at a leading resort hotel at Punta del Este, with a reputation for exquisite cuisine, the dinner was marginal.

March 13 / Montevideo:

A few hours sleep revived our spirits, and I departed to meet the client representative, Captain Pigni. Since Pigni works at home, and there are not any other Institute offices, we will be using a camera (office) provided by maritime interests. The camera is located in the Corregidor Building on Misiones.

For the initial discussion, we were joined by the Instituto Commission President, Captain Ravena, and another commissioner, Americo Deambrosi (droves of Italians settled in Montevideo) who is president of a maritime shipping company.

Senior Deambrosi had been informed of our accommodation plight. He took us to the Lafayette Hotel on Soriano. The hotel is minuscule, with only three rooms on each floor, but the rooms are clean and operational, and we were appreciative.

I prepared a list of assumptions pertaining to the new university. We were not provided with any advance materials. As usual, new organizations are more at home with details than with substantive objectives.

The institute will confine the initial curriculum to three years, one less than a bachelor's degree from the respected National University. The basic purposes, as announced by President Lacaze of Uruguay, are to decentralize the national higher educational system, to utilize unexploited marine resources, and to prepare Uruguayans for middle-level public and private administrative positions to reduce the existing "brain drain."

The faculty will be part-time. The students will be recruited primarily from the Maldonado (Punta del Este) District. The government will not discharge any role in managing the Institute. Tuition will constitute the principal source of revenue. Research will not be included as an initial commitment. An old fort in the Punta del Este area will be refurbished by the Maldonado government for use by the institute. Scholarships will not be offered. The library will be limited to donations from universities in the United States. No student housing or student services will be offered. The basic curriculum will include careers (majors) in general administration, shipping economics, and fishing firm management. For the first academic year, beginning in March, 1994, approximately twenty students will be enrolled in each of the careers.

Dick Epply will focus on the marine sciences curriculum. I will devise an organizational structure, the additional required and elective courses, other than marine sciences, for each career, and prepare a credit system.

For a generation, the Connecticut-based International Executive Service Corps has provided senior executives from the United States to assist fifty developing countries with the creation and nurturing of private, entrepreneurial organizations. In most cases, the assigned executives discharge consultative assistance for a period of one to three months.

For the Uruguayan assignment, I was informed by IESC that we would be responsible for creating a "new university." The academic venture I have just described bears little relationship to a university in any frame of reference. After surviving as president of three universities (Long Island University, Clark University, and the University of Connecticut), I feel that my skills will be of little value in creating an institute charged with training pre-Bachelor's degree students for administrative assignments in fields related to maritime endeavors.

The culprit is the Uruguayan permanent representative of the International Executive Service Corps. He failed to negotiate the assignment with precision. Obviously, he did not have any interest in the projected Institute or the consultants who would assist it during the incubation period. At least, the responsibility for devising the institute's program, and departing before the faculty can choose up sides and before the students can riot, has unusual appeal.

March 14:

Dick Epply is a quiet academic who devoted his career to analyzing the effect of radiation on microorganisms in sea water. Most of his research was subsidized by United States government grants. Since my exposure to the marine sciences field is nonexistent, it is reassuring that Dick is competent to handle that phase of the curriculum.

My academic experience with the Spanish language was as a freshman at Cornell University in 1946. Brief assignments in Puerto Rico and Mexico kept the limited facility alive. During the past summer, I reviewed my college Spanish textbook. Unfortunately, an operation intervened, and the trip to Uruguay was postponed for six months.

Now, in Montevideo, for the first time in a half century, the requirement to speak some Spanish is forcing me to recapture minimal facility. The conjugation of verbs, with the exception of the present and future tenses, is presenting a challenge, but it is remarkable how quickly the basic vocabulary and essential social phrases return. Since the level of English facility in Montevideo is not exemplary, I have been encouraged to resort to Spanish. Although rapid-fire questions elude me, social interaction is being accomplished.

March 15:

The section of the new city where we are located is surrounded by slums. In Uruguay, there are not any indigenous Indians and very few Blacks. As you head north on the Rambla, low-cost housing is replaced by the inevitable high-rise apartments which cater to the aspiring.

The people of Uruguay are gracious and friendly. They are open with strangers, and lack the pseudo-sophistication which arises from insecurity. The Italian and Spanish admixture presents a cultural, religious, temperamental homogeneity which avoids the racial and religious conflicts which preoccupy most countries.

In Uruguay, violence is limited. The extended family is supportive. Although the extremes of affluence and poverty are manifested, there are basic cultural values which appear to transcend financial status. The gringo syndrome is limited because Americans, and most Europeans, have not discovered Uruguay. As a result, North Americans are generally welcome.

For a century, Uruguayans have doted on vintage automobiles. They are not only collected, but they are also used for daily requirements. I have seen hundreds of ancient vehicles on the streets most of which predate our 1962 Bentley. Each garage seems to include a few old cars which collectively require the unique expertise of a mechanic. Half of the population of the country seems to be involved with auto mechanics.

A few years ago, a double-decker bus from London was imported. On two occasions, I have seen it barreling along the Rambla.

At the Gran Cesar near our hotel, Patti and I enjoyed a delicious dinner with superb indigenous vino tinto. The pasta at the hotel has been outstanding. Although fresh fruits are limited, and leafy vegetables should not be consumed, we are enjoying the cuisine immensely.

March 16:

For the institute, I prepared organizational charts which feature a strong Academic Secretary (Provost); a weak Rector (President) who will be part-time and non-academic, meager support services, and the potential for additional majors in an expanded, more academically respectable, four-year program.

At the American Embassy, I arranged an appointment with Larry Moody, the Cultural Affairs Officer who had been informed by the United States Information Agency in Washington, D.C., of our pending arrival and our lecturing status. Two USIS speeches have been confirmed for me in Buenos Aires, and there will be at least one speech in Montevideo dealing with higher education.

March 17:

I have completed a basic curriculum for the institute. There will be five required courses in each of four terms with increasing commitment to management courses in the second year. The first year electives are confined to the humanities or sociology. In the second year the students would be able to take two electives in either public administration or industrial management. If they are specifically interested in marine applications, marine economics or a survey of oceanology will be offered.

In the third year, chemistry and physics would be required for the oceanology majors. For fishing and shipping majors, courses would be required in applied economics and management. Originally, the institute was planning to offer more than one hundred courses, which would have been patently ridiculous.

At the National Institute of Fisheries, the Director General briefed us concerning the marine research role of the fisheries program. Given the current cholera epidemic in Latin America, the daily testing at the Institute is vital. The Institute of Fisheries would be able to provide minimal assistance to the students of the new institute who will enroll in the marine science phase of the curriculum.

Pisano de Escardo, the Director of the International Executive

Service Corps in Uruguay, joined us at the office with Captain Pigni. Six days after our arrival in Montevideo, we are privileged to meet the person responsible for the details of our program.

March 19:

I asked the Public Affairs Officer at the American Embassy for the latest news regarding the devastating terrorist bombing of the Israeli Embassy in Buenos Aires. The spotty news reports are confusing, but the deaths and injuries are significant. The explosion was caused by a car bomb which ripped apart the embassy, killing 29 people and injuring 252. The pro-Iranian Islamic Jihad has claimed responsibility.

In the United States, Governor Bill Clinton is the winner of the Michigan Democratic presidential primary with Governor Brown of California, nudging Senator Paul Tsongas, a former Peace Corps Volunteer, for second place.

At a meeting with Ambassador Brown, we reviewed the potential of funding to support the new Institute including "President George H. Bush's Initiative" (ecology for debt swaps), the Fulbright Program, USAID, and the Conosur (regional common market) options. Since Uruguay is considered the best managed country in Latin America (in fiscal terms), only $80 million in debt would be potentially available for swap arrangements. In effect, the USA is penalizing Uruguay for competence.

Ambassador Brown was a former Deputy Chief of Mission in Montevideo. In an unusual career foreign service personnel action, he was reassigned to Uruguay as Ambassador. To illustrate his approach, I will cite one anecdote. The Ambassador said that when he rides his bicycle along the Rambla, he is tempted by an ocean swim until he realizes that "if he put his toe in the water, something would grow on it." In the presence of senior Uruguayan representatives, even the Public Affairs Officer cringed with that germ of sensitivity.

The new United States Embassy building in Montevideo was designed by I. M. Pei. I am convinced that a rejected project prepared by one of his least successful architecture students was mailed to Montevideo by mistake.

Of greater importance than the esthetic void, the security at the embassy is an excellent example of the doctrine of overkill. On the top of the high iron exterior fence, Uncle Sam, the bastion of freedom, has installed sharpened steel spikes facing upward to thwart potential terrorists. The shards, which look like glass, would not deter a terrorist, much less a ladrón, but they certainly project an unfortunate image for the sole remaining superpower.

The security system at the front entrance is even less appropriate. Four separate checkpoints culminate in a US Marine Guard who temporarily confiscates a guest's identification card. In order to pass the Marine Guard, it is necessary for a member of the embassy staff to accompany the visitor. We live in an insecure world; however, the security measures employed must be fitted to the ambience and the extent of the risk. With the present security measures, we can only be accused of overreaction, hubris and spurious planning.

March 20:

Louis and Susan Pigni hosted a buffet dinner at their attractive apartment. The guests were those of us affiliated with the new institute including Captain Yamandu Ubal Mundemurra who directs water systems at the Department of Public Works and who also serves on the institute's Commission.

We arrived at 8:30 p.m. The buffet dinner was served at 11:00 p.m. Dinner was finished at 1:00 a.m., and we left the premises at 1:30 p.m. Latin Americans have garnered the reputation for siestas and a "manana" approach to daily life. The reason is now clear.

For two centuries, Uruguay has been dominated by two political parties—the Reds (Colorados) and the Whites. There is no ostensible ideological difference. Generally, Uruguayans inherit political party affiliation.

In recent years, the Whites have been triumphant. The current Legislature and Administration are controlled by Whites.

In contrast, the City of Montevideo is controlled by the Socialists, the "Wide Front" which represents a consortium of Leftist-oriented splinter parties. The demise of the USSR has not altered their philosophical stance. Since half of the country's population resides in the capital city, and since the populist Socialist Mayor appears to be more interested in sinecures for his sidekicks than fixing potholes or collecting garbage, Montevideo is going to seed.

Unless the former president can rally the Colorados and defeat President Lacaze and the Whites in the national election scheduled in 1995, the prognostication is that the "Wide Front" will be reelected and Uruguay will experience further economic and social deterioration.

March 21 / Punta del Este:

At Punta del Este, we visited the former army barracks which will be the initial situs for the institute's faculty and students. The drive along the coast from Montevideo was beautiful. We enjoyed views of the dunes, the Rio de la Plata, and the Atlantic Ocean. We stopped to see Captain Pigni's attractive daughter and grandchildren and the summer homes of Captains Pigni and Ravena. The flowers were in full bloom. The local colors were stimulating. The local denizens were friendly and responsive. The prices for resort property were astronomical. The twelve-hour round-trip ride was confining.

In winter, Punta del Este serves as the permanent residence for 15,000 people. In summer, the population swells to 300,000. A significant percentage of the increase is attributable to affluent Argentinians, who lack beautiful beaches, but who have sufficient wealth to construct some of the most attractive homes we have seen. The houses are vacant ten months of the year. During that time, the Uruguayans enjoy their own resort.

The local fish luncheon at the Yacht Club was not distinguished; however, the sights of the town of Maldonado were stimulating. Jose Artigas, the George Washington of Uruguay, resided in Maldonado for a lengthy period. There are attractive relics of the colonial era including a quaint plaza, an ancient church, a broken statue of Artigas, and the pink stone facade of the army barracks. The barracks will be renovated by the city. In two years, the new instituto will commence classes. The interior courtyard will provide a quadrangle, and the exterior corridor will include offices and classrooms.

Returning to Montevideo via another route, we passed the beautiful estate where President George H. Bush resided as a guest during the Uruguay Round, the retreat of the President of Uruguay, and the club where the presidents of Chile and Uruguay meet to discuss affairs of state. At the estate, only two police officers constituted the security guard. The entourage was confined to a few cars and a single small bus. It is tempting to suggest that some countries have a security fixation until you recognize that the former Israeli Embassy in Buenos Aires practiced a relaxed approach to security.

In the remarkable sunset which was provoked by a major eruption of a Philippine volcano, and the pollution gap in the skies over Antarctica, we noticed the intricate telephone pole nest of the Rufous Hornero (Argentina's national bird), the Monk Parakeets on the wires, and the healthy cattle on the estancias (ranches). The rolling plains, with semiarid hills in the background, reminded us of the area east of Nairobi en route to the Kenyan coast.

March 22 / Montevideo:

After extensive discussion regarding the new institute, it is clear that there is little sentiment to create a university. Although management will be the curricular point of departure, marine sciences will probably emerge as the major emphasis.

During World War II, the Graf Spee, a battleship which invoked German national pride, was scuttled in the Montevideo harbor. For many years, the riggings of the vessel could be seen. The hull disappeared. It was discovered that the steel had been utilized for the underpinnings of a new building. If the hull had been raised, a unique bit of military history would have been preserved.

Patti and I toured the Mercado del Puerto (the Port Market) and investigated carefully each parrillada before selecting a luncheon spot. A parrillada is a fast food restaurant which includes an open grill, a view of other parrilladas in the market, stools and tables which are clean and inviting, local wine and beer in generous supply, and a remarkable array of meats and poultry, featuring lobo (filet mignon). Although the meat in Montevideo is acceptable, after residing in Europe, the comparison does not favor Uruguay.

At the Torre Garcias Museum in El Ciudad Vieja (the Old City), we paid homage to one of Uruguay's renowned painters. Like Picasso, Garcias had distinct periods, Paris and New York City. Although I consider Garcias' work primitive, and less than appealing, I salute his seminal impact on two generations of successful local painters.

Vacas, a disciple of Garcias died this week. In a commercial art gallery, we enjoyed a contemporary, modernistic Vacas work of art with distinctive use of color (yellow, orange, and black) and narrow, straight, lengthy lines.

Six o'clock tea at the Manchester was pleasant and reviving. In Uruguay, la siesta is generally ignored, as well as breakfast. but late afternoon tea is an established ritual. Rather than the inevitable English tea, with a scone or crumpet, Uruguayans prefer strong indigenous coffee either con leche (with milk) or Italian style (with hot, whipped milk). In addition, they make a feast of an amazing assortment of tarts, tortes, cakes and cookies, many of which assimilate tempting chocolate in diverse forms. The tea shoppe atmosphere is relaxed, and the clientele is amazingly quiet and well-dressed.

March 23:

The residents of Montevideo are a likable bunch. Young and old are kind to strangers on the streets, in the shops, and in the restaurants. Courtesy prevails, even in rush-hour traffic. Voices are generally controlled, and foreigners are not considered objects of curiosity or derision.

While running on the Rambla this evening, a middle-aged woman runner approached. Since the path was rather narrow, I stepped on the margin to allow her to pass. Eureka! Caramba! She smiled! After running on five continents, that is a first. When I say middle-aged, I mean forty, and she was attractive. There is still a place on earth where strangers are allowed to treat the opposite gender with civility.

To balance the ledger, I believe that the people of Uruguay have a collective inferiority complex. As the inhabitants of a small country among giants, they are paranoid about their national neighbors. Since winning the World Cup in soccer in 1950, and enjoying virtual parity with the US dollar during the same era, there have been few subsequent events to cheer about.

The country is flat, dull, and devoid of excitement, as perceived by the Uruguayans themselves. From my perspective, the undulating, forested hills are pleasant; the omnipresent sea is attractive; the pace is reassuring, and the people are kind. After six months in Montevideo, I would probably concur with the Uruguayan appraisal.

In Rhode Island, we are accustomed to frequent power outages, more than in the more civilized areas of the United States. In Uruguay, power cessation has become an art form, and it appears to be "off" more than "on."

During the hot, steamy, South American otoño (autumn), which is reputedly cool and refreshing and for which we brought appropriate clothing, the power is off daily for variable periods of time. When the outage occurs, backup generators are activated, and a single light for the separate system can be turned on in each room. The air conditioning is not operational, the bathroom is dark, clothes are not required in the increased temperature, and Rhode Island, by comparison, becomes modern.

March 24:

For the institute, I completed the core courses for nine major fields for all programs except marine sciences. Without academic respectability, and the requisite funding, the institute will probably never be launched. In spite of opposition from the leadership of the principal university, the curricula would fill many existing needs.

I walked the length of the main street in the new city, Diez y Ocho de Julio, which incorporates the principal shopping areas, to the situs of the Universidad de las Republica. The main building is a historic gem with two large atria surrounded by classrooms. Several classes concentrating on law and international relations were in session. I was delighted to hear occasional laughter (unusual when discussing contemporary justice and politics). Unfortunately, there was not any electric lighting in the dark classrooms. The chairs were crude (rural American one-room schoolhouse vintage), and they were relying upon mimeographed sheets rather than textbooks.

The university is free, public, and does not have to consider competition. There is a Catholic university, but even in a Catholic country, the standards do not match the public university.

At the university, there are 63,000 students. A very small percentage will qualify for graduate or professional degrees. The bulk of the students will enter the marketplace better prepared than the average bachelor's degree recipient in the United States.

With the exception of the classically beautiful main building which houses the law school, the University incorporates a congeries of office buildings covering a significant area.

On the same afternoon, I visited a secondary school in a lovely old Italian-style building with an inner courtyard, trees, and stone benches. The students illustrated the demeanor of typical teenagers except that all girls (and adult women) kiss as a form of casual greeting. There was no evidence of extracurricular activities, a library, or other support services, which North American students take for granted.

March 25:

At Parque Batlle (basically a sports complex) and Parque Rodo (with statues of Confucius and Einstein), we communed with our feathered friends. In Montevideo, the parks are small and geared for people pursuits rather than a rendezvous with nature.

At the American Embassy, we met with the USAID Director. With myriad needs, there does not appear to be any programmatic design for developmental assistance from the United States. The new institute may qualify for limited book purchase assistance but nothing more.

At dinner we enjoyed the second floor terrace of La Proa, an Italian-style restaurant adjoining the Mercado Puerto. The helado (ice cream) was outstanding.

March 26:

Dick Epply and I met with the Commission (Board of Directors) of the Institute. Captain Pigni reviewed our work to date which was confined to the organization, core curriculum, and major fields of study. The response was entirely favorable; however, I was dismayed that without discussion they decided to add tourism and hotel majors which would further debilitate the fragile academic reed.

March 27 / Montevideo to Colonia:

After a diligent search, I found the only commercial philatelist in Montevideo, a part-time stockbroker in the old city who until a few years ago was a security guard in New York City.

Eduardo Hoffman is able to communicate the language of philatelics in English, and I described my interest in obtaining Uruguayan airmail stamps. With Mr. Hoffman's assistance, it was possible to acquire all but six stamps on my "want list." In the United

States, even at auction, the issues available are limited, and the prices are exorbitant.

In late afternoon, Patti and I departed via bus for Colonia. The vehicle was air conditioned and semi-spacious. With reserved seats, and the absence of a prearranged schedule, we relaxed and enjoyed the countryside.

The rolling hills, small rivers, estancias with sheep, Holstein dairy cattle, and an occasional vineyard, presented a pleasant change of scenery.

The highlight of the trip was a quick glance at a flock (approximately twenty) of Greater Rhea browsing in an open field. The Greater, which is found in east central South America, is more than five feet tall, does not fly, and runs swiftly like the Ostrich. The Greater Rhea is not endangered; however, few are found in the wild.

In 1680, Colonia del Sacramento was settled by a small group of military and civilian Portuguese under the leadership of Lobo. A beautiful fort, with high stone walls; lovely homes; and cobblestone streets were constructed on the bank of the Rio de la Plata, one hundred miles west of Montevideo across the river from Buenos Aires.

For almost three centuries, the ruins of Colonia were ignored. During the past decade, many of the houses have been renovated. With external financial support, the city of Colonia has restored the fort and public buildings. It has managed to retain its quaint character, a small population, a plethora of antique automobiles, and a historic, leisurely ambience. Scores of open air shops offer attractive woolens and artifacts. Colonia, if it can control the mopeds and the population growth, will continue to depict the epitome of a historic village.

We were able to obtain a small but adequate room at the distinctive Posada del Gobernador. With ten rooms, and drains in the center of the bathroom floors, we realized that we were a considerable distance from the land of chain motels.

March 28 / Colonia to Buenos Aires, Argentina:

On the spur of the moment, we decided to take the ferry to Buenos Aires, Argentina. We were persuaded to take the trip after being reassured that the one-way journey would require a maximum of one hour. After a three-hour trip in cold, windy weather, without, as usual, appropriate clothing, we arrived at the huge, bustling, extremely dirty port of Buenos Aires. Because of the deplorable weather, only a few gulls and swallows welcomed us to another country.

Securing a taxi, we completed a one-hour tour of the downtown area including the American Embassy, the Florida district shopping areas, the port, the principal plazas, a few monuments, and several major hotels and office buildings. Our purpose was to secure an introduction before undertaking a lecture tour scheduled for next month.

The six-hour round trip commitment for the ferry was a mistake given the weather and the short time frame.

The sunset view of beautiful little Colonia from the river was enticing. Jamon and queso (ham and cheese) sandwiches at a picturesque konditorei in the old city restored our natural juices and sagging spirits.

March 29 / Nueva Helvecia:

A group of Swiss immigrants established a colony near Colonia in the early eighteenth century. Initially, the colony was called Suizo. The official name is Nueva Helvecia, and it is located forty-five minutes and two bus rides east of Colonia.

We were dumped, with two large bags, at the bus station which encompasses a small locked room on the main square. The plaza surrounds a powerful statue of several Swiss farmers pulling a plow.

In contrast to Montevideo, at 1:00 p.m. on a Sunday, the town was enjoying a total siesta. I was able to rescue a taxi driver from a huge glob of helado. He knew the location of the Suizo restaurant outside of town, and we arrived before the siesta doors closed.

To complement the houses in town, the premises were immaculate. The lady in charge spoke German, arranged for a bus to pick us up in two hours, and seated us in the dining room which was more Bavarian than Uruguayan.

Starting with cheese fondue and concluding with another excellent local white wine, we were grateful for our good fortune.

The twenty-acre plot at the restaurant was bulging with cultivated fields. After the recent challenge of several major urban areas, we strolled through the grounds admiring the bucolic surroundings.

March 30 / Montevideo:

En route to the office, Captain Pigni was signaled by a policeman to pull over. He checked the driver's license, registration, headlights, horn and brake lights. Sullenly, but without discussion, he waved us on. Luis informed us that because the two passengers in the front seat were wearing ties, and the automobile was relatively expensive, the police were required by the Socialist city government to stop and to inspect such vehicles. No other cars were stopped. If the lights failed, the fine would have been extensive.

Discrimination exists everywhere in variable forms. If Luis's interpretation is correct, Montevideo has devised a unique application.

March 31:

The Chairman of the Board of Trustees at the American University of Paris called from Paris to inform me that I had been elected president. The Chairman said that the university community had totally endorsed the selection. He suggested that we meet in New York City in early May to discuss major priorities. It is anticipated that we will report for duty in Paris on July 15th.

April 1:

The Cultural Affairs Officer at the American Embassy arranged a luncheon at his home in our honor. Larry Moody and his wife are a delightful couple who have lived and worked in the Third World (India and Niger) and who are discouraged by the negative impact of the Reagan-Bush era on US relations abroad. The guests included the head of the Fulbright Commission in Uruguay; the Deputy Rector of the university, and the Dean of the School of Chemistry and Engineering.

In spite of freedom of speech and the press, and the common knowledge that influential politicians in Uruguay have been unfaithful to their spouses, the Dean is convinced that, in contrast to the United States, the media would never cover the issue. Infidelity is considered irrelevant in judging political competence and integrity in Uruguay.

The approach differs fundamentally from the contemporary media practice in the United States.

April 3:

At the Solis Restaurant, which adjoins the Solis Theatre, we were reminded that the theatre has attracted distinguished performing arts individuals and groups for a generation.

At Lincoln Center in New York City, I was impressed by the number of international ballet and opera companies that had performed at the Solis.

We were scheduled to attend a symphony performance at the Solis next week; however, the Socialist mayor decreed that the performance would be free. The theatre can accommodate 500 patrons. Thousands of curious citizens who might not be able to distinguish a symphony orchestra from a gaucho serenade, and hundreds who would treasure the opportunity to attend, will storm the Solis in the quest for seats. Ignoring the fire potential, it is anticipated that there will be seating in the aisles and that there will be major traffic jams in the Old City.

April 4:

With the assistance of an arts and crafts devotee whom Patti met, I have been able to make arrangements to take private French lessons with a superb teacher, Senora Perla Vidal. Mrs. Vidal is a retired teacher who spent many years in France.

I have completed several hours of instruction, and Mrs. Vidal has prepared a cassette tape which I will be able to use on my own time. At my age, improving my French facility for acceptable use in Paris will require a significant commitment.

April 5 / Montevideo and La Paloma:

A cultural affairs assistant at the US Embassy arranged for us to spend a day on an ornithological safari. Our host was Hernan Sorhuet, a professor of biology. He writes a weekly ecology column for *El Pais*, the newspaper with the largest circulation in Uruguay (25,000 daily and 70,000 on Sunday). Dr. Sorhuet also serves as the World Wildlife Federation representative in Uruguay. For the trip, Hernan recruited a game warden from the Wildlife Department in the Ministry of Agriculture to serve as a guide. He also persuaded Alfred Gepp, a British Uruguayan who prepares daily bird counts, to join us. Since our new friends do not speak English, except for Mr. Gepp, our Spanish expertise was severely tested.

We drove 250 kilometers east of Montevideo, close to the coast, about 100 kilometers northeast of Punta del Este. From there we drove north along the Atlantic Ocean in the direction of the Brazilian border.

At a stream flowing into the Atlantic Ocean from Castillos Lake in the Rocha District, we transferred to a motorboat which conveyed us to the shore of Castillos Lake. The lake is generally fresh, but for a few months each year it is brackish which attracts variable birdlife including flamingos.

In a reserve, which is protected by the Ministry of Agriculture, we met the Warden and spent several hours viewing a remarkable array of exotic birds. At the lake, we identified thirty-eight new species in Uruguay including the Black-necked Swan, Black and White Monjita, White-crested Tyrannulet, and the Stripe-crowned Spinetail.

Local fishermen and hunters vitiate the reserve (which provides only limited protection for the fauna). The prodigious Baobab-like trees, the lush vegetation, the birdlife, and the pristine scenery are worth preserving.

On the return leg, we stopped at Pan de Azucar (Sugarloaf Mountain), which is a bump west of Punta del Este, to hike the lengthy maze of Estacion de Cria Cerro. The station is a large, well-designed zoo which includes the flora and fauna of Uruguay exclusively. The incarceration of mammals and birds induces deep depression for me, but our new friends did not appear to be disturbed. The odors were overpowering, but the inmates appeared to be well-fed.

In Solis, a remote suburb of Montevideo, we returned Alfred Gepp to his British colonial-style home replete with fruit trees and a vegetable garden. The Gepps have few material resources, but they are enjoying a beautiful natural world which transcends the modern realities which surround them.

April 6:

The institute is planning to arrange a press conference to announce the new academic venture. The commission members have asked the American Embassy to endorse the institute concept and the press conference. The Embassy has decided not to sanction the program.

At the American Library, I made a presentation to sixty college students and interested professionals about "US Society in Transition." The forthcoming 1992 presidential election was emphasized. The event was sponsored by USIS and represents my continuing affiliation as a lecturer.

In the speech, I stressed several contemporary US issues: economic justice, civil rights, foreign policy, free trade and the role of women and cited the policy positions of each of the major presidential candidates.

April 7:

An article appeared in *El Pais* concerning my speech at the American Library. Captain Pigni expressed apprehension that the American Embassy (USIS) would issue a press release pertaining to my speech but would not support the press conference dealing with the new university. I informed Captain Pigni that I was a USIS (AMPART) speaker, and that the US Government had an obligation to publicize scheduled speeches.

The American Embassy must reflect the position that a press release about the new university, endorsed by the Embassy, would suggest premature US Government support for the proposed Uruguayan academic program. Since the US Government will not make a grant to the institute, the American Government should not be perceived as a participating party.

The position of the Embassy was logical; however, in my opinion, the American Embassy had an obligation to state that the IESC assignment was indirectly funded by the US Government since IESC receives virtually all of its funding from USAID. At the same time, the American Embassy does not have any control over the substantive positions which IESC executives on consultative assignment might suggest regarding the new university.

The distinction is profound. The resulting confusion should have been clarified. Captain Pigni, and the others affiliated with the institute, would have understood the distinction including the fact that my USIS speeches were not related to the IESC assignment.

Our final commitment to the Universidad del Mar (the new name for the Institute) was to visit the Institute of Fish Research, of the University of the Republic, which is part of the Veterinary Faculty. The new university will be required to purchase virtually all equipment rather than being authorized to share equipment with existing organizations such as the Institute of Fish Research. This is another vital example of the lack of cooperation of the national university.

Two farewell dinners were arranged by the Institute leadership. Following precedent, both adjourned at 1:30 a.m. The second dinner was attended by the Minister of Education. Dr. Epply and I were each presented with a display of miniaturized pieces of Gaucho (cowboy) paraphernalia. The exquisite pieces range from saddles and knives to horseshoes and boots. Our wives received a book of Uruguayan lithographs.

April 8:

The major culprit in formulating plans for the Universidad del Mar is the local IESC representation. IESC did not negotiate the agreement and the resulting assignments carefully. The curricular and organizational advice required by the institute was marginal. IESC was unaware of the objectives of the institute. The institute leadership was anxious to receive potential financial support from Uncle Sam. Before the IESC agreement was signed, they should have been informed that such funding was improbable.

We enjoyed our brief exposure to Uruguay and to the Uruguayan people. As usual, American representation, both public and private, is seldom prepared for the realities of overseas assignments. I am doubtful that the Universidad del Mar will ever become operational, but hope springs eternal.

CHINA
Rare Cranes and Useless Chopsticks

May 24, 1992 / Narita Airport, Tokyo, Japan:

For the first time since 1978, I have returned to Japan. In 1952, following a psychological warfare stint with the US Air Force at the front in Korea, I was assigned to Tokyo to prepare a psychological warfare bibliography for the US Army and the US Air Force. For one month, I had the opportunity to enjoy the complexity and beauty of postwar Japan and to take a few short safaris, including a train trip to the impressive Great Buddha at Kamakura.

In 1978, Patti and I spent less than two days in Tokyo following a meeting of several state university presidents in Taiwan (at that time, I was President of the University of Connecticut). We returned to Kamakura and walked extensively in Tokyo; however, the obvious result of two short visits was merely to whet the appetite.

Currently, we are staying at the Tokyo airport motel en route to Beijing. We took a lengthy walk in the area which incorporates specialized flower and vegetable plots in a modern middle-class suburban complex adjoining the airport.

For the third time, I have been exposed to Japan without having the opportunity to absorb the national culture or to visit metropolitan areas other than Tokyo.

May 25 / Beijing, China:

In the past, our travels have ringed the People's Republic of China: Korea, Japan, Okinawa, Taiwan, Hong Kong, Macao, Vietnam, Burma, Nepal, India, and Pakistan; however, this is the first exposure to China per se.

The trip into Beijing, the capital for seven hundred years, was a revelation. Thousands of roses were in bloom along the major streets. The housing developments for low income families were immaculate. Virtually every citizen was dressed in clean, colorful, attractive clothing. With few exceptions, the populace represented the impact of meaningful diet and exercise.

There are eleven million people living in the Beijing metropolitan area. There are six million bikes which are pedaled effortlessly through the downtown streets on broad designated strips on both sides of the road.

The people of Beijing appear to be relaxed. There is no evidence of pressure. Smiles are worn as an integral part of the daily attire, and there is not any overt manifestation of repression. The inscrutable Chinese in Beijing are easy to fathom. The lot of the average person seems to have improved.

The evidence of security is minimal. Police are devoted to traffic duty exclusively. I have seen only one squad of soldiers jogging in unison and one truckload of soldiers returning from work detail.

The hotel windows are bolted shut probably to deter jumpers rather than to maintain security. In taking photographs, the response to the camera was uniformly friendly and nonthreatening.

Traffic moves without passion. Courtesy is the order of the day. Because the people of Beijing are generally used to foreigners, the stares are limited. Beijing, in contrast to many metropolitan areas, seems to "work" effectively and hope rather than despair is the dominant mood. In contrast to the United States, there is uniform pride in ancestors, family, history, and place. Relics are not only preserved but also admired.

It is relatively easy to describe the overt superficial projection of Beijing. The latent reality of collectivism and repression, in contrast to individualism and freedom, presents profound subtlety unless you are immersed in the culture.

In the West, the People's Republic of China is condemned for its systematic repression of civil rights. Tiananmen Square represents the zenith of totalitarian smothering of freedom. China claims that individualism is restricted so that the less fortunate can realize a modicum of economic security. Repression of civil rights is considered essential in order to avoid the abuses of individualism that would subvert the common good. According to the contemporary Chinese dogma, unless individualism is controlled, with violence if necessary, the blessings of collectivism would be in jeopardy.

In the West, protection of the rights of the individual transcends other issues including the abuses of capitalism. Since any basic limitation on freedom debases all other aspects of freedom, it should not be nurtured in shades or degrees.

Inevitably, collectivism will fail because it lacks the pluralism to weather all forms of challenge, and freedom is a more meaningful objective. Collectivism can survive the Tiananmen tragedy, but the seeds of Tiananmen will eventually doom the Chinese brand of collectivism.

Beijing is impressive. So are the people of Beijing; however, the repressive state will fail in China, as it has failed in most of the other substantial trials, including the Soviet Union.

May 26 / Beijing and the Great Wall of China:

In Beijing, the Summer Palace is located in a gigantic park encompassing 280 hectares. The imperial dynasties used the Summer Palace for rest and recreation. Kunning Lake dominates the scene and includes gilded, ornamented boats, a barque made of marble which reputedly floated, and a fleet of gondola-like craft for the sporting crowd.

The "Painted Walkway" is a wooden covered path with open sides which is decorated with more than seven hundred historic landscapes. From the summit of Longevity Hill, the lovely roofs and a breathtaking view of the lake are prominent.

The actual palace garden was barricaded, but the front facade of the palace reminded us that the structure was featured in the *Last Empire* movie. A mediocre ten-course dinner was served at the "Pavilion for Listening to Orioles" (none was heard).

The Great Wall of China (4,000 miles in length) is located forty-five kilometers north of Beijing. At 6:00 a.m., scores of tourist buses clogged the road to the Mutienyu section of the wall.

The wall was constructed in stages to protect ancient kingdoms from the northern hordes. Only a few sections remain, most of which have been rebuilt within the last several years. On the top of the wall, steps have been relaid. It is now relatively easy to walk to the highest point which affords a view of the line of the wall following the contours of hills and dales.

The Chinese tourists were loud, rude, and polluting the environment with discarded wrappers and bottles. Access to the men's room required a one yuan (20 cents) investment. The "airport art" hawkers and carnival atmosphere created a boardwalk mystique rather than that of an ancient Chinese culture.

Back in Beijing, we spent the afternoon at the Beijing Normal University, the leading university in the field of biology. Our host was Professor Zheng Guangmri of the Department of Biology. At luncheon, the natural history community was represented by the Chinese Academy of Sciences and the Museum of Nature.

In China, there are only three hundred and fifty persons who claim the affliction as birders. More than seventy are residents of Beijing. In the state of Rhode Island, there are more members of the local Audubon Society than the total number of birders in China.

May 27 / Beijing to Baicheng:

A ninety-minute flight deposited us in Changchun, the capital of Julin Province northeast of Beijing. With a population of 2.1 million, Changchun is known as the city where the first automobiles were manufactured in China. It is also considered a cultural city and the Hollywood of China. In contrast to Beijing, the attire is drab, the surroundings are less immaculate, and the impact of poverty is evident.

The six-hour train ride from Changchun to Baicheng was a memorable experience. Eighty-five people were crowded into a single car including fifteen seats which were devoted to baggage. The seats were hard with stiff backs and filthy covers. A small permanent tray was shared by six people. It served as a food and drink holder, refuse container, locus for personal belongings, and a conversation piece. To insure survival, the windows were fully opened which attracted the soot and dust from the outside world.

The rest room facilities were confined to a single slit in the floor which led directly to terra firma. For the trip, no food, water, or other services were provided.

The surrounding countryside deteriorated from relatively affluent, well-irrigated communal farms to bone-dry patches. We were exposed to rural and urban communities which were bypassed by the industrial revolution and the twentieth century. Pigs wallowed on front doorsteps, and the odors expressed the nonexisting plumbing. Since television sets are provided free, there was a television aerial on every roof. The single government-controlled channel insures that "duck-speak" will prevail. If the rural Chinese do not see the sins of materialism on the tube, the causes for rebellion back on the farm are less obvious than in other cultures.

China is an enigma—a monolithic, historic, homogenous, totalitarian, geographical, and political entity with elements of a common culture. Teeming with people, polluted, and superficially clean, China conveys a stereotype to the world outside. In fact, it is a collection of disparate, culturally related, flawed approaches to the life experience.

In contrast, the United States is a stable, superficial, inefficiently governed, materialistic cauldron of ethnic and racial groups in a seamless, democratic web which lacks cohesiveness or direction but represents hope.

Although cultural ties and devotion to history might assure voluntary control, China is ruled by fiat. The United States, the most effective democracy, represents a hint of anarchy with a vital veneer of protected freedoms.

In China, when the shackles of communism are discarded, the changes will not be profound. If the United States compromises with freedom, freedom will be in jeopardy everywhere.

Ninety-five percent of the Chinese people represent a single major ethnic and cultural strain. A mere five percent comprise the nationalities (read "minorities"). The minorities include both religious and racial components, e.g. Muslims in Xian, Tibetans on the steppes in Qinghai, and a scattering of Christians in the major cities.

In Beijing, a monolithic building pays homage to the nationalities.

In fact, the "nationalities" concept has been devised to discourage continuation of cultural and religious practices which distinguish the minorities. Chinese of Tibetan extraction are allowed to maintain innocuous small temples on distant hills, but the fire of tribalism is suppressed. Moslems are encouraged to wear Burkhas (women) and white skull caps (men). In spite of these minor variations, nationality rites and practices are not allowed to impinge on the burgeoning national holidays which depict a communal, sterile, colorless, facade of peace, harmony, and devotion to family values.

China tells the world that minorities are enjoying freedom while actually suppressing substantive differences. In the United States, minorities enjoy untrammeled freedom without the responsibility and restraint that will insure meaningful survival of traditions.

Baicheng in Julin Province is a city of 230,000. Arriving at the train station after dark, we were escorted to the Baicheng Guest House where we waited for more than thirty minutes to receive instructions regarding our rooms.

The small rooms were located on the second floor overlooking a busy street. If it were not for an insignificant fan, the noise and heat would have been oppressive. There is no longer sufficient time for packing and unpacking. As a result, we are learning to place a change of underwear and a toilet kit in an accessible corner.

May 28 / Baicheng to Xianghai:

Because sleep was impossible, I arose early to walk the streets of Baicheng. Before dawn in a desolate, provincial city, I was surprised to encounter hundreds of commuting bicyclists heading in all directions. The colors of the attire were subdued. The facial expression were camouflaged and little attention was paid to a gawking foreigner.

Without the impact of bombing, the cities in Julin Province appear to have escaped the ravages of war. The wooden shacks which serve as shops and houses have survived for centuries. The modern office buildings represent studied indifference to design, appearance, or utility. The drab sameness of the cities is enervating. Although children react with the curiosity and enthusiasm of youth, the adults convey a cultivated indifference.

A minibus was the last mode of transportation for the 130

kilometer trip to Xianghai Nature Reserve. A scientist from Northeast China Normal University and a security type accompanied us.

In China, most of our birding was confined to bouncing minibuses, which challenged pitted dirt roads, and narrow truck- and tractor-infested single-lane paved roads. I would not enjoy using binoculars from a moving Greyhound bus on a superhighway in the United States. Without stability or clean windows, our birding was less than systematic.

The trip to Xianghai was programmed for two and one-half hours. Although we stopped a few times for the call of nature, the trip consumed almost six hours.

Generally, the scenery was uninviting. Stands of poplar-like trees lined the roads and broke the view. The dust from the road obscured most of the local color. The final approach to the nature reserve was inundated with sheep, goats, cattle, and people doing their inevitable counter-environmental thing. The landscape was denuded from centuries of destructive cultivation, including the unique devastation caused by goats. The entrance to the nature reserve was unmarked.

It would appear that the reserve encompasses approximately 250,000 acres between the Xiang'an Mountains and the Songliao Plain. There are sand dunes, meadows, lakes, trees (not forests), and marshes; however, the theoretically attractive combination has been damaged by man's unthinking intrusion.

The Xianghai Guest House, where we spent two hot, mosquito-infested poorly-lit nights, was an abomination. Each guest was assigned a narrow, hard, wooden cot.

Unless you are willing to accept the "bare" necessities, do not be tempted by the tourist role in rural China. At the guest house (in fact, an abandoned school), there was one five-watt, unadorned bulb providing light in each room. There were not any chairs or other furniture, washcloths, mirrors, soap, running water, bathing facilities, screens, shades, curtains, or privacy. Water was obtained from a large communal jug which was always empty. The post-washing water was thrown out the window. In the absence of bathrooms, the tooth brushing ritual was conducted at open windows. For each of us, there was a napkin-sized towel. The acoustics were deplorable. Although my experience is limited, I would rate prison cells a star above the Xianghai Guest House.

Fifty yards from our sleeping quarters, there was a partially open brick building with two rooms which served as the toilet facility for men and women. In the men's area, there were two small holes in the cement floor; no water, and no toilet tissue. For many moons, the product had been deposited in the shallow open pit below without removal. Community access was assured to any local villager who wanted to see a North American in a posture of total submission.

Because of the cuisine, I became well-acquainted with the brick structure I have just described and with several local residents who stopped by to see me in action and to whom I intend to send holiday greetings.

Speaking of cuisine, I am tempted to be mute, but my commitment to science is paramount. We ate five meals at another structure, one mile distant in the village. The chef (rather the person who assembled the food) detested all forms of edible fare except fish bones, thrice-cooked vegetables, and stale bread. The same pieces of fish-bone were served stew-like at every meal, and the vegetables were cooked in unison until the individual species were indistinguishable. An inadequate supply of bottled water was provided which restricted the number of fatalities. Hot tea was offered in limited supply, and tasted foul, or possibly fowl. We were relegated to warm Chinese beer which had a semblance of flavor and which I assume was pasteurized.

Patti and I are used to "roughing it" in basic living conditions. For three years in Thailand, where I established the Peace Corps program, repeated up-country commitments reflected an unadorned lifestyle. In rural African areas, we experienced our share of casual accommodations. At our shack in Ontario, I reached maturity with a pump well, an outhouse, and gas lanterns.

Our disappointment with the living conditions in rural China is based on the absence of information, the callous indifference of our hosts, and the needless exposure to illness.

May 29 / Xianghai:

On my own, I explored much of the immediate area in Xianghai. The lake might have been attractive before the village polluted it. The desert might have been attractive before man, and his domesticated animals, occupied it.

The village was interesting. Mud huts protected the residents from the remarkable range of annual temperature. A few bureaucrats lived in more modern, wood-framed houses. All of the houses had straw roofs. There was no running water, but the village maintained a fire truck. Pigs ran loose in the front dirt patches of the houses. On the streets, an occasional bashful smile from one of the younger inhabitants forced me to recognize the fine distinctions in the plight of human beings.

Grain, usually maize rather than rice in this region of China, is stored in distinctive straw huts with domes that approximate mosques. The streets, pocked with deep dirt tracks, are impassable following any precipitation. At each shack, there is a tiny vegetable plot. I was tempted to introduce our chef to his neighbors.

Of the more than 9,000 species of birds in the world, the crane is admired particularly for its rarity and its beauty. Of the fifteen species of crane, six have been identified at Xianghai. The longevity of the crane exceeds one-half century. Chinese art and poetry reflect the crane's ability to capture the attention of mankind.

At Xianghai, we had the good fortune to see the Demoiselle and the rarer Red-crowned or Japanese Crane. Of the approximately, 1,300 Red-crowned cranes in the world, most of them are found in northeast China. It has been selected as the official bird of Jilin Province. Twenty-pair of Red-crowned Cranes, it is alleged by suspect authority, are permanent residents of Xianghai.

One of the highlights of the trip was a half-day visit to Inner Mongolia. From Xianghai, we drove through remote prairie country to the entrance of a special reserve about thirty kilometers into Inner Mongolia. At the border, the Jilin mesa ends, and Inner Mongolia spreads out into a vast, relatively verdant rift below. Water is ample. The seldom-traveled single-lane dirt road in Jilin becomes an almost indistinguishable grass track in Inner Mongolia. I experienced the unusual sensation of being in a truly different world.

The familiar Chinese physiognomy was replaced by the distinctive Mongolian features of the Inner Mongolian nomads. The generally dour Chinese appearance became the softened, disarming smiles of the adults and the children alike. The colorful black, red, and purple ensembles of the ladies and children provided sharp contrast with the open blue sky and the green marshes and fields which spread to eternity. The spirited dogs and miniature horses were omnipresent. Several of the itinerant farmers demonstrated their versatile, barebacked riding skills for our enjoyment.

The track ended. We were unable to proceed further. As we stood looking over the rift, several Red-Crowned Cranes were spotted in the distance. I had the distinct impression that we could travel hundreds of miles without seeing any visible sign of polluting civilization. I am now privy to the rationale for the Last Emperor's retreat to Mongolia.

May 30 / Xianghai to Baicheng:

The return trip to Baicheng again required more than six hours. We stopped for a standup picnic on the side of the road. The Chinese driver took most of the bottled water and threw half-filled bottles plus luncheon detritus on the side of the road. Collectivism does not necessarily begat courtesy or environmental concern.

The evening at the Baicheng Guest House recouped unfound memories of a prior sleepless night. This time, we were so tired and so grateful for a modicum of privacy, and an operational toilet with running water, that we ignored a major thunderstorm, a brilliant sunrise, and the inevitable noise from the street.

The six-hour train trip to Changchun, and the flight to Beijing, once again conveyed the pressure of population, the marginal development, the omnipotence of poverty, and the emerging, almost insurmountable problems of a gigantic nation out of control.

May 31 / Beijing:

Ned Hastings is from Providence, Rhode Island. He is seventy-six years old and a distinguished civil rights lawyer. Two years ago, as part of Equity for Africa fund-raising activities, Ned and I had lunch in Providence. He is exceptionally bright, very liberal, loquacious, and well-informed.

On the train to Changchun, Ned became ill and we attempted to provide assistance. Ned was adamant about his sterling constitution and insisted that he was well.

The medical diagnosis was pleurisy. Appropriate medication was administered. Until we returned to Beijing, Ned handled the acute pain stoically. He had a long-term arrhythmia. In his condition, he should never have made the trip.

I called the duty officer at the American Embassy. Upon arrival at the airport in Beijing, an ambulance, with a medical doctor, was in attendance. Ned was rushed to the hospital. At 1:00 a.m., the embassy duty officer and I negotiated his release from China with the Chinese authorities.

The following morning, Ned was evacuated to the United States. He recovered quickly and fully, and upon our return to Rhode Island, we were reassured to talk with him personally. When you travel in remote areas, it might be pertinent to inquire about emergency procedures.

June 1 / Beijing to Xinang:

Tiananmen Square is located in the center of Beijing. Three years ago, in May, 1989, freedom and then violence exploded at Tiananmen Square. China and the rest of the world have not recovered.

Today is Children's Day in China. Thousands of children were lined up in platoons to participate in the ceremony at the square. Before 8:00 a.m., the square was crowded. Myriad military and police units had assembled to maintain order.

I walked the length and width of the enormous square taking pictures of the children and the colossal structures which reflect minimal architectural diversity. At the same time, given the size of the square, the buildings seem to be appropriate for the locus. The principal buildings are the Gate of Heavenly Peace (north); the Museums of Chinese History and Revolution (east); the Great Hall of the People (west), and the Chairman Mao Memorial Hall and Monument to the People's Heroes (south).

Without notice, military units suddenly installed ropes and armed guards to partition the square so that the groups of children could be aligned for the formal ceremonies. Nonparticipants were turned away by armed soldiers. It was impossible to return to the bus by any logical route.

The bus was scheduled to depart momentarily, and I ran more

than two miles to the opposite side of the square and through the adjoining streets. Since the bus was leaving for the Forbidden City, and then the airport, those of us who did not have a direct path to the bus might have been stranded. At the bus, I notified the driver of the change of plans, and he waited for the late arrivals. My shirt was ruined, and running in street shoes is not recommended; however, I was able to complete at least one jog in China.

At the north side of Tiananmen Square, the Gate of the Heavenly Peace serves as the entrance to the Imperial Palace or the Forbidden City. The city covers 180 acres. Most of the 9,999 rooms were constructed in the early fifteenth century. The anecdote regarding the 10,000th room has been lost to posterity. The Ming and Ching dynasties, which included twenty-four emperors, resided there. The inner city was occupied by the Imperial family. The outer city is still used for ceremonial events.

At an unspecified historical date, 100,000 eunuchs (not 99,999) lived in the city. With ten eunuchs allocated to each room, it is amazing that the dynasties survived for centuries.

In 1911, the Ching dynasty was overthrown. The young emperor went into exile in Manchuria.

It is difficult to describe the intricate, varied, tasteful beauty of the Forbidden City. Brass incense holders represent each province. The red, brown, and ochre color combinations are exquisite. Each piece of art has been preserved with tender care. At the Imperial City, five hundred years of tradition have been perpetuated with consummate devotion.

Before leaving Beijing, as a former ambassador, I was asked to tape an interview for the China News Service. The questions were routine and focused on the natural history aspects of our visit to China. Upon returning to the United States, I received a copy of the interview which appeared in a few newspapers.

I was quoted as saying that "there was a bright future for animal watching tours to China; that I would like to tell the people in the United States that China has many birds that are well protected; that there are many people in China who do research on birds, and that there will be more tourists coming to China to observe birds." None of these statements was made in the taped interview. In fact, the thrust of the interview dealt with the status of wildlife conservation in East Africa where I had served.

When an interview concerning flora and fauna in East Africa becomes a propaganda pitch for apocryphal statements about the potential of wildlife tourism in China, I am tempted to tell the true story of the Xianghai Guest House.

Arriving at the Lanzhou Airport in late morning, we were transferred immediately to a bus to complete the four-hour ride to Xining.

Lanzhou is located in Gansu Province in north central China. We climbed gradually from Lanzhou to Xining following the old Silk Road.

Buddhist shrines with prayer flags flying were perched on the tops of hills. The paved roads became shale less than an hour west of Lanzhou.

On the high plateau, farmers grow wheat and potatoes. Rice paddies are nurtured by the origins of the Yellow River at the base of brown hills. There are extensive rows of poplar and a few willows. The flat roofs of the adobe huts serve as space for drying wheat and for the inevitable television antennae.

As we approached Xining, Moslem headdress was in evidence, and fruit trees appeared in great profusion. In a coal mining area, there were slag heaps, stone walls to prevent rock slides, and the constant population and poverty refrain.

In Xining, the center of Qinghai Province, we were taken to the Qinghai Hotel. We had traveled 370 kilometers from Lanzhou. In spite of the inevitable poor cuisine, we were grateful for a quiet, restful evening.

The Hue people who live in Xining represent a rich culture of more than 2,000 years. One of the oldest cities in China, Xining is known for its nature reserves, dry climate, and chemical and paper factories. The Yangtze River runs through the city.

June 2 / Xining to Qinghai Reserve:
On the main road to Lhasa in Tibet, we traveled three hundred kilometers to the Qinghai Lake Hostel. The plateau which we traversed

183

is the highest on earth. The route which borders a fast-running stream includes the Tang Dynasty Wind Tunnel Watchtower which was an early trading center for Qinghai and Tibet. According to fable, Princess Wen Cheng observed the scenery from this tower en route to Tibet to marry the king.

There was snow on the gorgeous mountains in the distance; yaks on the hillsides, and at every turn a crude brick-making enterprise. The terrain was progressively more arid. Gates and fences sport decorative deer, in contrast to cranes in northeastern China.

In the villages, a large stone is placed on each corner of the house roofs to prevent access by evil spirits (not the ravages of the wind).

As we approached Qinghai Lake, the largest lake in China, vegetation became sparse. At 10,000 feet, roving herds of yaks were predominant. The rivers that feed the lake have their sources in the Himalayas. Since there are no outlets from the lake, the water is salty. Through evaporation, the lake is gradually receding.

The Qinghai Bird Island Hostel has a commanding view of the lake. As you approach, the natural beauty and the rustic charm appear inviting. In reality, the bed and board offerings were only a marginal improvement over the deplorable hostel at Xianghai.

Patti and I were fortunate to be assigned twin "beds" with pillows made from rocks, heavy comforters and woolen blankets. The temperature was close to freezing, but the misleading odors of the pending dinner were only temporarily restorative. The food was the least appetizing on the trip.

The mattress was so thin that the cold air exuded from the floor through the mattress in waves. Sleep was difficult. As the temperature dropped, in spite of the blankets, shivering and coughing were early warnings of pneumonia which was nurtured in Xianghai and reached full maturity upon my return to the United States.

There were no curtains on the windowless openings. The bathroom deserves precise description. Ice water was available from the tap for washing but not for drinking. There was an inch of cold water on the floor. The commode was inoperable. There was a single soiled dish towel for each of us (for bathing purposes). The floor and walls had gaping holes. A single, low-wattage light bulb provided illumination. The generator ceased operating at 9:00 p.m., not a deprivation because it was too cold to read.

June 3 / Bird Island:

Today was devoted to birding. Our initial stop was at Bird Island at the lake which is merely a peninsula. The Great Cormorant Rookery was noisy, dirty, and the foul odors extended for several hundred yards. The other feature of Bird "Island" is a pillbox with fifty-eight windows which is dark and cold. The origins or purpose of the pillbox are unknown.

In the afternoon, we took the high road west en route to the Gobi Desert. Except for a few trucks and yaks, the lovely terrain was ours to enjoy. We stopped frequently to climb the adjacent hills. In the fields, there were larks and Demoiselle Cranes. At higher elevations, we spotted the Himalayan Griffon, accentors, snow finch, Wallcreepers, and Lammergeiers.

The hills were inviting, with a hint of green. The air was clear and crisp. The few Tibetans along the roads were inquisitive, friendly, colorfully-dressed, and red of cheek.

Getting to Qinghai was difficult. The food and accommodations were terrible. The local Chinese were basically unfriendly; however, in early June the Tibetans, the air, the birds, and the scenery overrode the inconveniences. If you make the trip, take your own sleeping bag and food.

June 5 / Xining:

After a full day of travel, we returned to the Qinghai Hotel. Except for the quality of the cuisine, we perceived a paradise.

At the Xining Carpet Factory, we observed women weaving sculptured pile carpets. The workers are paid 300 Yuan (approximately $60.00) per month for six eight-hour days per week. Working conditions are marginal. Ventilation and lighting are inadequate. Rest facilities are nonexistent. The supervision appears to be arbitrary and harsh.

In contrast, the local free market was clean, busy, and well-organized. There was a realistic pace associated with ready smiles.

At the Xining Airport, hundreds of Chinese were lined up at the borders of the runways to see the planes (Chinese government ownership and operation) depart. Currently, there is one flight per week to the big metropolis in the East, Xian, which may explain the remarkable interest of the populace. Upon arrival in Xian, we were taken to the Dynasty Hotel.

This evening, we attended a performance of *The Soul of the Terra Cotta Warriors* at a large theater which is in an integral part of the hotel. With a carpet, comfortable seats, and a red-velvet curtain, we were convinced that we were in nirvana. There were four acts and an epilogue. The initial dancing, staging and direction ran a close second to the typical high school production. As the story evolved, the quality of the performance improved appreciably.

The excellent female lead, who was a superb dancer, loved a warrior who lost his life defending the emperor. She sculpted her lover's image. The emperor was impressed. He requested comparable sculptures of each of his warriors. If this fable were true, it would explain why each terra cotta face has a distinctive physiognomy.

In the finale, all of the dancers wore masks and padded coats resembling the actual warriors. The performance was an intriguing blend of the traditional and the modern. There was not a hint of Chinese Communist indoctrination.

Speaking of indoctrination, a tourist sitting next to me who was an ordained minister informed me of his negative reaction to "the overt Buddhist indoctrination" in the Terra Cotta Warrior play. He assumed that the sculpted image was Buddha, and he was appalled that the Chinese would use religion for political indoctrination. When I pointed out his error, he did not have the graciousness to admit it.

Xian is a modern, prosperous city of six million people. The discovery of the terra cotta warriors by a farmer digging a well in 1974 has created a major tourist center with corresponding excellent accommodations. The wall in the center of the city was constructed in the thirteenth century during the Ming Dynasty. For more than two centuries (eleven dynasties), Xian was the capital of the central section of China. Eight rivers surround the city; hence, the lucky number in Xian is eight. There are several free markets (where private enterprise flourishes) and a few night markets, a recent innovation. The "Silk Road" to the east originated in Xian.

In China, if the external temperature reaches 40°C, the workers are given a day off. It is very peculiar, but in recent years, the temperature has never exceeded 39°C.

Early this morning, we journeyed to Li shan Mountain east of Xian. Prior to 1931, when Japan invaded Manchuria, Chiang Kai-shek, who directed the Chinese military forces, enjoyed a summer home at the base of Li Shan. At the time of the Japanese threat, Chiang's two deputy military commanders argued about the composition of the Chinese force to oppose the Japanese. The Communist general won the argument with the non-Communist general who wanted to consolidate all Chinese military forces.

Since Chiang Kai-shek was opposed to Communist domination of the army, the Communist general attempted to have him arrested. Chiang escaped by jumping over the wall of his summer home and hiding on the mountain. A shrine, reached by ascending 1,000 steps (not 999), marks the hiding place where Chiang was captured.

Since the anecdote was related by a communist functionary, the authenticity may be doubtful. Climbing the mountain was not particularly edifying, but at least, we have the anecdote.

Returning to Xian, we visited the museum which provides access to the terra cotta warriors. Two centuries before the birth of Christ, the first emperor of the Qin Dynasty built a sculptured terra cotta army, composed of approximately 6,000 warriors to guard his tomb. The warriors, including a few officers and cavalry, were discovered in formation in three pits ten feet beneath the surface. The columns were covered by wooden roofs and a thick layer of clay.

The excavation of the largest pit is covered by a gigantic glass bubble. Upon entering the site, you are confronted by thousands of well-preserved warriors stretching for one hundred yards. The impact is breathtaking. Different warrior specialties (archers, foot-soldiers, officers, charioteers) have been reproduced to perfection.

As mentioned previously, each face is distinctive. Masks were probably made of each living soldier which were then molded and affixed at final assembly. Since colors were added before submitting the mold to the kiln, many remnants of color have survived.

The manufacturing process has not been clearly identified. Since each figure weighs several hundred pounds, the technology was demanding.

At least two additional mounds in the Xian region, including the tomb of the first Qin Emperor, have been discovered but not excavated. Before excavation, it appears that the Chinese government is maximizing the tourist potential of the present digs.

The gallery of the rich and famous who have visited the terra cotta museum is extraordinary. For once, the hype that surrounds a special place does not transcend the wonders of the site. The terra cotta warriors of Xian are unbelievable and unforgettable.

June 6 / Xian to Shanghai:

Shanghai, the largest city in China with twelve million people, is located at the mouth of the Yangtze River. Until the late thirteenth century, Shanghai was a mere fishing village with another name. Following the opium wars in the mid-nineteenth century, Shanghai opened its doors to the outside World. It has become the largest port and the economic hub of China.

In rough approximation, Shanghai is the New York City and Beijing is the Washington, D.C., of China. Shanghai has preserved traces of the Boxer Rebellion. The French, American, British, and Chinese concessions have disappeared except for a few architectural remnants; however, commercial, pseudo-Western traits are prevalent.

In contrast to Beijing, poverty is not disguised. A narrow funnel of capitalism exudes, for a few, the modern trappings of private enterprise.

The busy port affords a window to the world. A ghetto of modern hotels includes watering holes and lovely grounds for increasing numbers of affluent Western tourists.

The New York City of China embodies comparable diversity. In contrast, the Washington, D.C., of China is a major city with a single industry—government. That industry has created, through repression, an active volcano which may erupt into another, more catastrophic Tiananmen Square.

June 7 / Shanghai:

Departing from the Hua Ting Sheraton Hotel at sunrise, we journeyed to the Fengxian Swamp on the seacoast sixty kilometers south of Shanghai. After walking along the irrigation ditches for several hundred yards, and enjoying a "celebration" of Common Cuckoos (an example of the venereal game captured by James Lipton in "An Exaltation of Larks"), we scanned the flats of Hangzhou Bay.

At the Shanghai Normal Technical College, the classroom buildings were marginal. Student services were not visible, and student laundry was hanging from every dormitory window. The grounds were overgrown with weeds, and trees and flowers were in short supply. The lack of basic facilities at an important college was disappointing.

Before our departure from China, I joined Patti at the Shanghai Friendship House which caters to the shopping whims of tourists. After living in Asia, and visiting several countries in the region for extended periods, I was amazed by the infinite variety of junk that tourists were willing to acquire at exorbitant prices.

June 8 / Shanghai to Narita Airport, Japan:

Courtesy of China Eastern Airlines, the meal served on the flight to Japan was the most appetizing on the entire China trip. It would appear that you must be up in the air to be exposed to enticing Chinese cuisine.

In the United States, our first priority will be to visit a Chinese restaurant. After all, Chow Mein and Chop Suey were invented in the United States.

COSTA RICA
Rain Forest Supreme

March 16, 1995 / San Jose, Costa Rica:

In January, after almost three years as President of the American University of Paris, I resigned. My prostate cancer had returned with a vengeance. The doctors advised me to return to Brigham Hospital in Boston for treatment. The 1991 prostatectomy had produced temporary positive results; however, hormonal therapy was now prescribed. Of partial importance, I am now 66 years old, and I believe it is time for the next generation to assume management responsibility.

As a break from therapy, we visited Costa Rica. The airport in San Jose was excessively crowded, dirty, hot, and in a general state of disrepair. Three immigration clerks manned eight windows while three huge jumbo jets disgorged hundreds of tourists simultaneously. The customs process was remarkably quick.

Costa Rica is a country the size of West Virginia (a comparison repeated to distraction). It is stable, viable, and beautiful.

On the Atlantic Coast, near the City of Limon, Columbus "discovered" Costa Rica in 1502. Because the Indians greeted him with gold trinkets, the name of Costa Rica seemed appropriate. The heritage of Columbus has been sustaining. From the language, to the culture, to the designation of the currency (Colones), Columbus made an impact.

In 1563, Coronado appeared on the scene. He established his headquarters on the Pacific Coast and proceeded to exterminate virtually all of the indigenous Indian population. As a result, the current racial mix is predominantly Spanish.

In 1856, a mercenary from the United States named William Walker staged a rebellion which was thwarted by the intervention of a teenage messboy named Juan Santamaria. Juan sounded the alarm. Costa Rica's Spanish heritage was preserved. Santamaria became a sanctified national hero. The country was "ripe" for United Fruit.

The thoughtless management of United Fruit destroyed much of the unique natural habitat of Costa Rica. Initially, the banana plantations were confined to the tropical lowlands on the Atlantic Coast. Where bananas grow, all other vegetation is in jeopardy. Jamaicans were imported to construct the commercial railroad. Their progeny altered the color and language of the populace permanently. Company towns imposed virtual servitude on the workforce. When the soil lost its fertility, United Fruit moved the entire operation to Golfito on the Pacific Coast. The same sordid process was repeated.

Reflecting the absence of racial strife, in 1889, Costa Rica conducted the first free election in Latin America. With the exception of the 1948 example of Calderon, who failed to honor the election results, Costa Rica has been a working democracy for more than a century. In the same year, the military establishment was abolished. Costa Rica was tightly squeezed between two volatile neighbors (Panama and Nicaragua). Bananas and other commercial pursuits induced the United States to apply the heavy hand of the Monroe Doctrine with unprecedented success.

In 1987, President Arias, manifesting the peaceful heritage, won the Nobel Prize for his efforts to promote pacification among warring factions in Central America. As a relatively young man, Arias is now enjoying the status of a private citizen; however, he continues to serve as a prototype for Carter-like, post-presidential behavior.

Because of relative economic stability, more than 30,000 retirees (pensionados) from the United States have settled permanently in Costa Rica (predominantly in and near the capital). Estimates vary from twelve to thirty percent; however, approximately one-quarter of the country has been designated national parks (compared to three percent in the United States). The parks and reserves protect the unique flora and fauna (including more than eight hundred species of birds). As a result, tourism is a major industry.

In the absence of Panda-like critters to induce donors to contribute from abroad, the delightful natural ambience, including sunny beaches on both oceans, is attracting increasing waves of tourists.

The Ticos, the local Spanish name for Costa Ricans, subsist on rum, beer, tourist dollars, and Gallo pinto (a staple dish of beans and rice to which an egg is added for the breakfast meal).

March 17:

The seedy capital of San Jose serves as home to one million urban residents in a total population in excess of three million. Borrowing from the practice utilized in many metropolitan areas, numbered avenues run east and west and streets north and south.

The monotony of hastily-constructed wooden shops and hovels is broken by the painted cement homes of the moderately affluent and a few attractive city parks and colonial-style buildings. Reflecting the Catholic dominance, the churches are old, beautiful, omnipresent, and seem to attract city parks as neighbors.

During a long weekend, Patti and I explored the city with generous breaks for swimming at the spacious Herradura Hotel pools. As a senior citizen, I can attest to the deleterious impact of high elevation and tropical sunshine coupled with slight cloud cover, and thirty minutes of exposure, to promote cutaneous mayhem.

After a tasty open-air luncheon at the majestic Gran Hotel at the Plaza de la Cultura, with a marimba band providing background music (an instrument which I attempted to solve), we covered a significant component of the downtown area en route to the Museo del Central Bank (not a romantic designation) which houses extraordinary pre-Columbian gold exhibits. The gold jewelry depicting birds and animals represents astonishing artisan skill, and an advanced culture, which flourished without the prosaic influence of Christian religious icons.

A stroll through the open air artisan market afforded displays of the worst examples of airport art.

On our first full evening in San Jose, we responded without gusto to a mediocre dinner at the Bougainvillea Hotel in suburban Santo Tomas. The cuisine had been endorsed by an American culinary writer. We were reassured to return to the Herradura which incorporates diversity, anonymity, and basic essential services dispensed with courtesy and a smile. Without exception, the Ticos are friendly and civil. It is tempting to suggest that the disappearance of the military is the magical ingredient.

March 18:

After a run at the golf course near the hotel, Patti and I returned to the Plaza de la Cultura to attend a piano concert at the Teatro Nacional. Because Europeans expressed concern that there was not an adequate performing arts hall in Central America, the Costa Rican landed gentry inspired the construction of the theater in 1897. The small Baroque facility accommodates three hundred guests and reveals an architectural jewel.

On this occasion, the British Embassy sponsored a pianist countryman who began with a slow motion version of Beethoven's Sonata Number 14 (the Moonlight Sonata). From that point, the quality of the performance deteriorated. His choice of Liszt's "Venice and Naples," "the Iberia" by Albeniz (to please the Spanish-oriented audience), and Chopin's Sonata Number Three represented minimal virtuosity and a disquieting lack of diversity. More importantly, each selection was played with the verve of a funeral dirge and the pace of a snail. Without demonstrated talent or stage presence, the pianist received few plaudits.

March 19:

On the final day before departing on an up-country safari, we visited the Simon Bolivar National Zoo and the extraordinary annual orchid show. For a nation trading on the preservation of remarkable flora and fauna, the zoo was a disgrace. One Bengal Tiger and one Lion paraded in filthy, lonely splendor while assorted local species of mammals, fish, and birds endured squalid conditions. A few of the colorful indigenous songbirds were incarcerated in a dark, exceedingly small aviary.

In contrast, the orchid show was unbelievably lovely. Thousands of orchids were displayed at "the largest orchid show in the world."

Scores of entries bore prize ribbons from the recent judging. Since orchids grow in great profusion in the canopies of the tropical rain forest, it is fitting that Costa Rica should be the situs for a remarkable display in San Jose.

March 20 / Carara Reserve:

Heading West from San Jose, we passed through terraced, hilly country en route to the Pacific lowlands. Slightly after dawn, within a few kilometers of the Pacific at a river bridge adjoining the Carara Reserve, we saw a flock of elegant Scarlet Macaws flying overhead. The flock is resident at Carara and represents a large percentage of the Scarlet Macaws which are now confined to the Pacific slope.

The Carara Reserve was created in 1978. With the exception of a minimal number of tourists from the few cruise ships which stop at the Costa Rican Pacific Coast, there are minimal visitors.

Deferring our visit to the Reserve itself, we arrived at the Dundee Ranch which is located in the most arid section of Costa Rica northeast of the Reserve. The ranch is newly-constructed, and the arid terrain is unique in Costa Rica.

After a refreshing swim in the ranch pool, where we were observed by a large iguana, we drove to a remote valley where we descended on foot. Howler Monkeys were screaming at a high decibel level until a downpour intervened. The vehicle became stuck in the mud. In heavy rain, we walked approximately five kilometers back to the Dundee Ranch. During the night, the vehicle was towed to the ranch by tractor.

March 21 / Monteverde:

The following morning, we returned to Carara. The walk on the trail in the tall moist rain forest yielded a charming little red and blue Poison Dart Frog. Ancient Indian tribes used the poison to tip arrows which became remarkably deadly. As usual, the protective coloration disguised a lethal kick.

From Carera, we drove north on the Pan American Highway to Monteverde. The highway was confined to two lanes and the trucks were troublesome. The views of the Pacific were infrequent and obscured by trucks. We were delighted to leave civilization and to head into the dry hills approaching Monteverde.

Following World War II, the region was developed by American Quakers. The foothill scenery with deep gorges was wild and stimulating, but the trucks continued to appear.

The village of Monteverde is perched among tropical, wooded hills. Several Americans have retired in the area. The houses are basic, remote, and unattractive. The local artisan products lack distinction. The plethora of motorcycles and "hippies" detracted from a lovely ambience.

The Monteverde Cloud Forest Preserve is privately owned and managed by the Tropical Science Center. More than 26,000 acres are incorporated. The tract is split by the Continental Divide. On the east side, the flora and fauna are distinctly Caribbean, and the cloud forest is relatively wet. On the west side, the limited Pacific rains provide an appropriate habitat for a different genre of flora. The extensive hilly trails on both sides of the Divide were particularly enchanting.

For several years, Patti has suffered from deteriorating knees. The cartilage has been destroyed, and the pain is acute. In the next few months, she plans to have both knees replaced. In the meantime, her movement is restricted. Today, she decided not to accompany me on the Caribbean-slope trail.

On the walk, I had the privilege of seeing the secretive and colorful Resplendent Quetzal. During the return leg on the Pacific slope, I was greeted by the elusive Three-wattled Bellbird. The bellbird is heard more often than it is seen, and the wattles are incredible.

At the hummingbird gallery, a number of feeders attract a dozen species of hummingbirds. Since there is only one species in the Eastern United States, the array in Costa Rica is noteworthy.

Unfortunately, tourism is affecting the Monteverde Cloud Forest adversely. The crowds were crass, uninterested in the surroundings, and addicted to beer. The trails were crawling with noisy hikers.

March 23 / Cerro del la Muerte:

Two hours south of San Jose, the Cerro del la Muerte montane forest averages an elevation of 7,000 feet. In a few sites, the giant oaks disappear above 11,000 feet. In this habitat, the flora and fauna are unique. Unbelievably, for the second time, I was able to get a glimpse of the Resplendent Quetzal, featuring an unmistakable crest, a white tail with long green tail coverts, and a red lower breast.

March 25 / La Selva Verde:

From San Jose, we climbed to Volcan Poas National Park which is north of the capital and is still located on the Pacific side of the mountains. Poas is one of three active volcanos in the San Jose region. At elevations above 8,000 feet, high green hedges and coffee farms prevail.

Continuing northeast, we descended the Caribbean slopes and stopped at an attractive waterfall in the Sarapiqui River headwaters.

Two hours from San Jose, in the humid, tropical, Caribbean lowlands, we arrived at La Selva Verde Lodge at the confluence of the Sarapiqui and Puerto Viejo Rivers. The lodge accommodates eighty guests in screened rooms on concrete pillars with encircling porches. Each room contains a hammock, a fan, and two small beds. After a refreshing dip in a Sarapiqui River pool, reputedly without creature threats, we departed for the rain forest.

The Field Station, which is affiliated with Duke University, abuts the Carillo National Park. The station encompasses 3,500 acres. The elevation varies from one hundred to four hundred feet. In thirty years of operation, thirty-one miles of trails, including four miles of cement walks, have been constructed. Sixty percent of the tract constitutes original Neotropical rain forest.

The lowland rain forest sustains 1,700 floral species including 1,200 species of orchids and innumerable species of the philodendron family. One half of the bird species in Costa Rica and ten percent of the earth's butterflies are also found at La Selva Verde.

The Field Station operates as a base for biologists of all stripes who have prepared more than 1,300 publications pertaining to the natural history of the area.

In preparation for the trip, we read *Tropical Nature*, a 1984 layman's view prepared by biologists Forsyth and Mujata, which captures the "feel" of the tropical rain forest. Even Forsyth's unique writing ability fails to capture the diversity and grandeur of the forest.

The rain forest represents another world where the nuances of green shriek in distinction. The high canopy projects perpetual darkness. The seemingly unlimited species of flora and fauna defy description.

The other reading orientation which proved invaluable was

Alexander Skutch's 1989 seminal work, *The Birds of Costa Rica*. Skutch was an ornithologist with the Cornell University Laboratory who, in recent years, has resided in Costa Rica. He has prepared definitive descriptions of 830 species accompanied by color plates by Dana Gardener. The book provided an introduction to Costa Rican birdlife.

In the rain forest, we hiked across a gigantic pasture to a secluded wooded stream. In the middle of the stream, a Boat-billed Heron family watched us calmly. The stocky, large head; huge eyes; and gigantic shoe-shaped bill were unmistakable.

At La Selva Verde, the animal world was represented by a white-nosed coatimundi, a rabbit-like agouti, an ameiva lizard, and a bivouac of bats which exploded from the innards of a gigantic tree. The insect world upheld its laurels with a score of blue morpho butterflies which initially might be mistaken for birds.

March 29 / Rain Forest Aerial Tram:

In 1986, Donald R. Perry, the first biologist to concentrate on the canopy of the tropical rain forest, wrote an exciting book, *Life Above the Jungle Floor*. Based on the success of the book, and his intrinsic entrepreneurial instincts, he was able to finance construction of the first Rain Forest Aerial Tram (unfortunately, saddled with the logo "RAT") which opened recently. The tract is located on the main road from Puerto Limon on the east coast to San Jose, about one hour's drive from the capital.

Arriving before the tourist deluge, we took an open truck to a narrow bridge and a footpath over the bridge to another truck which deposited us at the tram.

The aerial tram resembles a ski tow which carries six passengers in a green metal open cable car one hundred to one hundred and forty feet above the ground. There are twenty appropriately spaced cars which complete the 1.5 mile circuit with a stop half way. The lift system and specialized cars were manufactured by Superior Crown in Spokane, Washington. The pylons were installed with the assistance of Nicaraguan (Sandinista) Air Force helicopters which lowered the pylons from above the canopy.

The RAT is a profit-making venture which sponsors an excellent educational program. The enterprise is managed by Michael Shelly, a former Peace Corps Volunteer in Costa Rica. More than 2,000 local school children have access to the tram every year.

Patti and I were in the first car with a local guide. Through radio contact, the car can stop at any time for thirty seconds. Unfortunately, all of the cars must stop simultaneously, but for safety purposes, that aberration is vital.

Above the highest trees, we were transfixed by 1,000 acres of silent, magical sights in a tropical rain forest.

A gentle rain was falling. For a few brief minutes, we were exposed to a wonderland of shades of green, epiphytes growing in exquisite profusion, parrots sailing through the openings in the foliage, and glimpses of the distant ground through light gaps created by free-falling trees. If trees did not fall naturally in a rain forest, the sunlight would be inadequate to sustain the diversity of flora at ground level.

Following the tram ride, we took a walk with Freddie, an outstanding Costa Rican guide who was trained by RAT. Through Freddie's eyes, we were able to see the trail of a 350 pound Tapir (only one of 135 mammals found in the tract). The area also serves as home to 118 amphibians; 300 birds, and 50,000 species of insects. Since the tropical climate does not change by season, the growth of trees approximates seven feet per year. Because of the extraordinary growth, there are no annual rings on the trees.

Heeding Freddie's explicit warning, we stayed on the path to avoid a confrontation with the small, deadly, well-camouflaged Fer-de-Lance snakes. To illustrate the realities of a tropical rain forest, while we were resting on the trail, a small branch hit my shoulders and Patti's arm after a one hundred foot fall from the canopy.

Before departing from the tropical rain forest, one depressing fact must be shared. When primary growth rain forest is cut, 90% is lost for eternity. Unfortunately, preservation of the original rain forest, everywhere on earth, represents a lost cause.

March 30 / Tapanti:

After a delicious night's sleep at the hotel in San Jose, we drove south through the attractive old capital of Cartago to Tapanti National Park. The park is located two hours from San Jose in the Amistad

National Forest approaching the extensive Chirripo National Park.

In a Swiss-like glen, we watched scores of Swainson's Hawks circling in the thermals to obtain the requisite elevation to begin the northern migration.

For perspective, most of the migratory birds in North America are merely engaging in a short-term nesting commitment before returning to their permanent residencies in Central America. As Americans, we assume that "our" birds are returning "home."

March 31 / Tortugero:

At the hotel in San Jose, which now seems like home, we slept late, swam, lunched at the pool, and recovered our equilibrium.

Gluttons for punishment, we departed for the relatively inaccessible Tortugero region on the Atlantic Coast near the northern border with Nicaragua.

We took a minibus down the Caribbean slopes almost to the coastal Puerto Limon. Before reaching Limon, we turned north on a dirt road, past an operational Del Monte banana plantation, en route to the man-made canal which leads to Tortugero.

A profusion of banana trees destroys the natural cover. The plantation areas become sterile. When the soil has been denuded of nutrients, the fallow land will support only undesirable secondary growth.

When a ripe stalk of bananas, weighing in excess of fifty pounds, is cut, the base of the stalk dies, and a new stalk appears at the base of the trunk. To facilitate growth, plastic bags are placed over the unripe bananas. When the bananas are mature, the plastic bags are discarded. They are then strewn throughout the area and become formidable hazards for fish and wildlife.

Economically, the Costa Ricans working on the plantations are paid "almost a living wage." They live in squalid company towns, and few escape the cycle of poverty, On the Atlantic Coast, most of the plantations have disappeared. The impoverished terrain remains.

Since there is not any land access to Tortugero, and air service is restricted to small aircraft from Limon, we boarded a wooden river boat at the canal which was constructed for banana shipments. After a few miles, the canal joins a fresh water river which separates the

Tortugero strip from the mainland, The river has spawned scores of smaller rivers and canals. For two and one-half hours, we enjoyed "the main road" of Tortugero. Along the route, several breachways allow brief views of the ocean and access for limited salt water.

North of Tortugero Village, we arrived at a private tract which was a former banana plantation called Mawamba Lodge. The bare wooden cottages were uninviting. The beds were small and lumpy. The walls were paper thin. The amenities were nonexistent. The food was marginal. In oppressive heat and constant rain, we still felt privileged.

René, our guide, received a degree in biology from the University of Costa Rica. As a result, he had become a self-proclaimed expert in a number of specialties including ecology, zoology, and ornithology. During a slide presentation and an afternoon walk, he admitted that his botany expertise was not exemplary; however, that did not deter him from identifying more species than could be substantiated.

From the river to the black sand beach was a short walk. Because of the documented threat of sharks near the shore, and a powerful riptide, we were advised to avoid taking a dip. The natives followed their own advice.

The riverside town of Tortugero, a ten-minute walk from the lodge, offered a one-room community store, active beer halls, and brightly painted huts.

On two successive evenings, we enjoyed two-hour motorboat trips on the river including several small streams. Using a searchlight and the skills of a local motorman who knew the river, we were richly rewarded.

In spite of the rain, for which hooded ponchos were provided, we saw an Anteater, several Three-toed Sloths feeding high in the canopy, a Spider Monkey, a River Otter, and a clutch of Long-nosed Bats which resembled black leaves on a tree trunk. Lacking bone structure, the heavy sloths are remarkably slow, but fascinating to watch in a slow-motion mode.

On the final evening, while floating on a river inlet, we saw a Great Potoo, a night bird of forest canopy, on a horizontal tree branch five feet above the stream. The potoo assumes a head and body vertical stance resembling a stick. Normally, the Great Potoo perches higher on the tree. On this occasion, because of the abundance of insects in the rain, he must have been motivated to hunt from a lower vantage point.

On the morning of our departure, we arranged a final river excursion. The driver/guide took along breadcrumbs. When he reached the proper spot, he flung some breadcrumbs overboard. Three four-foot caimans responded to the bait. The same bait attracted a school of sardines, which in turn seduced a Snowy Egret, with missing claws on one foot, to share the meal. These unfolding scenes occurred within five feet of the boat. An equally famished Green-backed Heron followed a few feet behind, and both birds joined us for several crumb stops.

April 2 / San Jose to Tiskita:

As we passed through the Pavas District of San Jose, which is the situs of the American Embassy, I was reminded of a recent editorial which was written by the incumbent Ambassador and appeared in the local San Jose English-language newspaper.

The editorial was generally negative and stressed the Costa Rican government's recent decision to expropriate a limited amount of private property. Given the democratic credo, sound economic policies, and demonstrated performance protecting the principle of private ownership, the editorial was troublesome.

Upon inquiry, I discovered that during Colonel Oliver North's heyday, the Contra forces acquired land in the Northwestern corner of Costa Rica in the Guanacaste District. In Guanacaste, an operational airport was constructed on the land which served the Contras in ferrying munitions and supplies to Nicaragua.

Now that the Contra issue has been resolved, private interests covet the land. Those private interests would like to develop a private resort near Pacific Ocean beaches.

In contrast, the Costa Rican government would add the beautiful tract to the Guanacaste National Park (depicted in an excellent MacArthur Foundation video).

Senator Jesse Helms is an influential member of the private group attempting to acquire the former Contra land. It would appear that the incumbent American Ambassador is assisting private American interests by alleging that the Costa Rican government may be contemplating expropriation. Banana Republic American foreign policy is still alive and well.

In the one-hour flight from the San Jose City Airport to the Pacific Ocean, the twin-engine, five-passenger plane afforded an excellent view of central and southwestern Costa Rica. The plane touched down at Puerto Jimenez on the Golfo Dulce and the Oso Peninsula. Don Perry, the Aerial Tram biologist, climbed his first gigantic canopy tree near Puerto Jimenez.

After a ten-minute return trip to the mainland, we landed at a narrow beach airstrip at Tiskita Jungle Lodge. The lodge is located in the isolated Punta Banco area of Burica Peninsula which is only a few miles from the Panama border. With the exception of the airport at St. Bart's in the Lesser Antilles, or a confrontation with any New York City airport, the beach runway at Tiskita takes the prize for inducing passenger hysteria.

After World War II, Tiskita was purchased by a Canadian engineer who raised a family in San Jose. Fifteen years ago, he deeded the 350-acre private tract to a son who has launched an experimental farm. The farm contains fruit trees from many continents, medicinal plants, and scores of herbs. A few years ago, the son opened the lodge. He has also added 125 acres which adjoin the original property and which abut an extensive Indian reservation. To solidify the relationship, the name Tiskita was borrowed from the Indian dialect. Tiskita means "Osprey."

The 475-acre plot includes more than 200 acres of virgin rain forest. Crude trails have been constructed (the wettest and most dangerous we had encountered in Costa Rica).

A daughter of the owner greeted us at the airstrip and introduced us to the narrow gravel road to the lodge, 300 feet above the ocean. The lodge is attractive; however, as usual, the cottages were not exemplary. The open air bathroom was located at the rear of the cottage. Patti and I did not object to land crabs in the sink and lizards in the shower; however, when we were directed to put used toilet tissue in the trash, because of inadequate water pressure, we were nonplused. To be charitable, the food at the lodge was mediocre.

The lengthy walk to the white sand beach was rewarding. Because of treacherous riptides—a national condition—and a recent near fatal accident, we swam in shallow water as the tide was receding. The variety of swaying tropical palms along the beach was appealing, and we were at home in the ambience of a deserted tropical beach.

During the walk into town, farther down the beach, we met the sole teacher at the clean, utilitarian school; noted that the health clinic had received a donation from a California Rotary Club, and ascertained that the refuse of the village was being disgorged into a freshwater stream that flowed into the ocean.

A walk with the lodge's resident naturalist, who concentrates on flora, was edifying. Hundreds of esoteric fruit trees, many with medicinal and hallucinogenic qualities, have been planted. I was fascinated to learn that there are ninety-six species of mango and seventy-six species of guava in Costa Rica. On the Pacific Coast, the paucity of essential minerals in the soil makes fruit tree cultivation problematic. We tasted several of the fruits, including the Star Apple, and admired the diversity: brainfruit, eggfruit, java; Water Apple; Barbados Cherry; White and Red Ginger; breadfruit; cashews; cacao, Lemon Grass, and acres of others.

The humidity was oppressive. It was difficult to focus binoculars on dark-colored bird species in the rain forest canopy, but the handsome Blue Dacnis was worth the travail.

April 5 / Tiskita to San Jose:

On the return flight to San Jose, we landed at Golfito, an insignificant port two and one-half hours from Tiskita via automobile. Golfito was made infamous by United Fruit. The surrounding country still bears the scars.

Costa Rica was a joy, but we will not be tempted to return. Population increases, and the abuses of capitalism, will systematically destroy the natural wonders of the country. Even with a meaningful percentage of the land enjoying government protection, it is estimated that the rain forest will disappear within a generation. On Earth, one hundred acres of rain forest are being destroyed every minute. In three and one-half minutes, a plot the size of the original forest at the Tiskita Lodge will be obliterated.

HUNGARY
The Iron Curtain Lifts

May 17, 1995 / Rhode Island to JFK to Paris:

My exposure to Eastern Europe has been limited. As a former President of Radio Free Europe/Radio Liberty headquartered in Munich, Germany (1978-1982), I was not authorized to travel in Eastern Europe or the USSR.

In December, 1990, after the "iron curtain" opened, Patti and I crossed the Czech border and visited Pilsen. We also spent a few hours in the area near Dresden in Eastern Germany.

May 18 / Paris to Budapest:

Since I had been invited to Paris to receive an honorary degree from the American University of Paris, we left Rhode Island early to complete an abbreviated trip to Hungary before returning to Paris.

Americans tend to ignore the favorable impact of isolation on the development of the United States. Since the fifth century, the Hungarians have been forced to endure subjugation by their powerful neighbors. In that century, the Huns invaded. In the ninth century, the Magyars, who had permanent impact, followed the Huns. In the thirteenth century, the Mogols invaded, and in the sixteenth century, the Turks.

The recorded history of the Hungarian people is limited prior to the birth of Christ. During that period, the Romans were occupiers for five centuries. In the first century B.C., the Buda side of the Danube River constituted the outer limit of the Roman Empire.

In recent history, the Hungarians were the subjugated partner in the Austro-Hungarian Empire which led to disastrous results in World War I. In the Second World War, Hungary was occupied by Nazi Germany.

In 1945, the Russians replaced the Germans. For one-half century, Hungary was a satellite of the USSR. For the past six years, the Hungarians have been exposed to the strange winds of freedom.

Between the World Wars, Admiral Horthy (the Hungarians had access to the sea when they controlled part of Serbia) ruled with an iron hand. Prior to revolution in 1956, Nagy attempted to introduce a few semi-democratic reforms. From 1968 to 1988, Kadar represented the most liberal force in Eastern Europe.

For twenty centuries, with few exceptions, the Hungarians have been dominated by powerful repressive nations. In attempting to evaluate the impact of freedom, during the last six years, the absence of a relevant heritage has been critical.

In 1990, the first free elections in forty years were conducted. Many former communists have emerged as leaders. The media are state controlled. The abuses of capitalism are manifest. Yet, the most influential political party, the Hungarian Democratic Forum, and the opposition Alliance for Free Democrats, have been able to implement a modicum of reform.

Inflation has been a major deterrent to development. In 1992, $1.00 was worth 77 forints. Today, $1.00 has an exchange value of 125 forints.

In spite of the fact that approximately one-half of all Western economic support to Eastern Europe has found its way to Hungary, IMF guidelines are being ignored. The changes have been superficial. For example, foreign controlled hotels, advertising agencies, fast food chains, and women engaged in the oldest profession have made the most significant progress.

To compound a felony, a major component of the talent of Hungary left the country permanently following the 1956 Revolution. One-third of the population, at the time of the Revolution, now reside in other European countries or overseas.

In 1873, industrial Pest and imperial Buda were merged. The stereotyped distinction prevails; however, in reality, flat Pest has many charms and hilly Buda spawned drab Moscow Square, "Stalinesque" housing units and other trappings of communist urbanization.

Upon arrival at the international airport in Pest, we were informed that our luggage had not arrived. We proceeded to our Panzio (pension) in the Buda Hills, passing a ritual horde of McDonalds and Pizza Huts. Since the major hotels were charging exorbitant rates, and did not differ from comparable establishments in Western Europe, we decided to stay in a Panzio and to observe a bit of the local color.

After settling down in the clean former home, which has been converted to a Panzio, we departed for Pest via taxi. At lunch, to honor our current commitment, Patti chose Hungarian Goulash, and I opted for Hungarian Bean Soup. Each dish was excellent. Before midnight, our luggage arrived. With one exception, I was ready for Budapest.

Before leaving the United States, I had developed a roaring case of the flu. My overseas experiences have featured significant confrontations with flu bugs. We debated the cancellation of the Hungarian phase of the trip. The decision to proceed was wise; however, the flu germs also made the trip.

May 19 / Budapest, Hungary:

Through the good offices of the Panzio clerk, we requested a long-term, low-cost, careful, knowledgeable, English-speaking taxi driver (imagine the odds against realizing that combination). Fortunately, we secured the services of Andrasi Gyula, "Julius," a taxi driver who doubles as a driver for special tours. Our initial priority was to concentrate on the attractions of Buda.

The hills on the right bank of the Danube River served as home for several waves of royalty. The thirteenth century Buda Castle, constructed by King Bela IV, dominates the scene. Admiral Horthy lived in the castle for thirty years. It now houses three museums and the National Library.

Adjoining the castle is the remarkably attractive Matthias Church, a Gothic structure where a number of Hungarian kings were crowned. The premier of Lizt's "Coronation Mass" was presented at the church in 1867. One year ago, a terrorist's bomb, for which no group has claimed responsibility, destroyed several stained glass windows. They have not been replaced.

Behind the Matthias Church, the parapets of the Fisherman's Bastions overlook the Danube and the stately parliament buildings on the Pest side of the river, the left bank.

The historic Castle District is protected by UNESCO under the international historic preservation program. The specialized agency of the United Nations was unable to protect the medieval Dominican Monastery from the ravages of the Hilton Hotel chain. Ignoring the preference of the Hungarian people, who wished to preserve their heritage, the powerful politicos allowed the Hilton to convert the monastery into a typical, modern American hotel.

Further south, at the last rise in the Buda Hills, the Citadel overlooks the river and miles of urban decay featuring the usual Stalin era apartments. Under the prior regime, the apartments were provided free to communist workers.

Until 1989, the Citadel housed a gigantic Russian military statue and a commemorative plaque. When the Soviet regime departed, the statue and the plaque were removed immediately. With the exception of the hideous, monotonous, apartment houses, there is little evidence that the Russians occupied the city for forty-four years.

At the base of the Buda Hills, the ancient Roman thermal baths, which were reinforced by Turkish royalty, have become the focal point for the spacious, esthetically pleasing, Gilbert Spa Hotel. In contrast to the sterile Hilton, the Gilbert Spa is quaint and inviting.

Buda and Pest are connected by six famous bridges, the most renowned of which are the Chain Bridge, the first permanent bridge to cross the Danube, and the Elizabeth Bridge which was erected in 1903.

Since it was raining, we drove quickly through Pest to the city park and the Bagolyvar Restaurant which is one of two well-known restaurants modernized by George Lang.

In New York City, on the West Side near Lincoln Center for the Performing Arts, the Hungarian immigrant, George Lang, created the Café des Artistes, which was considered one of the finest restaurants in the area. During my stint as President of Lincoln Center, following evening performances, we enjoyed the Café frequently and became acquainted with George Lang.

Following the departure of the Russians from Budapest, Mr. Lang returned to his homeland and created the two beautiful restaurants adjoining the city park—the flagship Gundel and the smaller Bagolyvar.

After this advertising pitch, you might have anticipated the evaluation. The meal was mediocre and extremely expensive.

Following the luncheon, we walked through the park in the rain. We observed a few of the inmates at the zoo and admired the small ponds, one of which becomes a public skating rink during the winter months.

Heroes Square adjoins the city park. On October 23, 1956, the first manifestation of rebellion surfaced with a massive student procession. On November 4th, after several days of hints of freedom, Russian troops smashed into Budapest to quell the "revolution." Unarmed students were confronted by Russian tanks. The tactics were totally effective, and the uprising was quashed. The square is named in honor of the students who led the revolt.

That evening, we attended a reception at the residence of the American Ambassador to Hungary, Donald Blinken, and his wife Vera. During our residency in New York City, Donald was serving as Chairman of the Board of the State University of New York. Vera, a native of Hungary, was a leader of the International Rescue Committee with which Patti was affiliated.

The majority of the guests were participants in an ethnic conference. Before we departed from the reception, the Ambassador expressed interest in acquiring the Hungarian broadcasting tapes from Radio Free Europe.

During my Presidency of Radio Free Europe/Radio Liberty in Munich, the Radios were broadcasting to Hungary eighteen and one-half hours per day. There were two and one-half million listeners every day, and three hours per day were devoted to news, per se. During that period (1978-1982), more than half of the radio listeners in Eastern Europe were following the broadcasts of Radio Free Europe.

The Hungarian Service of Radio Free Europe during my term of service was directed by an outstanding civil servant, Joseph Szabados, who subsequently retired to California. His replacement in the 1980s was Lazlo Ribansky with whom I played tennis regularly in Munich. Both Joe and Lazlo became good friends. I have deep respect for the competent array of talent which they recruited to discharge the fundamental and effective broadcasting commitment to Hungary.

After leaving Budapest, I contacted the incumbent leadership at Radio Free Europe/Radio Liberty. They were receptive to the idea of donating the Hungarian tapes to Hungarian academic authorities in Budapest.

May 20 / Visegrad and Esztergom:

Julius drove us to the Bend of the Danube about fifty kilometers northwest of Budapest. En route, we strolled through the village of Szentendre (St. Andrew) on the Danube. Szentendre was settled by Serbians and has become a colorful artists and artisans colony. The Margit Kovacs Museum was particularly stimulating. Ms. Kovacs lived from 1902-1977. She is considered the master ceramicist of Hungary. She captures a unique combination of pathos and humor representing the basic emotions of ordinary people.

At Visegrad, we roamed through the ruins of the Royal Castle built by Bela IV in the fourteenth century. Chiffchaff and Greenfinch (birds, you know) were cavorting in the treetops below the castle ramparts. In the distance, the remains of the Brezhnev attempt to dam the Danube River were evident. Fortunately, the project was eliminated before the historic river was permanently disfigured. On the opposite bank, small villages in the Republic of Slovakia were visible. For his initial foreign service assignment, Senator Claiborne Pell of Rhode Island, with whom I worked on higher educational issues, was stationed at the American Consulate in Bratislava on the Danube River which was then part of Czechoslovakia.

At Esztergom, we visited the Basilica which serves as the center of the Roman Catholic Church in Hungary. The small Basilica is constructed of Italian Carrara marble. In 1991, it provided a stopover for Pope John Paul II.

In the crypt, the tomb of Archbishop Mindszenty is prominently displayed. As Cardinal, Mindszenty opposed both fascism and communism in Hungary. In 1949, he was convicted of treason by the communist regime for his failure to secularize the Catholic schools. He was sentenced to life imprisonment.

During the 1956 Hungarian Revolution, Cardinal Mindszenty was freed. Before he could be recaptured, he found asylum at the United States Embassy in Budapest where he was under house arrest for twelve years.

Cardinal Mindszenty served as a symbol of freedom for all of Eastern Europe.

Sunday, May 21 / Eger:

From Budapest, Julius drove us to the old city of Eger which is located one hundred kilometers northeast of Budapest. Settled by the Romans as Agria, Eger is the wine and tobacco center of Hungary. En route to the city, we passed through the edge of the Hortabage Plain.

From the walls of the castle, which withstood a Turkish siege, we enjoyed an entrancing view of the old city. Many of the surviving buildings were built in the thirteenth century. The wrought iron windows and gates by Henrik Fasola are distinguished.

Returning to Budapest, we passed a nuclear power plant named in honor of Yury Gagarin, the Soviet cosmonaut. The red poppies and white daisies were in bloom. The agricultural crops appeared lush and prosperous.

Julius offered to take a slight detour to see his weekend retreat at Fishing Lake, a reservoir near Pelotas Village. On a plot of land 50 feet wide and 150 feet deep which is backed by a state forest, Julius has constructed a twenty-five foot square cabin which includes open doorways to two very tiny bedrooms and a closet which might become a bathroom. There is no water. The dirt roads have a single track made by previous vehicles. Scores of plots of approximately the same size have been staked out, but very few cottages have been constructed. Theft is endemic. There are no screens, no community activities, and no stores in the immediate area. The "lake" is small and muddy. There is not any swimming, and the fishing is not productive. With great pride, Julius showed us his "retreat."

May 22 / Budapest:

The sunshine has returned, my flu is developing nicely, and we have resumed our exploration of Pest.

After passing St. Stephen's Basilica and the Opera House, we glanced at the Royal Crown and jewels at the National Museum. During World War II, the crown was incarcerated at Fort Knox, Kentucky. More than thirty years later, through the good offices of Secretary of State, Cyrus Vance, the crown was returned to Hungary. Only the small museum room which housed the crown was open to the public. The lighting was deplorable. There were not any signs. The crown was poorly displayed. Since every Hungarian child knows the saga of the Hungarian Crown, historic notations and adequate lighting are probably unnecessary.

We walked through the partially covered central market on the Vaci Utca, on the promenade which is the situs of the Atrium Hyatt and Marriott Hotels, and sampled a bland pastry at the Gerbeaud Patisserie at Vorosmartyr Square which reputedly was visited by Queen Elizabeth of Great Britain. In honor of that occasion, I trust that the pastry chef came out of retirement for the day.

On the evening before our departure from Budapest, we were exposed to another mediocre meal at Gundel's. The duckling and rabbit entrees were tough and overcooked. The sauces were distinctly non-French, heavy, and tasteless. German and Japanese business types occupied most of the tables. The prices were astronomical (in Hungarian terms).

On the Buda side, we visited the Bartok Museum. Although I do not fully appreciate Bartok's music, he is associated with some very distinguished Hungarian Colleagues: Franz Liszt, who is buried in Austria, and Eugene Ormandy.

Bela Bartok was a concert pianist who wrote one opera and several string quartets. Between the world wars, he devoted his talent to folk music. As a relatively young man, he died from leukemia in New York City.

Hungary, while experiencing a fragile transition period, is being bombarded by external forces. The weapons are economic and slightly more subtle than cannon; however, the impact may be devastating.

The relatively liberal communist Hungarian regime prior to 1989 was not entirely counterproductive. The agricultural cooperatives were efficient. Since the departure of the Russians, the emphasis on "free private markets" has been exploitive rather than productive. The abuses of uncontrolled capitalism are omnipresent. Irrelevant goods and services are being foisted on Hungary without the benefit of a sustaining plan. The few affluent folks are becoming very rich, and the masses are becoming poor. A McDonald's overcooked hamburger; a Mercedes taxi with an altered meter; an advertising agency utilizing antiquated techniques, and an invasion of prostitutes from Russia, do not represent a viable formula for national advancement after half a century of repression.

Hungary requires a freer press, honest elections, and meaningful external economic support to develop useful goods and services coupled with a few distinctive exportable products.

Hungary will need a generous dose of enlightened leadership and sora bona (good luck). Based on the grand total of four and one-half days in Hungary, our conclusions are heartfelt but dependent upon a modicum of exposure.

NEW ZEALAND
The Elusive Kiwi

April 8, 1997 / North Island, Auckland, New Zealand:

After losing a day to the International Dateline, we arrived at the Auckland, New Zealand, airport at 5:30 a.m. Because of the complexity of the route to the hotel, the automobile rental agent suggested that we take a taxi to the Hotel, and that the rental car would be delivered later that morning.

At the fourth-class hotel (First Imperial) which charged first-class rates, our room was not ready. We were informed that it might be available at any time within the next six hours, and that we should wait in the lobby. Beating a hasty retreat, we returned to the airport; secured the rental car, and started early on our North Island itinerary. This was the only frustration regarding reservations and facilities on the New Zealand safari.

Following Route 2 to the Firth of Thames, we headed for the "Seabird Coast" at Miranda. At the nature center, the Director, Keith Woodley, shared tidal information which was germane to the appearance of shorebirds. After securing a motel room, I returned to the nature center at the appropriate tidal hour. High winds, rain, and cold weather intervened. The most exotic species had decided to wait out the storm.

Our motel was located at Thames on the Coromandel Peninsula. In 1626, Captain Cook sailed up the adjoining river. Since it reminded him of home, the name was selected. After a gold-mining spree, the region is now dominated by logging trucks and the motel by a bowling group.

April 9 / North Island, Thames to Rotorua:

Breakfast at a dairy bar in Paeroa was a pleasant surprise. The freshly-cooked bacon was superb, the fried eggs were prepared with care, and the freshly-baked bread was special.

We observed the clean-cut, attractive, uniformed, exclusively White students walking to school. In the absence of racial diversity, except for Maori pockets, major societal transition problems have been reduced. At the same time, a lack of diversity may become suffocating.

L&P (Lemon and Paeroa), the New Zealand national soft drink, was launched in Paeroa. No additional civic attribute needs to be cited.

Following Route 2 to the northeast coast of North Island, we spent a brief period of time at the clean, attractive city of Tauranga. At the port, Mount Maunganui, we admired the beautiful beach and the absence of crowds in early fall.

The industrial area of the city was amazingly well-planned and managed. Each factory, warehouse, depot, and store included manicured grass, well-kempt flower beds, and the requisite paint. Civic pride was in evidence.

Heading south through small sheep ranches and rolling hills, we passed Lake Rotoiti en route to our Rotorua destination.

Rotorua is the center of Maori culture in New Zealand. Because of the Maori Center, and a beautiful lake, Rotorua has become a tourist Mecca.

The cultural traditions of the Maori, who are indigenous Polynesians, are obscure, and the documentation is limited. Although there is a renaissance in wood carving and weaving, the arts lack appeal or definition. In contrast to the American Indian, who in spite of poverty and prejudice has nurtured a culture that has continuing pertinence, the Maori have preserved few of their customs. Undoubtedly, systematic discrimination and lack of support have telescoped the process of degradation.

The Maori people, of all ages, are generally sullen and obese. Belatedly, the government of New Zealand is now providing minimal financial resources to support Maori families. Unfortunately, the remedial emphasis centers on assigning title to huge tracts of marginal land without annual stipends.

At the Maori Center, which is staffed entirely by Maori employees, some of the employees were demonstrating on the main highway for increased wages. Their current wages are three times higher, on the average, than the full-time wages of Maori employed in other endeavors. The Maori leaders are attempting to eliminate the disparity, without increasing the wages of the Center employees. This approach provoked the Center employees to demonstrate. The demonstrators were noisy, rude, obtrusive, and dirty.

In New Zealand, there are too few Maori (nine percent) to gain effective political power and too many for equality or absorption.

The city of Rotorua represents a cultural void which has been fostered by tourism; however, the lake is lovely, and it afforded us a memorable experience.

We hired a powerboat which took us to Mokoia Island in the center of the lake. The Maori own the island, which is used occasionally for pseudo-religious ceremonies. There are no permanent residents, but the skipper of the boat is allowed to take a few short-term day visitors to the island.

Two virtually extinct indigenous New Zealand birds reside on the Island—the North Island Saddleback and the Stitchbird. We were fortunate to be able to see several of each species in the deep woods. The setting was magical. In the absence of other humans, we felt privileged to share the situs of the two remarkable avian species.

After returning to the mainland, I walked along the lake shore to the Sulphur Point Refuge and enjoyed the shorebirds including the endemic New Zealand Dabchick (a small grebe).

April 10 / North Island, Rotorua to Wellington:

The long journey from Rotorua to Wellington, via Route 1, was monotonous, tiring, and devoid of interest. It was windy and raining, and the traffic on the principal highway on North Island, with only one lane in each direction, was formidable.

Lake Taupo is a tourist trap. The desert in the Tongariro region is dismal. The beach on the Southwest Coast from Levin to Wellington (including Kapiti Beach) is dirty and unattractive, and the ocean is unbelievably sullied. Because of the weather, we missed the lovely rolling hills and horse breeding ranches around Palmerston North.

Wellington, the capital of New Zealand, is a beautiful, modern metropolis of 400,000 compared to the 1.3 million in the Auckland complex. Approximately three-quarters of the people in New Zealand live on North Island.

Lambton Harbor is well-protected and distinctively beautiful. The abbreviated history of the area, slightly more than one and one-half centuries, is being preserved. The superb buildings and natural beauty of the city, and the vitality of the people, are gratifying.

The parliament buildings complex includes the Beehive (the executive wing), the Parliament, and the National Library. The wharf area contains a new performing arts building (the National Ballet is outstanding), and the National Archives which features the Treaty of Waitangi document which allowed the British to euchre the land from the Maori. Wellington represents a tempo and an ambience which are unique for a national capital.

The people of the North Island of New Zealand are warm, open, uncomplicated, and friendly. The population explosion, and the high unemployment rate, present major hurdles. The natural scenery, tourism, and a commitment to preservation may buy essential time.

Currently, in spite of traffic and urban sprawl, the North Island embodies a meaningful scale, pleasant surroundings, and manageable complexity. It is fighting to retain a simpler way of life.

April 11 / Wellington to Kaikoura, South Island:
Departing from picturesque Wellington Harbor via ferry, we entered Cook Strait bound for South Island. The distance is only nineteen kilometers. Until Captain James Cook sailed between the islands in 1770, the Strait was considered a bay. On occasion, the winds in Cook Strait exceed two hundred miles per hour.

The entrance to Marlborough Sounds on South Island is the beginning of the ten kilometer ferry ride to Picton. There are several islands and a long peninsula that borders the channel to the terminus.

At Picton, we rented an automobile (rental cars were not allowed on the ferry) and began our South Island trek. Following Route 1 to Blenheim, we were forced to rely upon McDonald's for an overcooked hamburger.

En route to Kaikoura, our night's destination, we stopped to admire a fur seal colony which was dozing on the rocky shore. The northeastern tip of South Island is extremely dry. The highest craggy peaks to the southwest were covered with snow.

At the attractive town of Kaikoura, we secured a room at the White Morph Motel. After a solid dinner at the Green Dolphin, we drove to the end of the Kaikoura Peninsula to observe Fur Seals "up close and personal."

April 12 / South Island - Kaikoura to Christchurch:

We boarded the whale watch boat at Kaikoura. For the first time, we saw whales at a realistic distance. Three Sperm Whales took in a new supply of oxygen while we marveled at their size and beauty. The boat was equipped with sounding devices. While we waited for a whale to surface, we were entertained by Bottle-nosed Dolphins which performed their exuberant maneuvers.

Driving south to Christchurch, the most populous city on South Island, we registered at Eliza's Manor, a historic home with charming rooms. Then, we spent a few hours exploring the center of the attractive downtown area. We strolled along the magical Avon River with its thirty-nine bridges and walked around Cathedral Square which has served as the heart of the city since its founding.

The Anglican Cathedral is preeminent. Our positive reaction to the square was marred by the presence of a gang of teenage Oriental hoodlums who were loud, rude, and involved with drugs.

An antique tram, which was built in 1925, provided a remarkably satisfying one-hour tour which included Hagley Park, the museum, and New Regent Street where the houses were constructed in the 1930s in Spanish Mission style. A rewarding day was capped with an exemplary dinner at the Clarendon which is designated the finest restaurant in Christchurch.

April 13 / South Island, Christchurch to Twizel:

In early morning, we visited the museum in Christchurch which served formerly as a university building. The Maori artifacts were superior to those in Rotorua. At the museum, a gigantic Japanese tour group was obnoxious and literally running up and down the aisles. The Natural History Museum and the Botanical Garden restored our equanimity.

Christchurch is a captivating city which has proudly maintained its British heritage including the parks, gardens, and buildings which reflect that heritage.

After several hours driving in the rain, we lunched at Fairlie, which is near the center of South Island. In the clouds, the snow-capped New Zealand Alps appeared. We hurried past Lake Tekapo. As the scenery became more arid, we arrived at the southern shore of Lake Pukaki. In the late afternoon sun, the clouds parted, and we were treated to a magnificent view of Mount Cook at the northern end of the finger lake.

Mount Cook is the highest of a lovely series of snow-capped mountains which hug the western shore of South Island. The mountains of Kashmir, Nepal, the Swiss Alps, and the Rockies inspire awe and inspiration. Mount Cook can hold its own in that illustrious crowd.

Twizel serves at the gateway to Mount Cook. It is a quaint village in MacKenzie Country (named after a vagabond who stole some sheep). The terrain in the area is dry and basically dull. After a superb sleep at the MacKenzie Country Inn in Twizel, we were awakened by helicopters at the pad outside our window. The incongruity of travel is truly astounding. Wherever you perch on earth, it appears to be impossible to escape the omnipresence of machines of all flavors.

April 14 / South Island, Twizel to Queenstown:

At first light, we drove sixty miles north along the west bank of Lake Pukaki to the base of Mount Cook. Backpackers and campers dominated the immediate landscape. We took a long walk along the braided Ahuriri River (in this context, braided means multi-channeled). The views of Mount Cook were enchanting.

We then drove southwest to Lake Wanaka where a fish and chips luncheon featured shark which was delicious.

In the late afternoon sun, Lake Dunston was pristine and lovely. Since there was still adequate light, we decided to continue to Queenstown on Lake Wakatipu.

The setting for Queenstown is unparalleled. It is placed on the shore of a long narrow lake fringed with beautiful towering evergreens with views of the Alps in the distance.

Developers have partially destroyed the idyllic setting. Minuscule box houses, without character, are crammed along the shore. Resorts of doubtful merit crowd the town and the adjoining shores. Traffic was a major factor, and "fast food and airport art shops" dominated the scene. Tourist buses were parked in profusion. We were dismayed at the extent to which a uniquely beautiful setting had been disparaged.

April 15 / South Island, Queenstown to Te Anau:

The drive from Queenstown traversed the unspoiled southeastern finger of Lake Wakatipu to Kingston at the southern tip of the lake. We then headed southwest to the eastern border of Fiordland National park and to our rustic motel at the crossroads of Te Anau on the shore of the lake bearing the same name. Since the weather report for the next day was discouraging, we drove the 121 kilometers to the end of the road at Milford Sound, which is on the Tasman Sea (Pacific Ocean) at the northern end of the park.

We were able to book passage on the last cruise of the day. The village of Milford Sound is the only settlement in the immense Fiordland National park, and it is the only sound (fiord) accessible by land.

In two hours of cruising, we went to the open sea and returned to Milford Sound village. A light rain prevented views of the highest peaks; however, the lower elevation views of the sound and the surrounding steep cliffs were astounding. Innumerable falls dropped several hundred feet into the sea. Seals and dolphins accompanied the boat. The elevation of many of the sheer cliff faces exceeded 1,000 feet which created a magnificent wonderland. There were very few passengers on the last cruise of the day.

In a constant rain—Milford Sound has one of the highest annual rainfalls on earth—the captain shared his remarkable knowledge of the flora and the fauna of the park.

Milford Sound is a scenic treasure. It is reassuring that the designation of a national park may preserve that treasure for posterity.

April 16 / Te Anau to Stewart Island:

From Te Anau, Mark Hanger, a local ornithologist, introduced us to a few extraordinary birding spots en route to Milford Sound. On a sunny, chilly morning, the scenic highlight was a very small, but very exotic, Lake Gunn. On a narrow inlet of the lake, we saw a dozen relatively rare songbirds which were colorful and confiding. After returning Mark to his home, he called to arrange for our accommodations on Stewart Island.

We drove to the city of Invercargill at the southernmost tip of South Island and left our automobile in the port parking lot. An attractive ferry conveyed us the eighteen kilometers across the treacherous Foveaux Strait to Oban Township on the northeastern shore of Stewart Island. Stewart Island encompasses less than seven hundred square miles. It is approximately forty miles long (north to south) and thirty miles wide (east to west).

Oban, at Halfmoon Bay, is the only settlement on Stewart Island. The population of Oban is four hundred, in the summer months. There are only nine miles of paved roads which are confined to the Oban area. In Oban, we spent two nights at the B&B owned and operated by Peter and Jeanette Goomes.

On the first evening, we enjoyed a fish dinner at the South Sea Hotel, the only hotel on the island. With the exception of the southern tip of South America, it is the southernmost point on earth (with the obvious exception of Antarctica). The South Sea Hotel claims the distinction of being the southernmost of its ilk.

Stewart Island is subjected to unpredictable weather which creates severe winds, of high velocity, and driving storms. It is also one of the few remaining homes of the Brown Kiwi.

April 17 / South Island, Stewart Island:

After dark, Phillip Smith, a Stewart Island denizen who enjoys nature, took us via a small boat to a remote beach on a secluded bay. It was our unreasonable expectation that we might see a Brown Kiwi. There are no dirt roads, or even distinct trails, at this eastern location on the island. We beached the boat, and after a trek of more than an hour, over a putative trail, we reached the beach where Phillip had occasionally seen a kiwi.

The Stewart Island Brown Kiwi is one of three sub-species found in New Zealand. One, which is seldom seen, is confined to a heavily-forested area of North Island. The second is restricted to the South Island, and a sighting has not been reported for a significant period. The third sub-species is found exclusively on Stewart Island.

There are two other distinct species of kiwi which were found in New Zealand. The Little-spotted Kiwi is rare and is alleged to still exist in the deep forest of Southern Fiordland on South Island. The Great-spotted Kiwi was identified on the northern part of South Island but is now adjudged exceptionally rare. If we were to see a kiwi, our option was restricted to a Brown Kiwi on Stewart Island.

For an extensive period, probably an hour, we waited patiently on the beach. Phillip used the indirect beam of a low wattage flashlight for spotting. Kiwis are nocturnal and very skittish. We were advised to remain quiet and still. The flashlight was seldom utilized.

Voila! A Brown Kiwi was discovered at the edge of the sand and vegetation line searching for grubs in seaweed with its long beak.

The Brown Kiwi is twenty inches in length. Evidently, it is a descendent of the Emu and the Ostrich. It spends its life, at night, on the forest floor, and occasionally on the beach, searching for insects. The grubs which reside in seaweed provide its favorite meal. It is greyish-brown with an exceptionally long bill and tactile bristles around the mouth. Since the kiwi's eyesight is severely limited, it depends primarily on the bill and the bristles for assistance in searching for food. Its sense of hearing is remarkable, and it is easily startled. Although the indirect light did not reveal the color, it is lightly streaked with reddish brown and black.

The male kiwi makes a whistle that approximates, you guessed it, "Ki-Wi."

For several minutes, while the Brown Kiwi speared grubs, we were transfixed. It disappeared in the vegetation, and we felt elated. Unbelievably, while catching our breath, two more Brown Kiwis appeared near the same clump of seaweed.

Periodically, Phillip Smith has conducted this nocturnal quest with occasional success. He appeared in a recent New Zealand television documentary depicting the current status of the kiwis on Stewart Island. Feral cats are a serious predator, but Phillip feels that the Brown Kiwi has a reasonable chance for survival.

In the near future, hundreds of thousands of kiwis may be discovered in a trash dump near Christchurch. In the meantime, we will savor our unique introduction to one of the most remarkable bird species.

April 18 / Stewart Island to Otago Peninsula, South Island:

While waiting for a weather change that would allow the ferry to leave Stewart Island, we enjoyed the quaint maritime museum which featured the early settlers (whalers and loggers). Subsequently, we took an auto tour of the nine paved miles with an array of small huts. Before boarding the ferry, we relished a long walk on the single lane track east of town which follows the contour of Halfmoon Bay.

Stewart Island is a special nugget which combines a proud history, interesting residents, and exciting scenery.

Returning to the mainland, we picked up our vehicle and visited the Southland Museum at Invercargill. The indigenous Tuatara Lizard was sleeping in an enclosed "cave," but we found the historic Maori artifacts from the South Island diverse and appealing.

The southern scenic route, from Waipapa Point to Nugget Point, leading to Dunedin on the southeast coast of South Island was disappointing. The Catlin Hills comprise a native forest, but the distinctive views are generally inaccessible from the road. A large section of the road is unsealed, and the trucks and campers make life miserable. Our luncheon at the "wild west" cattle town of Balclutha completed a less than satisfying reintroduction to South Island.

Arriving at Dunedin, which nestles in a lovely spot at the end of a bay with a beautiful view of the Otago Peninsula, we completed a quick round-trip tour of the unattractive city with a proud Scottish heritage. Scurrying to the Peninsula, we secured a cottage at the attractive Homestead which is located two kilometers beyond Portobello. Sheep grazing at the base of green hills overlooking the picture-card harbor reminded us of the old sod where some of our progenitors got their start.

At dusk, we arrived at the penguin preserve on an eastern Otago beach and watched more than one hundred Yellow-eyed Penguins emerge from the ocean to roost. The yellow-eyed are large, and their lumbering walk on the beach to their enclosed burrows on the hillside was spectacular. To avoid confrontation, when two males approach each other they throw back their heads and chests and assume "I did not do it" postures. Even hordes of Japanese tourists with photographic flashes igniting every two seconds could not sully the joy of a unique experience.

At Taiaroa Head we visited the Royal Albatross Conservation Project. We were fortunate to see a chick on the nest. The parents were away for the weekend. With a quarter of a century of protection, the colony has expanded to more than one hundred adults. It is unusual for the albatross to nest near habitation. Predators (predominantly wildcats) are a constant threat.

Only one egg is laid and both of the parents share the incubation responsibility. After a year of fledgling care, the parents will depart for a year at sea. The immature bird will spend three to six years at sea before returning to the colony to breed. With a wingspan in excess of nine feet, the Royal Albatross is a unique specimen.

April 19 / Otago (Dunedin) to Auckland:

Returning to Auckland via air, we took a quick tour of another less than inspiring metropolis. The bulk of our time was devoted to the extraordinary museum which captures the early Maori tradition. A Maori ceremonial canoe, more than eighty feet long and hewn from a single log, was the highlight of the exhibit. It is unfortunate that the contemporary situs of the Maori culture, Rotorua on North Island, does not emphasize the history and cultural uniqueness of the Maori people rather than featuring the arts and crafts of their contemporary existence.

The total South Island mileage of 2,359 kilometers contributed to the New Zealand total of 3,840 kilometers. In twelve days, the beauty of the country and the innate kindness of the people were displayed.

Without a damaging race issue, an immediate population crisis, a considerable incidence of poverty, or aggressive neighbors, the people of New Zealand have time to be civil and the security to be kind. The relative lack of diversity, complexity, and intellectual stimulation is frustrating, but greater diversity will emerge.

New Zealand is isolated, predominantly rural, and the antithesis of a "melting pot." At the same time, current national priorities appear to be reactionary. Political change will become essential. For six years, a left of center coalition, represented by the Labor Party, has failed to carry a national election. Now that the nuclear threat of US naval warships has been eliminated, and the only menace from Uncle Sam is increased tourism, the Labor Party platform of economic justice and education for all may generate enhanced appeal.

Given its geographical isolation and limited size, it is unlikely that New Zealand will warrant world attention. How fortunate for New Zealand!

SABAH, MALAYSIA
Orangutans Up Close

May 21, 1997 / Brisbane, Australia, to Singapore:

The Qantas flight from Brisbane to Singapore was lengthy and tiring. For most of the flight, it seemed that every seat had two occupants. From a previous era, the Qantas acronym represents "Queensland and Northern Territory Aviation Services."

In promoting the extraordinary growth of the last few years, attractive beaches were filled in to construct a plethora of golf courses for Japanese tourists who are now less addicted to duty-free shopping. The attractive scenes from the supreme court building (which I remember vividly from a previous trip in 1957) have been replaced with modern, high-rise, carbon copy office buildings. The supreme court building now serves as the Performing Arts Center.

Chris Lingle, a writer for the *International Herald Tribune* was excommunicated from Singapore for reporting the truth about the strictures on civil rights in Singapore. The *Tribune* was sued by the government of Singapore for documenting corruption. Surprisingly, even our taxi driver had the courage to cite the repressive acts of the current Singapore government.

May 22 / Singapore:

A nostalgic visit to the historic Raffles Hotel revealed a restored facade which has preserved the gardens and courtyards but has created a sterile environment with seventy upscale shops in a new arcade. The "Singapore Sling" (gin and cherry brandy) cocktail which was concocted at the Long Bar at the Raffles during World War I is still served. More than one hundred rooms are available with a price range from $500 to $3,500 per night. Rudyard Kipling dined at the Raffles regularly, and Charlie Chaplin, Somerset Maugham, and Noel Coward were honored guests.

The Bum Boat River tour, with its trite, canned commentary, did not inspire fond memories of a city which now relies upon conspicuous consumption. In a generation, I am confident that Singapore will forfeit its appeal to the next batch of entrepreneurs.

May 23 / Singapore to Kota Kinabalu, Sabah, Malaysia:

Arriving at Kota Kinabalu, the state capital of Sabah (which is part of East Malaysia in Northern Borneo), we proceeded to the Tanjung Aru Resort Hotel.

In 1865, Brunei leased Sabah to an American company, and a small American colony was founded. The company failed. The mainland of Sabah was occupied by the British in 1877. In that year, the territory was leased to the Dent brothers as a private reserve. In 1881, the British North Borneo Company assumed control and ran the country until World War II. In the same year, Roman Catholic missionaries arrived.

In 1888, Sabah became a British Protectorate. In 1895, Sabah's national hero, Mat Salleh, led a rebellion against the British North Borneo Company which almost succeeded. In 1898, the present boundaries with nine hundred miles of coastline—Sarawak to the southwest and Indonesian Borneo to the south—were established.

In 1963, Sabah was granted self-rule by Great Britain. In the same year, Sabah voluntarily became a state in the constitutional monarchy of Malaysia (composed of eleven states on the Malay Peninsula and two on the island of Borneo or Kalimantan).

With long-term ties to the Philippines, the state of Sabah was known by Sulu pirates as the "land below the wind" (signifying that it was located south of the typhoon belt). With the exception of the flat, relatively affluent western coast, the population of 1.7 million is not dense. Coconut, rice, and oil palm are the principal crops. Natural resources are confined to poor quality coal and limited bauxite.

Sabah incorporates a medley of thirty distinct cultures and eighty languages and dialects. The three principal languages are Kadazan, Malay and English. To illustrate the language diversity, the daily newspapers in Kota Kinabalu are trilingual.

The largest ethnic group is the Kadazan who reside in the interior. The second largest group is the Bajau who reside at the coast and who are also indigenous. In addition, there are the Malay (Moslems) and the Chinese, each of whom approximate fifteen percent of the population. The Kadazan are overwhelmingly Christian.

During World War II, the British seaport of Jesselton was destroyed by the Japanese. Following the war, with Australian assistance, it was rebuilt and Jesselton was renamed Kota-Kinabalu.

Kota Kinabalu ("KK" as it is known) is home for 300,000 people. Although the city is relatively new, intelligent urban planning was not a factor. Lovely tropical shorelines have been filled and extended into the ocean to accommodate potential country clubs and resort hotels for predominantly Japanese tourists.

Given the Moslem code, casinos will not be launched. With Japanese tourism no longer a significant factor, the new resorts may be in jeopardy.

"KK" has become a "boom town" with logging, manufacturing, and construction fostering the economy. The main coastal highway north to the second largest city of Kota Belud is modern and deadly. The Filipino open market is extensive. Having lived in the Philippines, we were impressed with the size of the Filipino minority, the common use of the Tagalog dialect, the distinctive Filipino fruits and wooden handicrafts which were available at the market, and the impoverished living conditions.

May 24 / Kota Kinabalu to the Danum Rain Forest:

After a restful night in "KK" enjoying the ocean breezes, we flew to Lahad Datu on the southeastern coast on the Celebes Sea. The crowded conditions reminded us of the rural Philippines. Lahad Datu is known as a "cowboy town." It did convey the atmosphere of the frontier.

After a four-hour bumpy van ride on unsealed roads through heavily lumbered forests, we arrived at the Borneo Rain Forest Lodge.

May 25 / Borneo Rain Forest:

Until a few years ago, Sabah was predominantly rain forest. Untrammeled private lumber interests have decimated the forest. Now, in a few areas, secondary and tertiary growth is prevalent. In most areas, the ground is bare and devoid of life except for a few unsightly tree trunks. The one exception is the Borneo Rain Forest Reserve in the Danum Valley Conservation Area. The reserve is huge (encompassing approximately one-seventh of Sabah). The reserve is owned by private logging interests. On a constant basis, gigantic logging trucks move out of the reserve to the ports near Lahad Datu. In contrast to the other logging regions, the removal of logs from the reserve is partially restrained.

As a condition for a governmental grant of a private concession for the lumber company to remove logs from the reserve, the lumber interests agreed to designate five percent of the total forest concession as a protected area for flora and fauna and for tourist development. Compared to adjoining areas which should also be protected, the plot surrounding the Borneo Rain Forest Lodge is very restricted in size. Because the only road passes through the "protected area," the ride to the lodge is illusory. As might be expected, the lumber company holding the concession is receiving plaudits for its "enlightened" environmental policy.

May 26:

Reputedly, the Danum River Reserve constitutes a home base for 275 species of birds. More than 200 species of trees have been reported in a single hectare. The Danum River flows through the reserve.

The Rain Forest Lodge, with ten cabins, was constructed in 1994. The facilities are adequate. The food does not meet that standard.

Since there are few places to visit in Sabah where tourist resorts are not the order of the day, we spent four days at the Rain Forest

Lodge, using the lodge as a base for day trips. For the four-day period, we looked up fifty to one hundred feet into the rain forest canopy. After our Costa Rican experience, the canopy was not unique. At the same time, the flora and fauna were vastly different and endlessly fascinating.

May 27:

We followed endless trails through the rain forest. The local employees of the lodge are friendly, impoverished, and dismayed by the rudeness of the foreign guests. Relatively affluent citizens from the urban areas of Sabah do not appear to be interested in the rain forest.

On the last full day, Patti and I completed a three-hour walk along the bank of the fast-moving river. We admired the diverse flora within reasonable proximity to the lodge.

Two evening rides in an open truck presented a few highlights of Sabah—Red Giant Flying Squirrels, a Leopard Cat, a Common Palm Civet, a Western Tarsier, and a Banded Linsang. The bulging eyes of the Nocturnal Tarsier reminded us of the Bush Baby in Kenya. In contrast to the Common Palm Civet, which was uniformly gray-brown, the Banded Linsang had a distinctive black and white barred tail, brown spots, and white on the face. Both species were very cat-like except that the long noses reminded us of foxes.

During the days, we saw Red-leaf Monkeys, Bornean Gibbons, and Common Barking Deer. The prize was awarded to the Orangutans, which we saw repeatedly, feeding in the high forest canopy.

The Orangutan is a remarkable animal. To see one in a zoo is a memorable experience, but to see them in their native habitat is sheer joy. The color is an unusual reddish-brown, but longevity may alter the coat to orange. The adult male can weigh in excess of 220 pounds. The female's call has been characterized as "a long belch," and the males seem to prefer loud roars. The Orangutan builds a nest of woven twigs and branches high in the canopy. If necessary for security, the female will build a nest for its progeny every evening. The only other primate which makes a nest is the Sun Bear which we have seen only in captivity.

The Orangutan was once plentiful in Borneo. Currently, as the result of extensive hunting and the logging of montane forests, the number has been reduced significantly. The Northern Borneo Rain Forest is one of the few areas where the Orangutan is observed frequently.

The small critters to which we had access in the forest were the Water Monitor, Flying and Long-tailed Lizard, House Gecko, Olive-spotted Skink, and the Giant Millipede.

In the bird world, we identified our share of exotics: several species of hornbill, the White-crowned Shama, the Asian Fairy-Bluebird, and the White-bellied Swiftlet. Probably the rarest and the most beautiful bird was the Blue-headed Pitta.

After standing still for an extended period on a very narrow path in the dense rain forest, a Blue-headed Pitta male quickly crossed the path in front of us. The conspicuous white bars on black wings were diagnostic, but the maroon-red back, bright blue crown and tail, and white throat were amazingly beautiful. The bird is endemic to Borneo. As it walked on the rain forest floor, I realized that I was enjoying a very special birding treat.

May 30 / Borneo Rain Forest Lodge to Sandakan:
For Patti and me, Borneo represented the epitome of tropical allure. We had never been exposed to Indonesian Borneo, but Sabah, one of the few accessible sections of Borneo, has lost much of its appeal. In reality, Sabah is a defaced tropical paradise which depicts the short-term greed of private entrepreneurs. The cash crops of tobacco and rubber, as well as lumber, have contributed to the demise of the pristine and unique ambience of Northern Borneo.

The three-hour van trip from the Borneo Rain Forest Lodge to Sandakan on the northeast coast displayed a nightmare of poverty and logging trucks. The roads were narrow and in a state of disrepair. It is unlikely that the requisite financial resources can be generated to improve the plight of the people while conserving the beautiful natural environment.

May 31 / The Kinabatangan River:
At dawn, we took a small boat across the Bay at Sandakan to the mouth of the Kinabatangan River, the only navigable river into the interior of Sabah. For more than two hours, we glided among the

mangroves observing the Borneo of the past. A Hairy-nosed Otter was swimming near the river mouth. Proboscis Monkeys with long, flexible noses cavorted in the trees at the river's edge, and Hose's Langurs (Grey Leaf Monkeys), with pink faces and white beards, swung through the trees.

Friendly natives, who waved with dispatch, dried and hung their fish catch on the decks of precarious stilt wooden houses. Others fished from small boats. With the rare exceptions of an occasional boat carrying coconuts to market, or a logging barge, the scenes could have been extracted from a previous era.

After lunch, and a nap on a hard cot at Ben's River Lodge, we bounced along in a small truck on a deeply-pitted dirt road through more scrub terrain en route to the bat caves. A female Orangutan, with a good-sized youngster clutching her stomach, scurried up the only first-growth tree in sight. For an hour, we listened to the chirps, or were they belches, of the mother Orangutan while she constructed a nest of branches high in the tree. The Orangutan's chance of survival, mother and child, in that environment is severely limited; however, for a brief moment Borneo came alive.

Since there had been a major rainstorm at noon, the birds had assembled to feed on insects. In the sparse, secondary growth, we saw a dozen new bird species.

At dusk we arrived at the caves in time to observe the thousands of emerging bats. Three rare Bat Hawks were attacking the separate bat clouds and emerging from the clouds with victims. Nature can be cruel, but the drama of the moment was electrifying.

Back on the river, in the dark, we returned to Sandakan.

June 1 / Sandakan to Mount Kinabalu:

Sandakan is a dirty, congested city which is a logging port, river entry to the interior, and residence for more than 100,000 people of Chinese, Filipino, and Malay extraction. Until World War II, Sandakan was the Sabah capital.

A visit to the new mosque, which looks and feels like a prison unfolded a pride of ladies in bright tribal dress. A taxi ride to the ornate Chinese temple overlooking the harbor partially restored our sagging spirits.

The Japanese invaded Sabah, at Sandakan, on New Year's Day, 1942. During the occupation, more than 1,000 Australian prisoners of war were incarcerated near Sandakan. On a forced march to the interior to perform slave labor, virtually all of the prisoners died. The Bataan "death march" appears to be a brief hike compared to the Sandakan disaster. Today, Japanese tourists visit Sandakan in droves. The local citizens seem to have forgotten the barbarity.

After the War, Australia supported the rebuilding of Sandakan (as well as Kota Kinabalu). Both cities were heavily bombed.

Before leaving Sandakan, we made an effort to locate the former home of Agnes Newton Keith, the American author. Patti continued the quest and found the house where Mrs. Keith resided with her husband and son prior to World War II.

There are three books by Agnes Newton Keith which deal with North Borneo and the Philippines. All three present the unique trials and tribulations, as well as the joys, of a foreigner living in this remote part of the world.

The first book, *Land Below the Wind,* was written in 1939 and received the Atlantic Nonfiction Prize Award. The book describes life in North Borneo (Sabah) for the Keith family (the British husband was in the Forestry Service). *Land Below the Wind* is not only the title of the book but also is the Malay traditional language translation for the land of North Borneo.

In 1946, Mrs. Keith wrote *Three Came Home* which was converted into a 1950 movie starring Claudette Colbert. In May of 1942, Mrs. Keith, her husband, and her young son were imprisoned in a Japanese prison camp on Berhala Island, a former leper colony in Sandakan Harbor. Mrs. Keith and her husband were forced to live in separate units. After unbelievable hardships, all three were released in September, 1945.

While in the prison camp, Mrs. Keith wrote the draft of *Three Came Home* on the labels of cans and the margins of old newspapers. The book is a poignant portrayal of her creative efforts to keep her son from starvation.

The final Keith book, which concentrates on the Philippines, is called *Bare Feet in the Palace.* It was written in 1955 as a tribute to President Ramon Magsaysay.

From 1951 to 1953, Patti and I resided at Clark Field on the Island of Luzon in the Philippines, where I served as a Psychological Warfare Officer in the US Air Force. During that period, the Hukbalahap (Huk) insurrection had succeeded in controlling a large portion of the rural Philippines. As secretary of Defense, Magsaysay brought civility and sustained pressure to the attack, and the Huk movement was curtailed. Subsequently, Magsaysay (the first Filipino of Malay, as opposed to Spanish, ancestry to be elected to the highest office) was elected president. The book is inferior to the two previously mentioned, but it is one of the few which captures the history of a few critical years in Philippine history.

Flying from Sandakan to Kota Kinabalu, we then completed a hazardous two-hour bus ride over treacherous roads with heavy traffic to Mount Kinabalu National Park. The three hundred square mile park extends to the top of the 13,455 foot mountain, the highest peak between the Himalayas and the Snow Mountains of New Guinea. The mountain was not climbed until 1857.

Mount Kinabalu is a figurative island of flora and fauna diversity with 300 species of birds and 1,200 species of orchids alone.

Our lodge at the park headquarters was named "Nepenthes," the Latin name for the nine species of pitcher plant, each of which can hold one quart of water.

In contrast to the Tropical Rain Forest, the Montane Rain Forest can provide a semblance of comfort; however, the light in the forest was limited, the birds were evasive, and the leeches did not distinguish high from low altitude.

June 2 / Mount Kinabalu:

During our visit, the Malay Moslems were enjoying a holiday (most holidays are extended for several days). Any child who started walking up the mountain was entitled to a commemorative ribbon. Thousands arrived to qualify for the honor. The resulting hordes of vans and buses were oppressive. Wisely, the fauna also decided to enjoy the holiday.

Mount Kinabalu without the crowds might be captivating. Because of its proximity to "K.K.," the crowds will continue. With variable holidays in every country, it is difficult to arrange a visit that will avoid peak periods of calamity.

June 4 / Mount Kinabalu to Kota Kinabalu:

After returning to the capital city, we collapsed at the Tanjung Aru Beach Resort and luxuriated with acceptable food, privacy, cleanliness, a large swimming pool, and spacious tropical grounds.

Generally, Malaysia and Indonesia have friendly relations. The major exception is the increasing concern in Sabah about illegal immigrants from Indonesia. Malaysia has been unwilling to assist with the problem.

In Sabah, there is sustained friction between the majority Kadazans and the controlling Muslim government in Kuala Lumpur. In 1987, the Malaysian government, without success, attempted to prevent the sitting of the newly-elected Kadazan Christian Party. Arabic is now being taught by law in all of the public schools, even if the student body is non-Malay. Currently, the Malay Islamic revival is reflected in religious-oriented legal prohibitions comparable to Sharia in The Sudan.

Recently, the government of Sabah has attempted to become semi-independent in the Federation of Malaysia. Sabah receives only a minuscule annual budgetary supplement from the Malaysian treasury.

Sabah does not entertain thoughts of seceding. At the same time, authorities in the Malaysian capital are becoming alienated by the divisive rumbles from Sabah.

Sabah's virgin forest can only survive for a few more years. Tourism is temporal. The exotic flora and fauna are in jeopardy. The survival of Sabah as a unique entity is problematic.

THAILAND
A Lost Weekend

April 2, 2001 / Los Angeles to Tokyo to Bangkok:

From 1961-1963, Patti and I and the three children lived in Bangkok, Thailand, where I established the Peace Corps and served as the first Representative.

In early 1961, I had left the management consulting field in Washington, D.C., to join the Peace Corps as Sargent Shriver's assistant for a variety of staff duties including the recruitment of Peace Corps Representatives. In October, I was recruited as the first Peace Corps Representative in Thailand. The Representative serves as the senior staff member in each country. He or she is responsible for relationships with the host country and with the relevant components of the American Mission, for the negotiation of Volunteer assignments, and for the ultimate supervision of the Volunteers.

In June 1962, after completing training at the University of Michigan where President Kennedy launched the Peace Corps, the first contingent of thirty-nine Volunteers arrived in Bangkok. I had negotiated individual up-country assignments for teachers of English in rural areas, for vocational agriculture assistants, for malaria eradication technicians, and for a few Volunteers who were assigned teaching duties at Chulalongkorn University.

Before arriving in Thailand, all of the Volunteers were trained extensively in the Thai language. After our arrival in Bangkok, Patti and I enrolled for five individual Thai lessons per week. In the Thai language, there are five distinct tones which distinguish otherwise identical words (high, low, rising, falling, and a middle tone). Thai is a beautiful language, but because of the tones, it is difficult to learn well. In spite of our limited previous Thai language training, our efforts in Bangkok proved invaluable for up-country travel.

Before the Volunteers were assigned to the field, they completed a refresher training program with Thai instructors at the rustic location of Chachangsao, seventy-five kilometers east of Bangkok. To support the Volunteers in Bangkok, we rented a small compound close to the downtown area which included a dormitory, a room for medical care, and an adjoining house which served the Peace Corps staff. In addition, we rented a Chinese-style house ten minutes from the Peace Corps compound which served as our residence and was used for informal Volunteer visits. Of greatest importance, there was a large, flat front lawn which served as the situs for touch football tussles in the era of the "New Frontier."

Utilizing a Toyota jeep, I visited the Volunteers at more than fifty up-country locations from Chiengmai in the north at the Burma border and to Songkhla in the south at the Malaysian border. The scenery, the people, and the cuisine were always inviting.

The most exciting trip pertained to the visit of Peace Corps Director Sargent Shriver. With the aid of a helicopter, he made several descents in rice patties where he greeted small groups of volunteers.

As the volunteers improved their Thai facility, the local populace was intrigued. Based on the overt activity of a few Communist action organizations, Peace Corps was translated as Nuay Santipaab in Thai. In essence, this translation implies that the volunteers were covert intelligence agents working in small units. The same accusation was made at several Peace Corps locations worldwide. Interaction with volunteers speaking the local language quashed those insinuations.

More importantly, as the years passed, the volunteer assignments in virtually all countries became more technical. USAID (US Agency for International Development) provided most of the technical equipment and occasionally support. In a few countries, the Peace Corps program was considered a junior appendage of USAID. The charge was inaccurate and did not survive, but for a few years the allegation was troublesome.

On June 1, 1962, the fifth contingent of volunteers arrived in Bangkok to discharge comparable roles including rural community action. At the time of our departure in the summer of 1963, a total of 226 volunteers were serving in Thailand, the second largest Peace Corps program. At the headquarters in Washington, D.C., I accepted the position as one of the Associate Directors. In the new capacity, I was responsible for volunteer selection, training, and support.

In 1979, while we were living in Germany, in response to the Cambodian refugee crisis, Patti returned to Bangkok and to the border camps between Thailand and Cambodia as a volunteer with the International Rescue Committee. At the airport, she recognized a "Mrs. Ferguson" sign. The Thai holding the greeting was Pradeep, who had worked with the Peace Corps staff in the early 1960s. Through the American Embassy, Pradeep had learned of her projected visit. For several weeks, she assisted with the education program at the refugee camps in northeastern Thailand.

Today, on April 2, 2001, after flying without a break from our home in New Mexico to Thailand, we arrived at 2:00 a.m. For me, this was the first visit in thirty-eight years; for Patti, the first in twenty-one years.

April 3 / Bangkok:

To resurrect the basic facts pertaining to launching the Peace Corps in Thailand two score years ago is not difficult. The paper trail is meaningful. In contrast, to capture our feelings about Thailand and the Thai people, without the benefit of periodic trips, relevant correspondence, or a daily written record of impressions is problematic. Fortunately, my memories of Thailand are acute and the depth of my positive reactions is indelible. Although a few days in Bangkok without a glance at the up-country scene is skewed, I welcome the opportunity to share my reveries in the context of contemporary Bangkok.

Thai history appears to be inordinately concerned with kings, Buddhist temples, and the independent thought and action that inures to the benefit of the only nation in Southeast Asia, and on most of the other continents on Earth, that has avoided the yoke of colonialism.

Architectural ruins in Central Thailand are omnipresent and visible. The Kingdom of Siam was created about 1350 with the capital located at Ayutthaya, north of Bangkok. The basic outlines of the capital remain intact including an exquisite, gigantic Reclining Buddha.

Four centuries after Ayutthaya became the capital, it was partially destroyed and ceased to function following a war with Burma. For Americans, the history of Thailand becomes a reality with the reign of King Mongkut which commenced in 1868. King Mongkut opened the country to Western ideas and influence. His memory has been enhanced by the written memories of Mongkut's English governess that germinated the musical comedy, *Anna and the King of Siam*.

From 1886-1910, King Chulalongkorn ruled with a sensitive and productive hand. In 1939, Siam was renamed Thailand. In World War II, Thailand was an unwilling ally of Japan, and it was occupied by Japan.

In 1946, the current King Bhumibol was crowned. He, and his attractive and community-oriented wife, constitute a new standard for modern royalty. Thailand is a democracy; however, the Prime Minister enjoys inordinate power and the major components of effective democracy are seldom in evidence.

With only a few exceptions, the influence of the United States in Thailand has been collateral and less than vital. One exception is Jim Thompson of Delaware who converted Thai silk making into a major industry.

Before our first arrival in Thailand, Mr. Thompson disappeared during a brief vacation at a hill station in Central Malaysia. Facts concerning his disappearance have never surfaced. Innumerable theories concerning his demise are still circulating. The most logical theory involves a criminal reaction to his intelligence experience in World War II including Bangkok service.

Thai silk was revolutionary. The worldwide response was remarkable. Jim Thompson became an authority on Thai art, built an authentic Thai-style house in downtown Bangkok, and became the most notable westerner in Bangkok and probably in Southeast Asia.

Thailand is approximately the size of Wyoming. It is 930 miles north to south and 500 miles east to west. In 2004, the population was estimated at 65 million. Ninety-five percent of the people are Buddhist.

The coastal resorts on both sides of the Gulf of Thailand and on the western side of the isthmus on the Pacific Ocean have become worldwide attractions. The wildlife is also a major resource and includes elephant, gibbon, leopard, and tiger. Tin is the major export. The parliamentary government is based on a constitutional monarchy. For at least two generations, the military has dominated the government and broadcasting is under government control.

Chulalongkorn University, built in 1917, is the oldest university and represents the highest academic standards. Thammasat University sponsors a more practical curriculum featuring law, public administration, economics and finance, business administration, and the social sciences. Both universities are extraordinarily beautiful, a significant number of foreign students matriculate, and the research results are substantial.

The Hill Tribes of northern Thailand constitute a major cultural attribute. In spite of proximity, and occasional involvement with the drug trade, twenty tribes have maintained their cultural identity. The Hill Tribe villages extend to the Burmese border and anthropological studies are still producing vital research.

Buddhism is divided into two critical wings: the Mahayana (Northern school) that is prevalent in Vietnam, Tibet, and North Nepal, and the Hinayana (Southern school) which is a major faction in Ceylon, Cambodia, and Thailand. Thousands of saffron-robed monks, of all ages, patrol urban and rural areas in a successful search for daily victuals from the supportive populace. Few Thais aspire to achieve nirvana (heaven); however, the monks set a vivid standard for all.

The artistic, esthetically-pleasing, picturesque Thai temples are enjoyed in myriad shapes and sizes. The colors are diverse and relaxing and the prevalent wooden Thai-style roofs, gates, and windows are gratifying. Buddhist temples are a source of constant appeal.

April 4:

At the Oriental Hotel on the Chao Phraya River, a major artery that runs through Bangkok, we were reunited with one of our favorite spots, registered, and were shocked by the baggage assistant who was a voluble "born again" Christian who set the stage for a difficult transition to modern Bangkok.

In 1963, the Oriental Hotel represented an acceptable scale. It was a premium hotel. The meals were excellent. The view of the spirited life on the Chao Phraya was unprecedented, and the historic dimension was distinctive.

In 2001, the original Oriental Hotel has been preserved in all respects. It has been annexed to a twenty-year-old modern wing that is architecturally pleasant but dwarfs its parent. The "old" wing still represents western-oriented history with photographs of Thai kings interacting with international dignitaries. The inviting author's lounge stresses former ties with Noel Coward, Graham Greene, James Michener, Joseph Conrad, and Somerset Maugham. I was tempted to ignore the paucity of former talent and to compose the definitive novel with an oriental flavor. The Oriental is still the most captivating hotel in Bangkok and probably in Southeast Asia.

After a delicious breakfast on the hotel terrace adjoining the river, that featured fresh local fruits we will always associate with Thailand (mango, papaya, kiwi, and pineapple), we enjoyed watching familiar species of birds frolicking in the trees. My thoughts returned to the birding experiences of one-half century ago.

Birding in Thailand is relatively recent. For twenty years, beginning in 1928, Herbert Deignan compiled definitive lists of bird species which appeared in a remarkable 1945 publication of the Smithsonian Institution, *The Birds of Northern Thailand*. Mr. Deignan's commitment merely laid the groundwork for further study. Modern field guides have been pioneered by my friend Boonsong Lekagu who published two comprehensive editions, the most recent in 1974, *Bird Guide of Thailand*.

Before leaving Thailand in 1963, I visited Boonsong at his aviary in downtown Bangkok. His research was fundamental, but the die was cast. In 1974, seventy-five percent of the forest cover in Thailand had been destroyed. At that time, more than half of the recorded bird species had disappeared. Reputedly, 849 species remained. For comparative purposes, the depth of birdlife in a small country can be illustrated by 452 species in Europe and in excess of 900 species in the continental United States and Canada. Unfortunately, my personal bird lists for Thailand were lost during international travel, and I am unable to resurrect a reliable total.

Following breakfast, we booked a traditional riverboat to the newly-constructed Skytrain. The Skytrain has transformed the City of Bangkok (Krung Thep in Thai). The Skytrain has two routes which intersect at the Central (Siam) station which is now an upscale shopping district at the beginning of Sukhumvit Road. Formerly quaint Sukhumvit Road, which facilitated access from the Peace Corps office to each of the two homes in which we resided in 1961-1963, is now solid "urban commercial" restricted to office buildings and modern apartments.

Taking the main northwestern spur from Siam Center eight stops to the approaches to the airport via the War Memorial, we did not recognize a single landmark. Returning to the Siam Center, we sped through nine stops to the southeastern terminal point. Reverting to Siam Center along Sukhumvit, without recognizing any point of reference, we recovered our composure with a glorious fruit punch, which gave prominence, again, to mango and papaya.

The Skytrain serves the exclusive needs of the professional yuppies who have created a way of life revolving around the new medium for work, residency, and leisure time pursuits.

We hailed a taxi to search for our Bangkok roots. The Soi (major side road) to our former Peace Corps office had been eliminated. Soi Promsit provided access to our Chinese-style home and to the succeeding Thai-style home on stilts. In 1963, it was semi-rural with large open tracts and klongs (narrow, manmade canals). It is now clogged with solid blocks of high-rise commercial and residential development. Not one scene was recognizable. The traffic was intense. It took us more than one hour to return to Siam Center on a route which used to require a maximum of ten minutes.

In "our" era, the Erawan Hotel, at the origin of Sukhumvit, was classical, spacious, convenient, and the Thai cuisine was superb. Ten years ago the existing hotel structure was razed and replaced with an elegant hotel which is attractive, modern, and dull. It attracts the "new" Thai generation that relies upon the Skytrain. For us, the modernity and crowds were shocking.

April 5:

Patricia (Trish) Young joined us for tea at the hotel. She was the wife of American Ambassador Kenneth Young, who served in Bangkok during our Thai residency. It was reassuring to reminisce, to compare notes, and to despair regarding the "modernization" of Bangkok.

Trish is an Asian art expert who advises the local art museums and maintains her apartment, via the Skytrain, in Bangkok. Her husband was an excellent Ambassador. During his term of service, Thai-American relationships were exemplary.

Three years ago, Bangkok experienced a severe recession. Hundreds of office buildings and apartment complexes were not completed. Given current economic trends, that condition is unlikely to change.

At the Oriental, two commemorative suites on our floor reminded us of the early 1960s in Bangkok. Kukrit Pramoj, who was a patron of the first Peace Corp Volunteer contingents and who became prime minister, and Jim Thompson, the silk entrepreneur, were designated.

In the afternoon we hired a river boat. As the only clients, we spent ninety minutes on the Chao Phraya. In addition, we traversed the large surviving klong, which bisects the old city and which was the situs of the floating market. The klong still incorporates the "feel" of life one-half century ago when the klongs were the arteries on which the populace depended for recreation and livelihood.

On the river, we relished the gilded Buddhist temples which have been maintained with tender loving care including the Wat Arun and the Grand Palace, Thammasat University, the boathouse for the Royal Barges, and the omnipresent Buddhist monks who inhabit virtually all of the historic premises.

Thailand is a remarkably beautiful and satisfying country. Since the current trip did not include an up-country visit, the reveries of the provinces now blend with the current urban development in Bangkok coupled with the unchanging Chao Phraya River ambience.

The flora and fauna are still varied, exotic, and exciting. Invariably, the people are kind, friendly, and reflect attractive characteristics. The Buddhist temples are exceptional works of art. The complex culture and the savory cuisine are exemplary.

After an absence of two generations, my facility in the Thai language returned reluctantly. I was able to communicate in basic Thai; however, my spouse, Patti, had few inhibitions.

A final episode from our residency in the 1960s. The family cocker spaniel, Taffy, was shipped by sea to Bangkok. A few days after her arrival, she wandered off into the adjoining neighborhood. We placed advertisements, with a photograph, in the local Thai and English papers. A call from a Thai informed us that Taffy had been staying with a family downtown several kilometers from our residence. We brought her home, and our family was reunited. That remarkable saga would not have occurred in many countries.

The current trip to Bangkok has documented profound changes in the urban culture. Comparable changes are occurring in most of the countries on Earth. The "big cities" now present major negative characteristics. Fundamental cultural values are disintegrating everywhere.

I do not intend to discourage a reader from pursuing an initial safari to Thailand. There are always nuggets of beauty and enjoyment.

Sawaddi khrab (good day sir or madam from a speaker of the masculine gender).

BHUTAN
Shangrila in Retreat

April 6, 2001 / Bangkok to Paro, Bhutan:

Having retired at 6:45 p.m., we arose at 1:45 a.m. to prepare for a pre-dawn departure for Paro, Bhutan via Druk airways. If it were not for the Chao Phraya River and the wonderful Thai people, the City of Bangkok in the year 2001 would have presented an entirely new experience. Thirty-eight years is a fleeting moment. During that period, in this modern age, virtually all visual landmarks can be destroyed and/or replaced.

Approaching Paro through a high mountain pass, we recognized the rationale for the utilization of the special British aircraft (BAE-146) which is maneuverable and which can climb and descend with precision and alacrity.

Until the late 1960s, the only access to Bhutan was via mule train. Currently, there is one plane per day to and from Bangkok and one plane per day (the same vehicle) to and from Katmandu, Nepal.

At the Paro Airport, we were impressed by the majestic snow-capped mountains, and the beautiful Paro Valley. The modern, yet classical, airport building provided efficient immigration and customs services. Paro Airport is the only airport in Bhutan. It also provides the only international transportation. There are a few domestic public buses which are seldom seen outside of the villages.

Depositing our luggage at the Kychu Resort Hotel (several miles outside of town), we visited the annual Paro Festival which is staged in the area adjoining the Rinpung Dzong. The Dzong houses the provincial offices and a monastery. In a city of 15,000, which is the only semi-modern city in Bhutan, the festival is well-known. Monks in colorful costumes and masks portray scriptural events with uninterrupted dancing for several days (two hundred monks participate in the ceremony). Hundreds of denizens in colorful dress observe the dancing from the hillside above the open courtyard where the male dancing is performed.

Purchasing a few Bhutan bird stamps from a knowledgeable vendor, we went to the National Museum, which includes intricately carved altars and a sacred Buddha with multiple arms. I had not remembered that the Buddhists, as well as the Hindus, rely upon multiple appendages for many of their icons. At the museum, we were surprised to see a few German and Japanese tourists.

Returning to the hotel, we stopped to observe a group of archers (archery is the national sport) participating in a contest. The course was 120 meters long. The target was a 30-centimeter slab of wood which is placed in the ground. Hitting the target requires consummate skill. Bhutan competes in the Olympics, but victories in archery have been confined to regional meets in Southeast Asia.

April 7 / Paro to Thimphu:

Admiring sacred, snow-capped Mount Jhomolhari, and the extensive apple and peach orchards and rice terraces, we ascended hundreds of steps to the main entrance of Rinpung Dzong. Because of the festival, the Dzong was crowded. The ancient interior and wooden courtyards were artistic and distinctive. The combination of secular and laic functions in the same structure is unique.

After a two-hour drive of sixty-five kilometers (imagine), half heading south towards India and half heading east, we arrived at the Bhutanese capital of Thimphu, the major city of Bhutan, with 70,000 people. In the 1960s, it was designated the capital. After checking in at the Hotel River View, Patti nursed a slight sore throat, and I attended a slide show conducted by the Nature Conservation Department of the Royal Government of Bhutan. Following the presentation, I met Nado Rinchhen, Deputy Minister of the National Environment Commission and a former Ambassador to India and to the United Nations Organization in Geneva.

At 7,700 feet, Thimphu is the only national capital without traffic lights. At the major intersection, a policeman directs traffic competently with hand signals. Thimphu is the only city with an operational hospital, and, most importantly for many visitors, the only golf course. The Royal Family resides in Thimphu. The principal foreign missions are confined to the United Nations, the Danes, the Swiss, and the Indians. Russia, the United States, China, France, Germany, and the United Kingdom have not been invited to send delegations. Bhutan wishes to engage in foreign affairs on a "small scale." The first limited foreign aid program was negotiated in the late 1960s. The incumbent Foreign Minister is Jigme Thinley, who was educated in the United States.

April 8 / Thimphu:

After an early morning walk in the city park (with hundreds of agricultural commuters boarding buses), a walk through the open market conveyed the usual smells from fish to meat to fish. The Memorial Stupa (Chorten) which was erected to honor the memory of the father of modern Bhutan, King Wangchuk, dominates the principal downtown artery. A weekend art studio introduced us to thirty young student volunteers from twelve to nineteen years of age who are programmed to traditional Buddhist art. The oldest member of the group, aged nineteen, seems to have broken the mold. He proudly displayed two of his scenic works, which were vivid and promising. A visit to the "zoo," which in fact was a fenced city park, displayed two Takin, the national animal of Bhutan. A Takin is a rough approximation of equal parts of yak and bison. We also spent a few minutes at the Handicrafts Emporium and were rewarded with a plethora of religious-oriented Buddhist artifacts.

The area in front of our hotel on the banks of the river displayed one of the most impoverished slum areas to which I had been exposed in Asia. Famine is not a current problem; however, the standard of living is so depressed that the poverty is particularly onerous.

Heading in the direction of a national preserve, we enjoyed strolling over an ancient covered bridge replete with religious flags and artifacts; ran into the art class that was cavorting for a few hours on a Sunday afternoon, admired the wild cherry, Mountain Plum, and several species of rhododendron which exhibited beautiful blooms in the early spring.

The Queen Mother's Palace was a remarkably attractive structure. Only one military guard was on duty at the entrance to the compound. In a gigantic building that houses the unicameral National Assembly and the King's Secretariat in one wing, the other wing is home for 2,000 fortunate monks.

With 6,000 monks in Bhutan, one-third, in a single building, enjoy royal patronage.

The separation of church and state has not been formulated in Bhutan. In the absence of a written constitution or bill of rights, the King and the National Assembly enjoy unlimited power. King Jigme Singye Wangchuk, fourth in the dynasty since 1907, was anointed in 1972.

In recent years, the King has manifested interest in partial reforms. He has introduced "values" education to the curriculum, which stresses politeness, respect for elders, and protection of the environment. He has taken the leadership in promulgating environmental reforms, imposed a dress code, and has replaced the Gross National Product measurement with "Gross National Happiness." In 1998, he removed the ban on neon signs. He lives in the Royal Palace with four wives.

In the area contiguous to the National Assembly, the King's prestigious military guard is housed in abject filth. Each family resides in a dilapidated box. Scores of young children run about in the mud which surrounds the boxes. The King of Bhutan receives plaudits from abroad for his modern approach and his concern for his people. Unfortunately, he has not allocated financial resources to basic support for the elite military guards.

On a mountain above the national preserve, at an elevation of 9,000 feet, there is a Shangri-la-like Buddhist retreat. In that setting, a highly selected group of young Buddhist monks is indoctrinated. The training is composed of three separate three-year blocks constituting the initial commitment to the priesthood. For each of the three-year periods, the immediate family of the fledgling monk is responsible for providing total support including food and clothing.

The Buddhist prayer flags are found wherever there is a slight wind. In rural settings, every house, independent of a wind source, has prayer flags hoisted. The prayer flags insure that the Buddhist faith will be disseminated far and wide by the winds. That belief requires faith. The number, size, colors, and condition of the prayer flags appear to be irrelevant.

April 9:

On the final morning in Thimphu, we visited the home and garden of a local naturalist and ornithologist, Rebecca Pradhan. Her garden was lovely. We saw a few exotic birds and she inscribed her book, *Threatened Birds in Bhutan.* Rebecca was knowledgeable regarding flora and fauna. She was warm, responsive, and shy. In Bhutan there are very few people who have expressed interest in nature, particularly birding. Rebecca has accepted a major educational challenge in her society.

Our subsequent visit to an arts and crafts school emphasized, as usual, Buddhist religious themes using the medium of wood. Pine was the species of choice.

A stop at the Zilukha Nunnery prompted a few frightened young nuns to appear. Their English facility appeared to be nonexistent. The average age may have been thirteen. I had not realized that women, in any Buddhist culture, qualified for the nunnery.

At the sole post office, I acquired a few bird stamps which I had not been able to find at the Dzong. For fifty years, I collected stamps from more than one hundred countries, with particular emphasis on the United States, Canada, and Kenya. Ten years ago, I liquidated my stamp collection except for a few bird stamps from a variety of countries. I found that philately required inordinate time which I preferred to devote to other avocational interests. It is amazing that many small countries issue remarkably attractive, diverse bird stamps while the offering in the United States is limited. Since the themes for new postage stamps in the United States are selected by a broadly-represented citizen panel, birding is probably low on the totem pole of interests.

At the bank, there was an extremely long line. Since I towered over the others in line, and since I was an obvious foreigner, a teller from another window beckoned to me. Since I was converting US dollars into Bhutanese Ngultrums (if you can pronounce it, you can spend them), a special teller was required. I was reassured that I was not receiving special treatment because of my elevation or pale coloration.

While Patti absorbed the arts and crafts in the local shops, I walked through the town past the clock tower and the river bridge to the hotel. The wind was fierce. Smell pebbles struck my face and head, and the dust permeated my clothing.

Rebecca Pradhan was so impressed with our commitment to birding that she took us to the reclamation flats (birds and humans have a tendency to select strange places to roost). Three Ibisbills were feeding on the narrow river flats. The Ibisbill has a black face and black breast band. The distinguishing feature is a long, downward-curved bill like an ibis. It is found near mountain streams and rivers in the high elevation foothills of Northern China, Southern Tibet, and Bhutan.

In the evening, we met several of the Canadian volunteers assigned to Bhutan. About a dozen are engaged in technical, environmental assignments. They are committed people, but they remind me of the technically-oriented, American USAID personnel whom we met overseas rather than the idealistic, people-oriented Peace Corps Volunteers who served in the early contingents.

April 10 / Thimphu to Punakha:

From Thimphu, we drove three hours north on the usual narrow, winding, mountain roads (only 75 kilometers were covered) to Punakha. Until 1955, Punakha was the Bhutanese capital.

At the Dochula pass (10,200 feet), we admired the sterling view of the snow-capped Himalayas and the hundreds of "broadcasting" prayer flags. The truck traffic was ample. The curved, narrow roads, without shoulders or guard rails, were, for peace of mind, ignored.

Built in 1637, the Punakha Dzong dominates the approach to the city and is located at the confluence of the Pochu (father or pa) and

Mochu (mother or ma) rivers. There are several rivers running north to south in Bhutan; however, none is navigable. In 1986, the Dzong was destroyed by fire. Currently, the destroyed rooms are being painstakingly rebuilt by craftsmen who are monks.

Walking along the narrow road on the bank overlooking the Mochu River, I enjoyed chatting with the young children who were returning from school. In Bhutan, the children wear uniforms designating their schools. Male adults, other than monks, also wear a gown, but the checkered tunic is tan with a sash and is worn with green knee socks. The children did not hesitate to use their blossoming English facility. Their overt curiosity was confined to my camera and binoculars.

The Hotel Zangho Petri, south of Punakha a few miles, was comfortable and relatively quiet, except for the worldwide barking dog menace. The food was tasteless and repetitive (rice and bits of chicken bone and barely potable tea). Dessert is not normally a component of Bhutanese cuisine.

April 11 / Punakha to Wangdi:

From Punakha, we traveled only forty-five minutes south to Wangdi, an attractive Swiss-like town with shops painted brown and white like Tudor houses. The central square was quaint. Although there were many tourists and hikers, the pace was reasonable.

The Wangdiphodrang Dzong unified western, central, and eastern Bhutan for many centuries. After leaving the western region of the country, Wangdi is the first town in central Bhutan. A side trip to the Phodrang Valley highlighted a number of Yaks climbing happily on the hills and a distinctive Indian village on the side of a low mountain which has provided a home for generations of manual laborers who emigrated from India.

The Kychu Resort served as our retreat for the night. It was the most attractive, clean, well-appointed accommodation we had experienced in Bhutan. Several cabins are located on a swift mountain stream. The shower was a distinct treat. The dinner offered several varieties of rice and stewed chicken.

April 12 / Wangdi to Tongsa:

Continuing in an easterly direction, we completed the longest travel day of the trip, from Wangdi to Tongsa, a distance of 180 kilometers. En route to Tongsa, we detoured south to the Phobjikha Valley, which is part of Black Mountain National Park. During the winter months, more than 300 endangered Black-necked Cranes are resident in the valley.

The farmers who reside in the valley head south for the winter while the cranes are in residence. When the farmers return from their winter retreat, the cranes have departed for northwest-central China. Although cranes are generally revered, if they fail to migrate, they are killed by the farmers.

On this occasion, the farmers had not yet returned. At a considerable distance, we were able to view distinctly one Black-necked Crane. The bird was a male with a black head and a red cap. The Black-necked Crane, which also winters in southern Tibet in small numbers, is endangered.

In 1992, while visiting China, we had seen a single Black-necked Crane at Qinghai in north central China. Although we were not recording a new species, it was a special treat to see this distinctive bird again.

From the valley to the main road (the only road) to Tongsa, we spent a few hours at the Gantey Gompa, a sacred monastery which was constructed in the seventeenth century.

The Buddhist religion is extraordinarily complex. One of the main theological branches, the Mahayana, is prevalent in Bhutan. The nuances of belief are myriad and esoteric. The Mahayana branch was introduced in Bhutan by a Tibetan lama in the seventeenth century.

Mayayana devotees manifest an exalted love for all living creatures. The Mayayana sect represents the Pan Asiatic form of the Buddhist religion. Celibacy is not strictly enforced. With the advent of foreigners since 1974, traditional practices of the faith are being eroded. Since the Chinese takeover in Tibet, Tibetan refugees have brought with them additional variations.

The Tongsa Dzong, founded in 1543, is a remarkable work of art containing twenty-three interior temples. Tongsa is the ancestral home of the Royal Family of Bhutan. The Crown Prince controls the Tongsa

Dzong until he ascends to the throne. As you approach the town of Tongsa from the west, the Dzong can be seen clearly at a distance of fourteen kilometers.

From above, the Ta Dzong watchtower protects the Dzong and houses several stupas and sacred relics. The traditional Buddhist architecture is unusually inviting with white rock walls and decorative brown wooden trim. The roofs are generally colorful. At Tongsa, they are a vivid yellow.

In Tongsa we roosted at the Hotel Norling, which was perched over the river bank in a row of low attached buildings. The Norling resides at the bottom of my Bhutan accommodations list. Our "suite" adjoined the dining room and incorporated a four-foot square "hall" with an adjoining bathroom. It may sound acceptable, but please reserve judgment.

There was not any running water. Except for two hours during the dinner period, there was not any electricity. On the bathroom floor, there was one inch of water emanating from the commode. That convenience did not flush.

The curtain on the window above one of the cots fell down upon our arrival and was not replaced during our two-night stay. The curtain and the bathroom had not been cleaned since the Crown Prince left to be crowned many years ago. There was one partially-clean towel for each guest.

The narrow porch from the dining room extended to our curtainless window. We were confronted frequently with loud, laughing, curious Japanese tourists who seemed to enjoy peering into our bedroom.

In the wall adjoining our little hallway, there was an open sewer pipe covered by a piece of plywood. Even with the door closed to the bedroom, the fumes were overpowering. Upon returning from dinner, a single candle was available for illumination. There was not enough toilet paper to blow one's nose. One small piece of soap, sans water, should not be considered a fringe benefit. There was not any maid service. The single towel per person was not replaced (without water it scarcely made any difference). Without water, we used the towels as rugs in the bedroom.

The toilet seat was loose. There was not any mirror. I could not recharge my electric razor which usually works on both 110 and 220 volts.

Inexplicably, the cuisine was the best we had in Bhutan. Small omelets, with toast you could break, were served at breakfast. Chicken "pieces" with chile, two kinds of edible rice, and mixed vegetables with flavor were served at lunch and dinner. The indigenous "Tiger Beer" was excellent. The local "Dragon Rum," at seventy-five cents a shot, eliminated many of our complaints except the open sewer pipe. Finally, our new Japanese friends retired. For every yin, there is a yang.

April 13 / Tongsa:

Although the first foreigners were allowed to visit Bhutan in 1974 (except for a few earlier British colonial representatives), only a trickle of tourists arrives in Bhutan. The government of Bhutan charges the tour operator $200 per diem for each foreign visitor. The tour operator then reimburses the innkeeper for amenities provided. The amount paid to the hotel, etc., is never revealed. Under this arrangement, the hotels may not be receiving a sufficient stipend to insure the requisite incentive. Currently, the government restricts the number of tourists to 5,000 per year. It is difficult to believe that only one million dollars is generated from tourism (excluding the miscellaneous meals and goods which the tourists may purchase).

This morning, we drove south from Tsonga toward the Indian border. Because of Indian insurrections in the national park which adjoins the border, the government of Bhutan has proscribed public entry.

Since 1991, 70,000 Bhutanese of Nepalese and Indian descent have emigrated to India and Nepal. They have received international refugee status, and the numbers continue to rise. The refugees are leaving as a result of the king of Bhutan's 1988 edict promulgated to induce Nepalese and Indian settlers to leave Bhutan permanently. In most cases, these settlers and their progenitors have resided in Bhutan for many generations.

In retaliation, a Gurkha Liberation Movement has been launched which stages armed raids into Bhutan from India and Nepal.

In the national park to which we were headed, there have been several battles between the insurrectionists and government troops.

The Indians are agitating for their own form of government and for their own elected representatives to the National Assembly. Without adequate military or security forces, the Government of Bhutan has been unable to control the insurrections. Currently, in Bhutan, there are only 5,000 members of the security forces.

In 1865, Bhutan came under the domination of the British Raj. In 1910, it became a British Protectorate. Until August 8, 1949, the British provided security and discharged the foreign affairs portfolio. On that date, the British negotiated a treaty with India that provided for Bhutan's independence. For more than half a century, India has been discharging security support for Bhutan. Obviously, the informal arrangements need improvement.

In Bhutan, there are three distinct ethnic groups. The Bhutia constitute sixty percent of the population. They represent a Tibetan heritage and they control the government, the economy, the schools, and the monkhood. Successive generations of the national royalty have been ethnic Bhutia. For centuries, the Druk Gyalpo (Dragon King) has been a Bhutia.

The Nepalese, who are Hindu, constitute thirty-five percent of the estimated 1.8 million people in Bhutan. They live in the western region of Bhutan, and they are the second largest ethnic group. The Nepalese include many Indians who provide menial and manual labor; are generally subject to discrimination, and may be treated as "untouchables."

The third, and smallest, group are the Sharclops, who are predominant in the southeast region. They are indigenous, well-educated, rural, and roughly comparable to the Hill Tribes of Burma and Thailand, except for the educational advantage.

En route to the national park, we passed through lovely forested regions devoid of population and brimming with unique flora and fauna. In the trees bordering a mountain stream, we observed a dozen endangered Golden Langur Monkeys. We had identified two species of langurs in Sabah. The golden is rarer and is restricted to a smaller range.

Returning to Tsonga for a sewer pipe reunion, we visited a school run by a monastery. The improvised recess games were fascinating.

Chatting with the students, we realized that the Bhutanese people are curious, aspiring, and friendly.

April 14 / Tongsa to Bumthang:

Sixty-eight kilometers east of Tsonga, after passing through the Yotong Pass at 11,500 feet, we entered the Bumthang Valley. Actually, there are four valleys. Passing through one as we approached the city of Bumthang, the road was bordered by buckwheat fields which are unique to this region of Bhutan. We also drove on the only stretch of straight highway in the country. For one kilometer, two narrow lanes, one in each direction, presented an unprecedented view down the pike.

In the Jakar Valley, we entered the quaint village of the same name. Jakar is a historic and a cultural center. The influence of Swiss developmental assistance is exemplified by a cheese factory where we acquired a delicious wedge of "Swiss" cheese.

We stopped at the Meebartsho (Burning Lake) Holy Spot; the Thogme Weaving Center, and witnessed the building of a stone and mud house by hand. At a Bhutanese house in Bumthang, we enjoyed tea with a family which was composed of mother, three daughters, and several young grandchildren. The father was working, but his family presented us with a glimpse of a shy, sheltered, confident, attractive, relatively affluent family. It was unique to witness a Bhutanese family in action, and we were grateful for the privilege.

The Bumthang Valleys are open and relatively large. They are havens for hikers, and the small villages are inviting. The pace is leisurely, the people are attractive, and there is no overt poverty. Although there are scores of young, foreign hikers, the limited numbers can be absorbed.

April 15 / Bumthang to Ura to Bumthang:

Traveling further east, after a forty-eight kilometer drive, we reached the village and valley of Ura. This was the easternmost point of our safari. Although we had not pierced the eastern region, the appearance of the people was charming. Sharclops were replacing Bhutia.

The pass into the Ura Valley is at 12,000 feet. The pine forests are superb. As you descend into the valley, the terrain becomes arid.

Ura village includes approximately one hundred houses all facing south toward the monastery which is located on a slight promontory above the town. The abundance of prayer flags blowing in the wind resembled windmills in action. After visiting the monastery, I perched on a rock to make a few notes. A dozen young boys were fascinated by my awkward southpaw penmanship and crowded around to enjoy the spectacle. Several minutes elapsed before I realized that they were fascinated by my fountain pen, and that my writing was irrelevant.

At the Ura Monastery, I recognized that the Buddhist celibacy rule was not practiced without exception in Bhutan. Within fifty feet of one of the entrances to the Monastery, the wives of the monks were seated on the stoops of several hovels.

When the women of Bhutan are young, they are well-dressed, lithe, proud, ruddy-cheeked, and attractive. The reddish-brown hue of their skin, and the high cheekbones, enhance the attractiveness. At age thirty-five, the constant wind and onerous toil alter that positive description. At a young age, the women appear elderly and even emaciated.

Disease in Bhutan has reached epidemic proportions. Women are the most likely to become infected. In fifteen years, infant mortality has been halved and longevity has increased by twenty years to age 66; however, women continue to suffer inordinately.

Returning to the main Bumthang Valley, and Jakar Village, we fell into bed while listening to the inevitable barking dogs and noisy children who seem to have reversed day and night.

April 16 / Bumthang to Punakha:

The return westward trek has begun. We have traveled the east to west dimension in Bhutan. With the exception of the high mountains in the northwest, we have been exposed to a substantial portion of the country.

In a country the size of West Virginia, only two percent of the land is arable; five percent is devoted to pasture. In excess of seventy percent is forested. Logging and home heating needs are depleting forest reserves rapidly. Water is the most prevalent natural resource.

Most of the hydroelectric power generated in Bhutan is being sold to India under a binding agreement. Some gypsum is exported, but other natural ores appear to be nonexistent or inaccessible.

India consumes ninety-three percent of all the exports of Bhutan. Imports from India to Bhutan are at the level of sixty-seven percent and include virtually everything that Bhutan needs: fuels, grains, machinery, and vehicles.

The most troublesome problem in Bhutan is not the severely increasing population growth, but the percentage of school age population. In a few years, the school children will be searching for nonexistent employment. In the short term, tourism cannot, and should not, increase to meet foreign currency needs. More importantly, in order to save the environment, assuming that the destruction of the forests can be curtailed, long-term tourist growth cannot be encouraged without imposing effective national controls.

In 1999, the King lifted the ban on television. Bhutan was one of the last countries to introduce the medium. Initially, the Bhutan Broadcasting Service enjoyed a monopoly which shielded it from foreign competition. Since the BBS local coverage was confined to Thimphu, foreign channels have now been authorized. As a result, one fifth of the Bhutanese people watch television every evening.

Although television is banned in the monasteries, young children have become addicted to Indian romantic movies and to lurid Western "real-life" episodes. The Web was becoming a minor attraction; however, that commitment is now being replaced by foreign television. The Center for Bhutan Studies is conducting a research study to determine the cultural impact of television on the youth of Bhutan, but the die is cast. With only one local newspaper, and no other competing attractions, television will prevail.

As we left Jakar, we observed the small local shops. At the rear of each shop, the owner's quarters are located. Bunches of small children enjoy access to the shop and to the family quarters.

The Jakar Hospital had ten beds in a small room. No nurses or doctors were in evidence. Families live with the patients. The families provide all of the food for the patient and for themselves. There is no evacuation plan. If specialty medical services are necessary, Thimphu is the only option.

In a single day, we made the trip from Jakar to Punakha. We

returned to the Hotel Zangho Petri thoroughly exhausted.

April 17 / Punakha to Thimphu:

In spite of the distinctive facades, the Dzongs of Bhutan are dirty, impoverished, in need of maintenance, and represent limited recorded history, except for religious myths which have been perpetuated by word of mouth.

As a religion, the Buddhism practiced in Bhutan concentrates on the monotonous repetition of selected doctrine and practices. For example, a monk is required to walk around the resident temple one hundred and eight times per day in a clock-wise direction. Clusters of monks are dependent on public charity.

Bhutan has a shortage of soap, toilet paper, hot water, towels, and wash cloths. These items may not be considered essential, but they are illustrative. There are only a few drug addicts or beggars. Handicapped people are not in evidence, except for a few elderly men with canes.

In Bhutan, we did not see an elevator. There are few passenger cars, and no ostensible aberrational behavior. There are only a limited number of schools. The single college is located in the capital city. When compared to a developed society, a few of these attributes are inviting, but time will erase these temporary advantages.

April 18 / Thimphu to Paro:

After a morning walk in the Thimphu Botanical Garden (no flowers displayed), we returned to Paro and to a cottage in the hotel where we began our Bhutan trip. I have been bitten by bed fleas on my hands and arms. I do not know to which of the resort areas I should attribute the condition, but I would postulate the sewer pipe retreat.

The travel requirements of the last few days have been demanding. An early hour for retirement was accepted with gratitude.

April 19 / Paro, Bhutan to Calcutta to Bangkok:

In early morning, we drove east of Paro on the highest paved mountain road in Bhutan, Chelia Pass at 12,300 feet. From the pass, the view of the Ha Valley was extraordinary. There is no road east of Ha to the Tibetan border.

We also savored views of the second highest mountain in Bhutan, which is located at the northwestern border with Tibet. Mount Jhomo Lhari, at 24,380 feet, was covered with patches of sun and clouds. Access to the border requires a one and one-half day trek from Ha. The Himalayas in northwestern Bhutan are not as lofty as Everest or K2, but they possess a grandeur and a sense of isolation which for me was unsurpassed. The high mountain vistas from a houseboat on Lake Dal near Srinagar in Kashmir were unprecedented, but comparable views in Bhutan are competitive.

After returning to Paro, we took the road east of town to Taktoang Monastery (Tiger's Nest) which towers 3,000 feet above the valley. From the valley, we were afforded with additional breathtaking views of the Himalayas.

During our visit to Bhutan, we did not see a policeman (except for the one directing traffic on the main street in Thimphu). Our exposure to the military was confined to the single guard at the Queen Mother's Palace, and a few Indian troops taking horses to the Tibet border who crossed a forest road.

Surprisingly, lamb is not eaten in Bhutan. Except for a dried-out serving of "fiddleheads," the vegetables were uniformly tasteless and dull. Cut watermelon is abundant, but because of the remnants of a dirty knife on several slices, the eating pleasure was deferred.

Invariably, breakfast was the best meal. The eggs were variable, fresh, and well-cooked (omelets, fried, boiled, and scrambled). Tea was the only safe beverage. All milk, sauces, and leafy vegetables were avoided. The tourists with minimal experience in the lesser-developed world regretted their willingness to partake of these culprits.

The Bhutanese language is Dzongkha. Dzong is a word of art. The meanings range from national and provincial monasteries and civic centers to word components that denote religious relevance.

The national bird of Bhutan is the raven which is found at high elevations and which embodies mystical qualities.

The airport at Paro fills most of the attractive valley. Fruit trees and semi-modern tourist traps surround the runway which can only accommodate small jets.

The survival of Bhutan is problematic. Within a generation, continuing exploitation, corruption, unemployment, the "brain drain," population growth, increased tourism, and the devastation of natural resources, particularly timber, will summon the death knell of a beautiful country.

After a three-hour wait at the airport, we departed for Calcutta. Since the temperature was 18°C, the pilot was forced to delay takeoff, because of air currents, until the temperature subsided to 16°C. In Bhutan, there are still a few quaint jewels in the disintegrating national crown.

Kuzu zangpo la (hello and farewell)!